A Practical Approach to
Pharmaceutical Policy

A Practical Approach to Pharmaceutical Policy

Andreas Seiter

THE WORLD BANK
Washington, D.C.

1818 H Street NW
Washington DC 20433
Telephone: 202-473-1000
Internet: www.worldbank.org
E-mail: feedback@worldbank.org

ISBN: 978-0-8213-8386-5
eISBN: 978-0-8213-8387-2
DOI: 10.1596/978-0-8213-8386-5

Library of Congress Cataloging-in-Publication Data

Seiter, Andreas.
A practical approach to pharmaceutical policy / Andreas Seiter.
     p. ; cm. — (Directions in development)
  Includes bibliographical references and index.
  ISBN 978-0-8213-8386-5 (alk. paper)
  I. Pharmaceutical policy. I. World Bank. II. Title. III. Series: Directions in development (Washington, D.C.)
  [DNLM: 1. Drug Industry—organization & administration. 2. Developed Countries. 3. Government Regulation. 4. Health Plan Implementation. 5. Health Policy—economics. QV 736 S462p 2010]
  RA401.A1S45 2010
  362.17'82—dc22

                                                                                    2010015420

Cover photo: istockphoto.com
Cover design: Naylor Design, Washington, D.C.

Contents

Boxes

Figures

Tables

Foreword

Recent decades have seen miraculous progress in developing drugs and medicines that save lives, treat illness, and protect families and communities from the devastating loss of parents and breadwinners. For people suffering from HIV/AIDS, malaria, tuberculosis, and pneumonia, as well as those with chronic diseases such as diabetes, cardiovascular disease, and cancers, timely access to life-saving treatment can make the difference between life and death or lasting disability.

Ensuring that people have the affordable, quality health care they need for healthy lives is a cardinal policy goal for governments around the world. To realize this goal, getting the details right is a complex process even by the standards of the Organisation for Economic Co-operation and Development, let alone in developing countries, where regulatory and pharmaceutical capacity may be stretched. For example, the pharmaceutical "value chain" that ensures that a patient gets the right medicine at the right time may be weak or broken. Manufacturers may decide against investing in developing or manufacturing new drugs for treating diseases that afflict poor people if they do not see a market for their products. Even if a potential market exists, regulatory barriers and other inefficiencies may discourage manufacturers from marketing their drugs in certain countries or may delay the launch of new medicines in others.

These potential breakdowns in the process show that pharmaceutical markets are not self-regulating, unlike those for many common consumer products. For example, policy makers must intervene frequently to set standards and subsequently enforce them through licensing procedures. They also need to provide financing in ways that counterbalance commercial incentives and ensure that doctors, nurses, and their patients get accurate information and knowledge about the medicines being prescribed and taken. Low-income countries need effective regulatory and distribution systems to make sure that donor aid for medicines can be made available to as many people as possible. This is no small undertaking. Consider that well-off middle-income countries' resources are also consistently under pressure to give their citizens wide access to the latest drugs and medicines within their existing, limited, health budgets.

This publication offers a compact "pharmaceutical field guide" for health and development policy makers in low- and middle-income countries. It offers analytical tools and practical advice, based on country case studies, of how to lay the groundwork for advancing smart policy solutions. The report also explores the political economy of reforms in the pharmaceutical sector. As we know from experience worldwide, governments that try to rein in health care costs by curbing drug coverage can face strenuous reactions.

As the world enters the five-year countdown to the 2015 Millennium Development Goals, this report will provide advice for governments, policy makers, development partners, civil society organizations, and others on the design and implementation of effective pharmaceutical policies—an essential part of the effort to improve the health of poor people.

Julian Schweitzer
Director, Health, Nutrition and Population
The World Bank

Preface

There is no shortage of literature about pharmaceutical regulation, pricing, financing, reimbursement, procurement, distribution, and all the other aspects that together define the pharmaceutical policy framework in a given country. However, what appears to be lacking is a "practitioner's guide" for navigating the complex field of pharmaceutical policy while considering the various challenges and limitations that characterize political reality.

Obviously, no "one size fits all" approach applies to pharmaceutical policy. Even two countries with similar objectives may need different sets of policies, depending on their starting position, preexisting laws and regulations, perceptions among providers and patients, and implementation capacity. Although high-income countries may find industrial policy and innovativeness hard to reconcile with cost containment in the health sector, choices may be even harder for middle-income countries that have to bridge the divide between a demanding urban population and large numbers of poor people in peri-urban and rural areas. Many low-income countries are struggling to provide basic essential drugs to their populations through still largely state-run delivery systems. At the same time, the growing private markets in these countries may be flooded with drugs of questionable origin and quality. In each case, policy makers and the implementing agencies need to select and combine their policy measures in a way that not only addresses the main problems conceptually but also is practically viable and sustainable.

This book discusses the wide range of challenges faced by policy makers in the pharmaceutical sector, presents the current know-how in terms of policy measures, and provides specific examples of policy packages that can be used in defined circumstances, even if one assumes a certain degree of political resistance and capacity limits on the side of the implementing agency. This book focuses on developing countries and tries to address the issues faced by both low- and middle-income countries. The book does not cover the vaccines market and its respective policies because too many differences exist between the markets for vaccines and pharmaceuticals to cover both subsectors in one publication of this type.

The book ends with an outlook on how things might evolve in the longer term. It assumes that some form of convergence will take place toward "models that work," thus reducing the fragmentation of policies and enhancing regulatory and economic efficiencies over time—one hopes to the benefit of all stakeholders in the sector and, in particular, those who, as patients, currently do not have reliable access to effective and safe medicines.

Who should read this book?

- Practitioners in national administrations, government agencies, insurance funds, and other bodies that deal with pharmaceuticals on a regular or occasional basis
- Staff members and consultants of international organizations, health sector nongovernmental organizations, and other professionals involved in health projects with a pharmaceutical component
- Academics and students in the field of public health and health economics
- Private sector professionals and all others interested in a better understanding of the complex pharmaceutical sector.

Acknowledgments

The following World Bank colleagues provided guidance and input during the concept stage of this book: Ekkehard Betsch, Mukesh Chawla, Heba Elgazzar, Armin Fidler, G. N. V. Ramana, Finn Schleimann, Juan Pablo Uribe, and Abdo Yazbeck. Peer reviewers for the book were Armin Fidler and Pia Helene Schneider, both of the World Bank.

The author would like to thank the following individuals for their thorough chapter reviews and constructive critiques, which helped correct several errors and omissions and provided many ideas about how to make this book more useful to its readers:

- Ekkehard Betsch (World Bank) and Juergen Reinhardt (UNIDO), the discussion of conflicts between industrial and health policies in chapters 3 and 4
- Kalipso Chalkidou (National Institute of Clinical Excellence), the discussion of innovation-induced cost pressures in chapter 3 and the discussion of decision making on formulary inclusion in chapter 4
- Agnes Couffinal (World Bank), the discussion of incentives and use of purchasing power in chapters 2, 3, and 4 and the Lithuanian case described in chapter 7
- Kees de Joncheere (World Health Organization Regional Office for Europe), chapter 5 on policy packages

- Henk den Besten (I+ Solutions) and Prashant Yadav (MIT-Zaragoza Logistics Center), the discussions of procurement, logistics, and supply chains in chapters 2, 3, and 4
- Richard Laing (World Health Organization), the discussion of drug pricing in chapter 3
- Ruth Lopert (Australian Therapeutic Goods Administration), chapter 8 on the pharmaceutical policy outlook
- Patricio Marquez (World Bank), chapter 1 on policy goals, chapter 2 on stakeholders, and the Russian Federation case described in chapter 7
- Andre Medici and Fernando Montenegro Torres (both World Bank), the section on regulation in chapter 3
- Zafar Mirza (World Health Organization Eastern Mediterranean Regional Office), the discussion of rational use of medicines in chapters 3 and 4
- Dena Ringold (World Bank), the discussions of corruption and governance in chapters 3 and 4, the dysfunction overview in chapter 3, and the introduction to the assessment tool in appendixes A and B
- Karima Saleh, Yi-Kyoung Lee, and Shuo Zhang, the country examples featuring China, Ghana, and Liberia in chapter 7
- Juan Pablo Uribe (World Bank), chapter 6 on implementation
- Anita Wagner (World Health Organization Collaborating Center on Pharmaceutical Policy at Harvard Medical School), the sections covering funding and financing issues related to health insurance in chapters 3 and 4.

Sincere thanks go to Ekkehard Betsch, Elizabeth Nyamayaro, and Sally Schlippert, who assisted with research and provided support for the preparation, review, editing, and production process.

About the Author

Andreas Seiter is a senior health specialist at the World Bank's Health, Nutrition, and Population Anchor. A medical doctor trained in Germany, Seiter worked for 18 years in the pharmaceutical industry before joining the World Bank in 2004. He is responsible for the World Bank's analytical and advisory work in all areas of pharmaceutical policy, such as regulation, governance, quality assurance, financing, purchasing, supply chain, and rational use. He has worked with World Bank teams, policy makers, and experts in several Bank client countries in Africa, Eastern Europe, Latin America, the Middle East, and South Asia.

Abbreviations

A4R	Accountability for Reasonableness
AIDS	acquired immunodeficiency syndrome
AİFD	Araştırmacı İlaç Firmaları Derneği, or Association of Research-Based Pharmacies (Turkey)
AMFm	Affordable Medicines Facility—malaria
API	active pharmaceutical ingredient
ATC	anatomical therapeutic chemical (classification)
cGMP	current good manufacturing practice
CIF	customs, insurance, and freight
CMS	central medical store
COP	community outreach pharmacy
DALY	disability-adjusted life years
EFPIA	European Federation of Pharmaceutical Industries and Associations
EU	European Union
FDA	U.S. Food and Drug Administration
FOB	free on board
GLP	good laboratory practice
GMP	good manufacturing practice
HIF	health insurance fund

HIV	human immunodeficiency virus
ICB	international competitive bidding
IEIS	İlaç Endüstrisi İşverenler Sendikası, or Pharmaceutical Manufacturers Association of Turkey
IFPMA	International Federation of Pharmaceutical Manufacturers and Associations
IMS	company that provides pharmaceutical market data in developed and middle-income markets
INN	international nonproprietary name
IT	information technology
KEMSA	Kenya Medical Supplies Agency
MeTA	Medicines Transparency Alliance
MOH	ministry of health
MSH	Management Sciences for Health
NCB	national competitive bidding
NDS	National Drug Service (Liberia)
NDSO	National Drug Service Organization (Lesotho)
NGO	nongovernmental organization
NHIS	National Health Insurance Scheme (Ghana)
NHS	U.K. National Health Service
NICE	National Institute of Clinical Excellence (United Kingdom)
ÖBIG	Österreichisches Bundesinstitut im Gesundheitswesen, or Austrian Health Institute
OECD	Organisation for Economic Co-operation and Development
OTC	over the counter
PBM	pharmaceutical benefit manager
PBS	Pharmaceutical Benefits Scheme (Australia)
PER	Public Expenditure Review
PETS	pharmaceutical expenditure tracking system
PFSA	Pharmaceutical Fund and Supply Agency (Ethiopia)
PPRI	Pharmaceutical Pricing and Reimbursement Information (initiative)
PSA	procurement services agency
QALY	quality-adjusted life year
R&D	research and development
Rx	prescription drugs
SDRA	state drug regulatory authority
SOP	standard operating procedure
SPF	State Patient Fund (Lithuania)
SSI	Social Security Institution

TRIPs	Trade-Related Aspects of Intellectual Property Rights (agreement)
UN	United Nations
UNICEF	United Nations Children's Fund
VAT	value added tax
WHO	World Health Organization

CHAPTER 1

Pharmaceutical Policy Goals

What Do Policy Makers Want to Achieve?

Policy, for the purposes of this book, is defined as the conscious attempt of public officials or executives entrusted with public funds to achieve certain objectives through a set of laws, rules, procedures, and incentives. With regard to pharmaceutical policy, the first question has to be "What are these objectives?"

The answer varies for countries of different income levels (see figure 1.1). For low-income countries, the most common objective is to secure the population's access to medicines necessary to achieve major public health goals. Such goals might include reducing maternal and child mortality or reducing death rates from AIDS, malaria, and tuberculosis.

Middle-income countries also must secure access to medicines for basic public health programs for the poor, who represent the majority of the population; however, these countries need to consider the demands of a wealthier urban population as well. The urban middle class in Beijing, São Paulo, or Bangalore increasingly enjoys a lifestyle similar to the middle class in high-income countries and expects access to a broader range of drugs than just essential medicines. This demand for innovative and more expensive drugs needs to be balanced against the limited funding available from public budgets or insurance funds, which tends to lag the growth of private incomes.

Figure 1.1   Emergence of Core Pharmaceutical Policy Objectives by Income Level

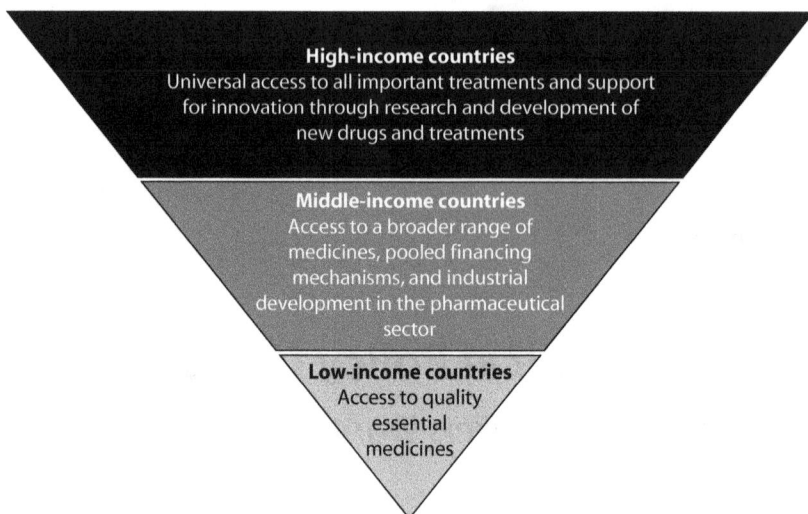

High-income countries
Universal access to all important treatments and support for innovation through research and development of new drugs and treatments

Middle-income countries
Access to a broader range of medicines, pooled financing mechanisms, and industrial development in the pharmaceutical sector

Low-income countries
Access to quality essential medicines

Source: Author's representation.

Most middle-income countries and several low-income countries have a domestic drug industry. For those countries, policy makers are pressured to ensure the prosperity of this industry, in particular if it is a significant factor in the national economy (as is the case in India and Jordan). This pressure creates conflicts with policy objectives that are based on public health goals: overprescribing and use of more expensive drugs are good for the profitability of the industry but bad for public health and public budgets.

In middle-income countries, pressure does not come from domestic manufacturers only but also from multinational companies. Occasionally, the trade representatives of their home countries support these companies; in negotiations of broader trade agreements, such representatives may be able to undermine domestic policy initiatives aimed at cost containment in the health sector by limiting access to expensive imported drugs. Pressure also comes from patient organizations and consumers, who through the Internet can access information on innovative treatment choices and demand that they be made available. Given the sophisticated cost-containment tools applied in developed countries, which still constitute the main markets for multinational drug companies in terms of size, middle-income countries have become the dominant markets for ensuring top-line growth for multinational companies. These companies, therefore, put significant resources behind strategies to influence political decision makers and to secure their growth opportunities in the larger emerging markets. Such conflicts between broader economic growth strategies and attempts to control drug expenditure in the publicly funded health sector add to the complexities of pharmaceutical policy.

High-income countries face the challenge of securing access to innovative, costly treatments for a broad population covered by health insurance while controlling the growth of health expenditure, which has become a macroeconomic risk factor for economic growth in many countries. At the same time, such countries want to maintain an economic incentive for the research-based industry to develop new treatments to address unmet medical needs. If the research-based industry is a significant factor in the domestic economy, maintaining the competitiveness of this industry becomes an additional factor of influence that is likely to reflect on the balance of policy choices. For example, Switzerland and the United States both allow higher prices for new drugs than the average allowed by members of the Organisation for Economic Co-operation and Development (OECD 2008).

All countries want to keep their population safe from untested, fake, or substandard drugs. Unfortunately, neither consumers nor health professionals are able to judge the quality of a drug under field conditions. Regulation of the market and all the players involved is therefore a cornerstone of drug policy. However, most countries are facing a huge gap between what would be needed to effectively enforce the rules and regulations for the sector and what they can afford or have capacity to do.

Figure 1.1 shows the typical emergence of core pharmaceutical policy objectives with growing income level.

Pharmaceutical Policy Framework

One way of describing a policy framework is to map the legal and institutional hierarchy that governs market and stakeholder interactions. Some countries have an explicit national drug policy or national pharmaceutical policy, usually drafted under leadership of the ministry of health with stakeholder input. The policy provides strategic guidance and defines overall objectives for the sector. Such a document usually does not have legal status in itself but is meant to inform the legislative process.

National legislation, issued by the legislative body (in most countries, the parliament) defines the rules and conditions under which the pharmaceutical sector operates. The executive branch (typically, the ministry of health) defines the technical standards and implementation guidelines for the law in bylaws or ordinances. The law may also provide the foundation for regulatory agencies under independent leadership. These agencies then take over most of the standard-setting and technical implementation responsibilities. Enforcing agencies develop all necessary administrative and technical procedures required to ensure full implementation of the law and bylaws.

Although the drug law and the enforcing agencies typically regulate all supply-side parameters of the pharmaceutical market (research, development, licensing of products and market participants, pricing, quality assurance, pharmacovigilance, marketing, and promotion), another set of legislative instruments regulates the demand side by defining who pays for which drugs under which circumstances. A health insurance law or a law defining a public health care system would fall into this category. In systems with government-financed health care, a general procurement law may regulate the purchasing of drugs for public sector health facilities. Other laws and regulations (such as trade laws and international agreements, antitrust laws, or laws governing environmental protection) may influence the pharmaceutical sector, and policy makers need to consider them as well when making policy decisions.

The pharmaceutical sector is highly dynamic and has a large number of distinct stakeholders (see chapter 2), all trying to promote their own interests. Laws provide a framework for decision making, but in most cases, the actual decisions require technical input from experts, who need room for interpretation of data and may disagree in their opinions. To assist in decision making in such an environment, commissions are formed that give guidance to implementing agencies or become decision-making bodies on their behalf. The work of such commissions is usually governed in the bylaws to the drug law and other laws relevant for the sector. Figure 1.2 shows the hierarchy of laws, regulations, and acting agencies that define the playing field for pharmaceutical policy.

This high-level view of pharmaceutical policy is necessary but insufficient to identify the levers that policy makers can use to address problems and to achieve policy goals, such as better access to drugs and better quality of care. Another, more process-oriented framework proposed by the originators of the World Bank–Harvard Flagship Program on Health Financing is built on five "control knobs" that policy makers can use in

Figure 1.2   Hierarchy of Laws, Regulations, and Implementing Agencies in the Pharmaceutical Sector

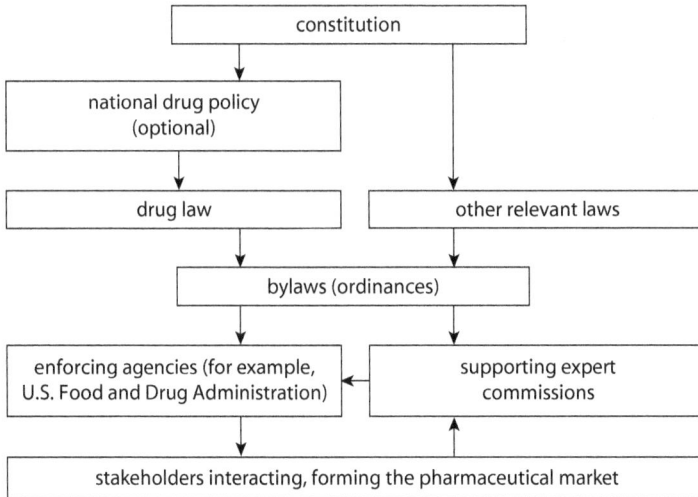

Source: Author's representation.

implementing reform. According to Roberts and Reich (2010), these control knobs are

- **Financing:** How is the money for pharmaceuticals raised, and how do those choices affect both what consumers use and the distribution of costs and use, among the population? How, in turn, do financing choices affect risk protection?
- **Payment:** How are both retail dispensers and wholesale sellers paid, and what are the implications of these for access, use, and cost burdens—and in turn for health and satisfaction?
- **Organization:** How are basic tasks in the pharmaceutical sector divided among public and private entities, and how do these divisions influence the incentives and processes that affect individual provider and worker performance?
- **Regulation:** What does government do to alter private sector behavior by imposing rules that are backed by sanctions? Note that this power can be delegated to private sector entities as well.
- **Persuasion:** How do governments influence the pharmaceutical sector by trying to persuade key actors (doctors, patients, dispensers, etc.) to change their behavior through educational and marketing initiatives?

This book does not specifically build on any of the preceding frame-works, which were developed for a different purpose. Instead, it tries to replicate the sequence by which policy issues are diagnosed and addressed in the World Bank's analytical work with clients such as ministries of health and health insurance funds. Stakeholder analysis builds the basis for understanding the actors and their motives. A "pattern recognition" approach helps in understanding complex problems, such as the following:

- Prevalence of substandard drugs and an informal market
- Lack of availability of medicines because of failing supply chains
- Misuse of funds and corruption
- High drug prices
- Inappropriate use of medicines
- Conflicts between innovation and cost containment and between public health and industrial policies

Such an approach is consistent with the real-world approach taken by many policy makers. Options for policy reform are presented in a way that matches the typical patterns found in the diagnostic process, emphasizing the connections that exist between different policy elements. Because the pharmaceutical sector is not usually a homogeneous block and therefore requires a combination of policies to address a given problem, a set of typical synergistic policy "bundles" is presented. These bundles need to be combined and sequenced to match the top-level, longer-term policy objectives.

Parameters for Monitoring the Effect and Progress of Pharmaceutical Reforms

Verification and quantification of reform progress is possible only if the implementing agency has access to data that describe the condition at the heart of reform. The effort to collect and process baseline data and monitor defined sets of data over time needs to be considered in reform planning and budgeting. In real life, the challenge is to develop a good representation of reality from data sets that can be sketchy or incoherent, complemented by anecdotal information from the field and a skilled interpretation of the "political temperature" of an issue. Decision makers get to "feel the heat" from stakeholders who are unhappy with the potential and real impacts of decisions. Depending on the political backing of a particular reform or actor, higher or lower heat levels can be tolerated. Reforms that have to cut into entitlements are often considered balanced if the level of protest from two opposing sides is equal. However, this approach overlooks the fact that commercial interests are usually much better organized and better able to express their interests than are normal citizens and patients. In particular, low-income and marginalized populations often have no voice in the political arena. To be effective, pro-poor policies, therefore, need monitoring based on objective metrics.

Metrics for measuring pharmaceutical policy outcomes linked to core objectives can be classified as input, process, and output parameters. For example, stock level is an *input* parameter: availability of a drug is necessary but not sufficient for the desired output—adequately treating a patient for a diagnosed illness. Deliberately, outcome parameters, such as mortality or disease incidence, are not considered in this context. Pharmaceuticals are a necessary input for health outcomes, but many other elements in the health system need to function well for pharmaceuticals to make their full contribution to these outcomes. An example of a *process* parameter would be lead-time predictability in procurement, which is important for optimizing buffer stocks and avoiding stock-outs but is not directly linked to an output. *Output* parameters relate to the services delivered, such as the number of treatments dispensed.

Parameters can be binary—a manufacturing site is either certified as meeting good manufacturing practices (GMPs), or it is not—or they can represent a value on a scale. For the practical purpose of measuring policy effect, the challenge is first to measure a baseline value of all parameters that are considered relevant and then to define a target value that stands for objectives achieved. Box 1.1 gives an example how this challenge is addressed in practice.

Parameters need to be chosen from data that can realistically be collected and that correspond as closely as possible to the specific reform goals. For example, collecting data on stock levels of certain essential drugs in public clinics may be relatively easy. (For the purpose of this example, assume that the clinics are supposed to hand out these drugs to poor people at no charge.) However, these data are not necessarily a good proxy for access of the poor to such drugs. Several other access barriers (such as distance, transportation costs, discrimination, unfriendly staff, inadequate diagnosis or prescription, and informal payments) mean that "free" drug distribution programs often benefit the wealthy more than the poor. Better parameters to judge access may be the percentage of people who leave the facility with the actual drug that was prescribed for their condition and the price (if any) that they pay for it. Collecting such data is possible but expensive. It requires specific exit surveys, which would

Box 1.1

Example of Target Setting in a Project Aimed at Improving Access to Medicines in a Low-Income Country

An exit survey at selected public health facilities shows that only 40 percent of patients get the drugs they need at the facility; the rest have to buy them in private pharmacies. The problem appears to be a combination of lack of funding and inadequate logistics management in the supply chain. Donors are willing to provide funding to double the budget available for essential drugs. A logistics consultant is asked to run simulations and come up with a realistic goal for availability of drugs given the available budget and the historic data on procurement and delivery lead times. The simulations show that with the doubled budget, availability can be increased only to a level of 62 percent, assuming no other logistics parameter is changed. However, if the project can modify the way drugs are procured and delivered, thereby obtaining more predictable lead times for the high-volume items, the availability level can go up to 75 percent with the increased budget because the need for buffer stocks decrease.

The responsible administration, therefore, sets the goal for the project in year 1 at 60 percent availability and coordinates with the procurement unit of the ministry and the central medical store to work in parallel to modify procurement procedures, inventory management techniques, and supplier contracts to make lead times more predictable.

Source: Author.

need to be repeated for monitoring purposes. In addition, the facility's staff may notice the survey taking place, and that information may influence their behavior.

A key factor to being able to access performance data when needed to plan policy measures or monitor implementation is the design of business processes that automatically generate data. For example, inventory management systems help manage supply chains in industries selling to retail customers. These systems record the movement of goods from one place to another and update the inventory data accordingly. At the end of each working day, the responsible manager can read stock levels at all warehouses and retail outlets and plan the dispatch of goods to restock as needed. Variations of such systems exist in countries where mobile phone networks provide the backbone of connectivity; thus, no technological reason exists for not using such a system in most low-income countries.

With a paper-based system, weeks may be needed to collect all the information; hence, by the time it is centrally available to decision makers, it is already outdated. Retrospectively looking at time series of data is very labor intensive, and data quality frequently is inconsistent from one place to another. Therefore, in reality, decisions often have to be made without access to useful and credible data.

The dominant sources of data on drug expenditure and use in middle-income and high-income countries are health insurance databases. As pointed out in chapter 4, all relevant data can be collected at the point of delivery, where the patient hands over the prescription to the pharmacist and receives the drug. In large markets, these transaction-based systems create huge amounts of data on a daily basis. Such data require a data warehouse and significant processing capacity to produce meaningful reports on relevant trends and outliers. However, the investment in hardware, software, and human resources needed to manage and use these data is still economical compared to the potential savings achieved by better control of fraud, errors, and system abuse.

Data on regulatory performance can be obtained from systems for drug registration and administration of drug licenses. The World Health Organization provides guidance for countries that want to upgrade their systems to make use of available technology. Data provided by such a system include, for example, the average time from acceptance of a dossier to issuing of the license. Other data that regulators typically provide are number and outcome of GMP inspections, data on regulatory actions against license holders in violation of rules and standards, and data on test results in national drug control laboratories. Most low- and many middle-income countries do not yet have capacity to introduce comprehensive pharmacovigilance systems or monitor drugs in circulation to identify illegal imports, counterfeits, and substandard drugs. Obtaining meaningful data in this important area should be a high priority for collaboration between donors and regulatory authorities in the countries that are most exposed to these problems. The costs and efforts are significant, because specific sampling, testing, and reporting protocols must be applied, and the necessary know-how may not be locally available. Without access to such data, however, a core element of successful policy is missing: trust in the authorities that are charged with protecting the integrity of pharmaceutical products and the health of a country's citizens.

The appendixes of this book provide tools that generate data (on performance of procurement agencies) or point toward typical sources of data that can be used to guide policy decision and implementation. The World

Health Organization and other technical agencies or consultant firms provide additional tools for policy makers (for example, Management Sciences for Health's [1997] *Managing Drug Supply* handbook).

References

Management Sciences for Health. 1997. *Managing Drug Supply*. 2nd ed. West Hartford, CT: Kumarian Press.

OECD (Organisation for Economic Co-operation and Development). 2008. *OECD Health Policy Studies: Pharmaceutical Pricing Policies in a Global Market*. Paris: OECD Publishing.

Roberts, Marc, and Michael Reich. 2010. "Pharmaceutical Reform: A Guide to Improving Performance and Equity." Harvard School of Public Health, Cambridge, MA.

CHAPTER 2

Introducing the Stakeholders

Many different actors populate what is known as the *pharmaceutical sector*. In an unregulated environment—for example, the United States before establishment of the U.S. Food and Drug Administration (FDA) or today's postconflict countries with shattered institutions—patients' need for some sort of cure for their ailments stimulates the emergence of a private sector, which initially consists of small businesses that make or import and sell drugs to satisfy the demand. In the preindustrial period, doctors, healers, chemists, or pharmacists compounded drugs in small labs on the basis of either available expertise or a "secret formula" gleaned from anecdotal evidence or the maker's belief system. Lack of reproducible efficacy and occurrence of dangerous or even fatal side effects finally lead to the creation of formal regulatory structures.[1]

Today, in postconflict countries, most drugs sold on the private market are imported from industrial countries—although with no assurance of authenticity or quality. The private sector establishes structures necessary to ensure supplies of drugs, such as importers, distributors and wholesalers, and retailers. If a manufacturing industry exists, it may try to compete with imports. However, it will have to import raw materials, which could put it at a financial disadvantage vis-à-vis importers of finished drugs. Such a situation is not conducive to maintaining high quality standards in the local manufacturing process. Depending on the conditions for running businesses and the topography of the country, the various supply-chain elements in the private sector are fully or partially integrated within single enterprises or, more typically, develop as independent businesses that interact with each other in buyer-seller relationships.

Once a regulatory function is formally set up, it creates barriers for market participants and products in the form of licensing requirements. These barriers put pressure on manufacturers and importers to build capacity for dealing with the product licensing requirements, resulting in a more structured private sector at that level. Physicians and pharmacists are recruited for expert commissions and as consultants to advise both sides of the regulatory process.

With the growing overall capacity of a country's government, the ministry of health (MOH) begins implementing service delivery programs that require supplies of commodities. The donor community increases its presence and switches from providing direct relief to giving financial support to public sector, nongovernmental organization (NGO), and private sector health projects. The need for organized procurement, warehousing, and delivery of drugs to a growing number of health facilities leads to the establishment of a new institution that combines these functions, frequently called the *central medical store*. Alternatively, if private sector capacity exists, the supply-chain functions can be contracted out. This option requires a public entity able to draft, monitor, and enforce contracts.

Once public procurement begins, international brokers and procurement agents may enter the field. Domestic private importers and manufacturers develop interfaces to do business with public buyers. Public sector drug supplies through public providers typically coexist with a private market for drugs for a long period during a country's development process, with patients using either one or both systems, depending on availability of affordable drugs, proximity to facilities, cash on hand, convenience factors such as waiting times, quality perceptions, and other factors.

In the transition from lower- to higher-middle-income levels, many countries introduce some form of reimbursement system enabling patients to use private health care providers without having to pay cash for the entire treatment. The typical vehicle for third-party financing is an insurance fund, which soon after its inception must define a reimbursement policy for drugs that prevents abuse and fraud and ensures cost-effective use of resources. In high-income countries, this management of the "drug benefit" part of an insurance package has become a service industry of its own, allowing multiple insurance companies or funds to pool their purchasing power and reduce administrative costs.

Figure 2.1 illustrates how the various functions of the pharmaceutical sector evolve when a country goes through the development process.

The following sections introduce the individual stakeholders in more detail and highlight their particular perspectives and incentives within the overall pharmaceutical sector.

Multinational Research-Based Companies

The large, global pharmaceutical companies that dominate the sector in terms of sales and market capitalization have their roots in the late 19th century, when their founders, usually pharmacists or chemists,

Figure 2.1   Evolution of the Pharmaceutical Sector in Countries of Different Income Levels

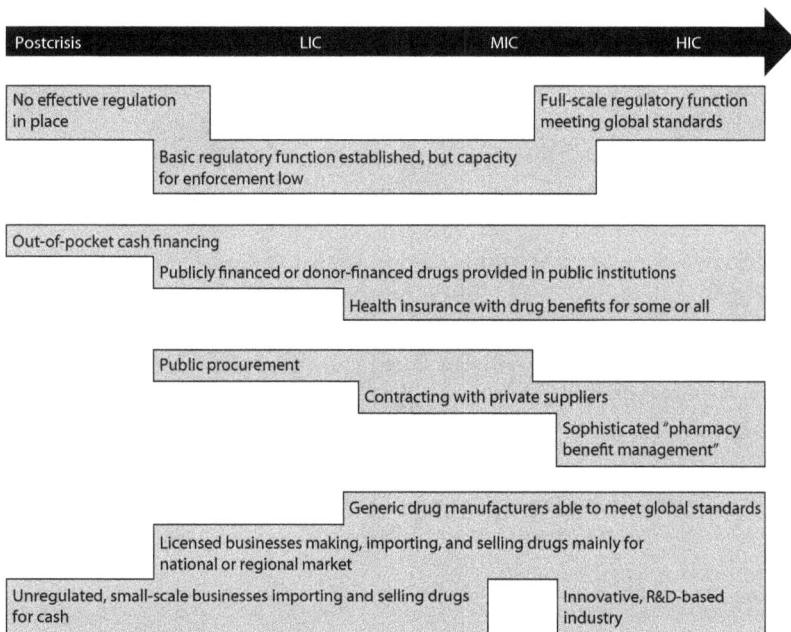

Source: Author's representation.
Note: LIC = low-income country; MIC = middle-income country; HIC = high-income country; R&D = research and development.

began industrial production of synthetic drugs. Most of these drugs were derived from herbal extracts with defined therapeutic activities. Advances in chemistry and later in information technology and robotics led to a multifold increase in research productivity for the labs of drug companies, which over time developed thousands of medicines, many of which are still available today even though the originator company may have disappeared and the original brand has been replaced by generic copies.

Clearly, pharmaceutical innovation, led by for-profit companies, has saved millions of lives and contributed significantly to the growth in life expectancy over the past century. The World Health Organization (WHO) recognizes through its "essential medicines" concept that a significant number of drugs are indispensible for adequately treating a wide range of life-threatening or debilitating diseases even under the most difficult economic conditions.

The costs for discovering, developing, and marketing new drugs are high, although critics sometimes question the numbers provided by industry sources, which go as high as US$2 billion (Masia 2006) for a new chemical entity.[2] However, there is no question that research productivity—that is, the relationship between investment in research and development (R&D) and output of successful new products—has been declining steadily in recent decades. Therefore, new drugs need to provide higher profits for the originator company to ensure long-term financial sustainability, which in turn leads to higher prices for new drugs.

No final consensus on the reasons for the decline in research productivity appears to exist, although a number of factors are likely to play a role:

- Increasing regulatory sophistication leads to higher barriers for market entry, making the studies necessary to provide all the documentation required more difficult, lengthy, and expensive to conduct.
- Certain therapeutic segments that have generated "blockbuster" products in the past now seem saturated (for example, duodenal ulcer, high blood pressure). Existing treatments are so successful that only marginal improvements are thought possible.
- New trends in biology pointing toward more individualized medicine may collide with the need to sell large volumes of identical treatments to recoup R&D expenses.

The business model of R&D-based pharmaceutical companies requires regular launch of patent-protected, innovative drugs that will have a monopolistic market position for about 10 years[3] (potentially longer for biologicals), during which they can command relatively high prices and margins and make enough money to finance operations and R&D for the next generation of compounds. When the patent expires, the market share and pricing power of the originator decline rapidly, faced with generic competitors who are able to sell their versions of the drug at much lower prices. Typically, the manufacturing costs for an innovative drug account for only a small percentage of the price. Thus, generic companies can still be profitable at prices that are only a fraction of the patented originator's price. With the entry of generic drugs, the originator has two choices: (a) keep the high price and lose almost all sales, or (b) reduce the price to a level at which the product is still competitive and can maintain some market share. In many markets, regulation limits these choices, forcing the manufacturer to cut the price.

If the research pipeline dries out, R&D-based companies, most of which are publicly traded, become vulnerable. Share prices are based on expectations of future profits and can drop long before a company's financial bottom line deteriorates. The ongoing consolidation of the industry through multiple waves of mergers and acquisitions is a symptom of the innovation crisis, at the end of which only a few survivors may still be able to afford large investments in R&D.

The lack of in-house research successes also leads to increased reliance on smaller biotech companies as providers of innovative compounds for the large firms that have the skills and resources to develop, register, and market these compounds. This system may reduce fixed costs for the big companies, but it also reduces profitability for new drugs because the inventor of the molecule demands license payments.

The limited time window available to earn back R&D expenses with a new drug causes drug companies to invest heavily in marketing and promotion. The marketing effort typically starts with medical education programs, which create awareness about the disease that a new drug addresses and introduce the new treatment option. In many countries, drug companies are the only providers of continuing medical education, which explains why physicians frequently appear biased toward the most recently introduced and expensive treatment options. Advertising, promotional gifts, regular visits by salespeople, free samples, invitations to conferences, and other tools are used with high levels of sophistication and clearly demonstrated effects. Most chief executive officers of large pharmaceutical companies started their careers in sales and marketing and were promoted because of their commercial success. Most international companies have pledged to follow the International Federation of Pharmaceutical Manufacturers & Associations' Code of Pharmaceutical Marketing Practices, but enforcement is difficult. In many countries, unethical practices, including bribery in various forms, are still reported as fairly common, although to what extent such practices are effective tools for building market share is not clear, even to industry insiders.

None of the pharmaceutical companies based in emerging markets has thus far been successful in rising into the ranks of the 20 largest multinationals. The largest drug companies in China have annual sales of less than US$5 billion;[4] the largest Indian manufacturer has about US$1.5 billion in sales, only a fraction of the sales of the global top 10 (see table 2.1).[5] Barriers to entry in the global market are high. Even if, for example, an Indian company discovered a breakthrough treatment that addressed a major medical need, it might not have the know-how and resources to manage a complex global development and registration process. Neither would it be able to organize the successful, parallel product launches in all major markets needed to fully realize the commercial potential of such a drug. The logical step would be a partnership with one of the existing pharmaceutical giants. In the longer run, provided that consolidation also continues in the generics industry, some of the Chinese or Indian companies might reach a size at which they could merge with or buy a majority share in a struggling multinational, eventually securing a position among the industry leaders.

Table 2.1   Top-10 Pharmaceutical Companies by Sales, 2008

Rank	Company	Pharmaceutical sales (US$ million)
1	Pfizer	44,174
2	Sanofi-Aventis	40,562
3	GlaxoSmithKline	37,810
4	Novartis	33,888
5	Roche	33,316
6	AstraZeneca	31,601
7	Johnson & Johnson	24,567
8	Merck	23,620
9	Lilly	19,285
10	Wyeth	19,025

Source: Scrip 100, http://www.scrip100.com/scrip_100_list.

Multinational R&D-based companies are, despite the erosion of their business model, financially strong and politically savvy. The following drivers of their profitability generally dictate their political agenda:

- Securing sufficient financing for drugs
- Maintaining strong intellectual property protection in key markets
- Keeping high regulatory barriers that delay the entry of generics
- Protecting their pricing power (absence of price regulation or price transparency)
- Obtaining market access for new drugs (limiting the effect of formal or informal cost-containment strategies)

For individual companies, the lobbying agenda may differ depending on their product portfolio. A company that has a new drug with a very convincing pharmacoeconomic value proposition may favor a value-based selection mechanism for inclusion of new drugs in reimbursement lists, although the general industry position does not necessarily support such selection criteria.

U.S.- and Europe-based major drug companies are politically well connected and have a record of successful lobbying for their goals. They are major donors to political campaigns in the United States. Their executives participate in official visits to discuss trade issues with international counterparts. They work through business associations and trade representatives in foreign countries to lobby for stronger patent protection and against pricing restrictions or market-access hurdles. Citizens (and consequently politicians) in developed countries value the contribution of the pharmaceutical industry in further advancing health care, developing cures for illnesses that cannot be treated successfully, and providing qualified individuals with well-paying jobs that support the local economy. As a consequence, the research-based pharmaceutical industry has shown that it has significant influence on pharmaceutical policy decisions in high-income and larger middle-income countries, and it is likely to remain a force to reckon with for politicians who want to reform pharmaceutical policies in their countries.

For multinational R&D-based companies, alleged misbehavior in developing countries can turn into a serious public image problem in their home markets. In 2001, after a large international media backlash sent shockwaves of public outrage into boardrooms, a group of 39 companies dropped a lawsuit against the South African government that was aimed at preventing the import of cheap generic AIDS drugs (United Nations

Foundation 2001). Repeated investigational reports and books detailing excessive marketing practices temporarily weakened political support for the industry. To reestablish a positive public image, the industry has, in recent years, started to rethink its business model for low-income countries. It has begun devoting substantial resources to expanding access to drugs and is trying to become a partner in addressing the health care challenges in these countries. For example:

- Companies have increased their investment in "good corporate citizenship" projects, including research focused on diseases of the poor, and are sharing intellectual property for neglected tropical diseases.
- They now provide certain drugs free of cost.
- They are building research facilities and capabilities in developing countries.
- They have developed flexible pricing and licensing schemes for drugs that are needed to fight major diseases in developing countries.
- They now subscribe to self-regulation in form of a marketing code.
- They disclose all clinical trials.

Health care reform in the United States, one of the key items on the 2010 agenda of the U.S. administration, could significantly affect the profitability of the R&D-based industry in that country. Given the high per capita costs of care in the United States compared to other countries, drug-related expenses may be an easy target for cost-containment measures. However, improving access for the previously uninsured population through some sort of public subsidy may benefit drug companies by extending their client base: many U.S. citizens have not been able to afford the drugs that would benefit them from an evidence-based medicine viewpoint. Whatever the outcome of the U.S. reform effort, the emerging economies—in particular the bigger ones—will become even more important for future growth of the industry, and lobbying pressure on the governments of those countries is likely to keep growing.

Multinational Generics Companies

Like their R&D-based peers, the top 10 global generics companies (by sales) are headquartered in high-income countries, although major Indian manufacturers such as Cipla are close followers and may rise in the ranks if they keep up their double-digit growth rates of previous years. Some of the leading generics companies, such as Sandoz and Ranbaxy, are owned by multinationals (Novartis and Daiichi Sankyo, respectively). So far, none of the major generics companies has a strong presence in all major markets. They all have certain regional areas of strength and weakness. On a global scale, overcapacity exists in manufacturing of standard dosage forms (tablets and capsules). Together with increasing competition in the generics market caused by reduction of trade barriers and convergence of cost-containment policies, this excess capacity is likely to lead to further consolidation of the industry.

The first generic that enters the market after an originator's patent expires usually get the highest market share and can maintain a higher price relative to later market entrants. Therefore, generics companies compete to be the first to launch a new product in developed markets. In some markets, a so-called Bolar provision in the patent law allows manufacturers of generic drugs to prepare and submit their registration files for a new drug while the patent is still active. In this case, they may be able to launch their generic version immediately after the originator's patent expires.[6]

The business model of relying on relative pricing power for newly introduced generics is vulnerable to strategies introduced by payers and providers with large buying power in high-income countries. These payers and providers offer generics companies a dominant market share in exchange for a low price. Some of these models work through direct contracting (for example, when a big hospital chain procures drugs for its in-house needs). Others include discriminatory co-payments for patients if they deviate from the default choice. For example, in Germany, patients have to pay €5 out of pocket for a prescription; however, if they accept a generic priced significantly below the market average under a contractual agreement between their insurance fund and the manufacturer, the co-payment is waived.

High-volume drugs attract many generics manufacturers, creating a situation in which the supply chain of wholesalers and retail pharmacies is overwhelmed by the multitude of equivalent options. To save costs, wholesalers and retailers carry only a fraction of the available products, which they select on the basis of demand from prescribers or patients and their own profitability considerations. Unless manufacturers of generics can secure their market share through price-volume agreements with payers or convincing marketing strategies for prescribers, they are frequently squeezed by wholesalers and retail pharmacists for higher margins or informal bonuses (typically provided in the form of free goods or favorable payment terms) in exchange for carrying and recommending their brands. In any case, the trend in the major generics markets is toward higher competitive pressure, which should lead to further consolidation of an industry that is still fragmented compared with other price-driven commodity industries.

Some generic drug companies make their own active pharmaceutical ingredients (APIs).[7] This backward integration of the business model increases in-house value creation and profitability, assuming that a company has sufficient economies of scale. However, almost all generic drug companies (and the R&D-based multinational companies) buy at least some of the APIs they need from other companies. Leading countries for the manufacture of APIs are Italy and, with growing market share, India and China (Bumpas and Betsch 2009). Pure API manufacturers are not stakeholders per se in the pharmaceutical sector, although those that sell to manufacturers in developed countries interact with regulators to obtain the so-called Drug Master File, a document used in the registration process to prove the origin and quality of the API. However, the separation of the API industry from the pharmaceutical manufacturers who put their labels on drug packages for sale creates a potential for quality problems, particularly in the case of smaller companies with limited ability to verify quality at the source of their APIs.

Some of the smaller generics companies, many of them based in China and India, focus on supplying developing markets rather than trying to compete in the large developed markets. Success factors in developing markets are, in addition to competitive prices, local knowledge and relationships with local buyers or decision makers. Quality requirements may be less stringent than in developed markets; in some cases, there is no quality control whatsoever, particularly in the private sector. Business risks include low payment discipline; bureaucratic hurdles and inefficiencies; corruption in the form of bribes, kickbacks, or other favors required to secure a business deal; and losses during transport or storage for which the supplier is responsible. These risk factors can be a deterrent for manufacturers when they consider entering a certain market or bidding for a public tender.

The political influence of generics manufacturers on an international scale and in major developed markets is significantly lower than that of their R&D-based peers. Over two decades of attempted cost control in the pharmaceutical sector, generics companies have benefited from measures that targeted mainly the originators, which was a disincentive for them to build similar lobbying resources. Given the commodity nature of their product, price has become the main parameter for differentiation, at least in strictly regulated markets with consistent enforcement of quality standards. Thus, the importance of the industry for developed economies is limited, which influences company bottom lines and forces the industry to keep overheads low, precluding it from buying political influence as the R&D-based companies do.

Lobbying goals of representatives of the generics industry are directed at patent rights, where they try to fight the originators' claims in favor of stronger intellectual property protection. The generics industry may also mobilize against attempts to introduce stronger price competition and increase market transparency for buyers.

National Generics Companies

Many smaller generics drug companies do business only on a national scale in their home country, sometimes even limited to a certain region within a country. Some of these companies operate with higher costs and lower quality standards than the global leaders. These companies typically buy their APIs from foreign sources and may find assessing the quality of the APIs difficult. Quality problems can also arise from poor packaging and use of insufficiently controlled excipients (inactive ingredients), as a tragic chain of events in Panama showed some years ago (see box 2.1).

Cost disadvantages for smaller national manufacturers can be attributed to limited volumes, insufficient purchasing power to secure good prices

---

Box 2.1

A Tragedy in Panama, Caused by a Toxic Ingredient in Cough Syrup

In 2006, cough syrup made by a government-owned facility in Panama killed more than 100 people (families reported 365 deaths but causal relationship to the syrup could not be established in all cases). The tragedy was caused by a mislabeled ingredient: through a chain of traders in Beijing, China; Barcelona, Spain; and Colón, Panama, a supplier from the Yangtze delta in China had shipped cheap, toxic diethylene glycol instead of glycerin. The manufacturer's quality control system should have spotted the toxic ingredient and rejected the shipment. It apparently failed to do so, and 260,000 bottles of cough syrup with the toxic ingredient were made and sold to Panamanian citizens.

Source: Bogdanich and Hooker 2007.

from suppliers of raw materials and APIs, bureaucratic hurdles, high taxes on imported equipment and raw materials, corruption, lack of access to financing, and other reasons related to the general business environment or specific parameters relevant for the pharmaceutical industry. However, in low- and middle-income countries with high unemployment rates and low attractiveness for investment in growth industries, protectionist policies are sometimes in place that allow such companies to charge higher prices, tolerate lower quality standards, provide direct subsidies, or create market-access barriers for international competitors. Strategic considerations might also override economic arguments: some governments want to preserve the possibility of procuring a range of essential drugs within the country (although most APIs would need to be imported because only few national drug manufacturers outside the big API-exporting countries have the capacity to make a limited range of APIs).

The political influence of local manufacturers can be significant, even if the industry is small by international standards. In some countries, political and economic conflicts of interest are prevalent: because of the high level of regulation, this sector is susceptible to corruption or influence peddling. Licenses to run drug businesses may be given to family members of politicians or used to create political allies. The lobbying of industry representatives is likely to be directed at maintaining a level of protectionism necessary to defend the home market against global competition.

These negative examples should not overshadow the fact that many national drug companies are well-run, honest businesses with high quality standards and good customer service. In many cases, they fill gaps in the public provision of drugs and contribute to access to medicines at least for the part of the population that can afford to buy drugs out of pocket. They may operate their own distribution networks and are potential partners for outsourcing the responsibilities of dysfunctional public sector supply chains. The local market knowledge of national drug companies makes them attractive targets for acquisitions or partnerships with international players. In the longer run, many of these companies can be expected to become parts of larger, regionally or globally operating groups.

Brokers

The term *brokers* is used here to describe traders specialized in selling drugs from smaller, unknown manufacturers to buyers with limited reach and purchasing power, such as procurement agencies of low-income countries. They play a little-known role in the international pharmaceutical trade and operate without meaningful regulatory oversight, from free trade zones or in countries such as the United Kingdom, where the national regulator does not control businesses that import drugs for the sole purpose of exporting them again. Brokers know the procedures of international procurement and the weaknesses of procurement systems in some low-income countries. They may bid for tenders shunned by other, more established suppliers and collaborate with small contract manufacturers that alone would not be able to put a bid together. Unfortunately, some reports (Forzley 2008) indicate that such brokers have provided documentation that appeared to be forged, shipped product that did not match the documentation provided with the bid, or relabeled drug packages in their warehouse (which would require a manufacturing license). Given their questionable business practices, most brokers keep a low profile and do not engage in political lobbying. However, one can reasonably assume that brokers use corrupt practices such as paying kickbacks to procurement officers or higher-level decision makers to secure their business.

Procurement Agents

Procurement agents are for-profit or not-for-profit intermediaries that bundle demand from smaller-scale or low-capacity buyers and provide a range of services, such as quality assurance, forecasting assistance, and logistics support. They are mainly used by public sector or NGO (institutional) buyers and fulfill a similar function as wholesalers in the private sector. The buyer can hire procurement agents in a consulting function (for example, to organize a specific procurement). They can also appear as bidders in a tender (like wholesalers), which can create an insider problem if the same procurement agent is involved in several parallel procurement processes in different roles. Procurement agents usually charge a percentage of the contract volume as overhead, but in some cases, a fee-for-service model is possible.

Procurement agents can be nationally oriented only (for example, the Tamil Nadu Medical Services Corporation in India) or work on an international basis (for example, Crown Agents, IDA Foundation, and Missionpharma). Some of the international procurement agencies offer consulting services as well, which gives them significant influence on policy decisions related to procurement regulation and practices. They also play a role in benchmarking prices of high-volume drugs, because some of them publish their prices either in a general form (price list) or based on specific tenders.

WHO developed a Model Quality Assurance System for procurement agencies that the World Bank used to create an assessment tool for pre-qualifying a procurement agency in India (WHO 2007). This tool is provided in appendix A.

Importers and Agents

Importers are private sector intermediaries that specialize in selling products manufactured in other countries to buyers in their country of residence. Their clients are typically wholesaler-distributors or larger institutional buyers such as hospitals, but they may also include retail pharmacies. Sometimes importers are integrated with national wholesale and distribution companies. Their special skills are in the area of handling import and customs procedures, registration, and marketing on behalf of the product manufacturer. Sometimes importers are also referred to as *agents*. Importers or agents may have exclusive distribution rights for certain branded products or a portfolio of products from one manufacturer, defined in a contract with this manufacturer and usually leading to higher pricing power. Exclusive agents may also have legal responsibility for safety issues with respect to the drugs they import. Depending on the national legislation, such exclusivity may not be fully enforceable if a competitor is able to open a parallel import channel, for example, by buying the drugs from a wholesaler in another country rather than from the manufacturer directly.

An importer or agent with exclusive distribution rights to a particular drug is usually also in charge of marketing and sales in the covered territory. For this purpose, importers may maintain a sales organization similar to those used by national subsidiaries of multinational companies. An international or regional marketing department of the manufacturer usually provides marketing support (promotion materials, training, and strategic guidance).

Importers, in particular those that represent multinational companies, usually have considerable resources and can be politically influential. Their lobbying interests will mostly be in line with those of the companies represented, focusing on patent protection, access to market and reimbursement, and suppression of competition from generics manufacturers. In addition, importers may try to block attempts from institutional buyers to establish parallel imports or may make deals directly with the manufacturer to get lower prices.

Wholesalers

Wholesalers are intermediaries that buy drugs from manufacturers, importers, or higher-level wholesalers and sell them to lower-level wholesalers, hospitals, or retail pharmacies. In high-income countries, the traditional wholesale model has given way to large logistics companies covering the entire distribution chain from manufacturer to retailer. These companies do not own their stock anymore (it remains in the possession of the manufacturer until it is sold at the retail level). Their business model is based on distributing for a fee. Large-scale and highly efficient logistics systems allow these distributors to operate profitably on small single-digit margins. Large markets such as France and Germany may have only a handful of pharmaceutical logistics companies, which are national subsidiaries of internationally operating corporations.

In developing markets, the wholesale sector follows the traditional model (buying and reselling) and is typically rather fragmented. In the absence of efficiently operating national players, setting up a pharmaceutical wholesale business is relatively simple, and profits are higher than in other trades. The business model of small wholesalers is usually built around personal relationships with a group of local or regional customers, who do not have the resources or competence to organize truly competitive procurement. In many cases, although hard to prove, personal links, clan or family associations, political alliances, or financial incentives may influence purchasing decisions and sustain business relationships even if they are not economically efficient.

Small, regionally operating wholesalers are not competitive in terms of operating costs once markets become more transparent and larger, better organized players enter the territory. Rapid consolidation through mergers and acquisitions is the logical consequence.

Sometimes governments introduce policy measures trying to cap drug prices through regulated maximum price or reimbursement levels for multisource drugs.[8] Such policies eliminate incentives for price competition and may put wholesalers into the role of "market makers" because they have limited capacity and can decide which brands they carry. Rather than lowering prices, manufacturers try to grow market share by crowding out competitor brands: they offer wholesalers generous payment terms or a bonus in the form of free drugs so that their brand is available everywhere whereas competitors' brands are not. Such policies increase the real profit margin for wholesalers (and retailers, who usually share the bonus with the wholesalers) and slow down the consolidation process.

Some wholesalers integrate forward or backward, or both, into manufacturing and retail sales to capture a larger share of the sector's value chain. The scope of possible vertical integration is defined by national legislation.

Wholesalers usually have limited political visibility and influence because the value they add in the supply chain is limited primarily to a logistics function. Consolidation in the subsector happens relatively quickly when the overall market conditions change.

Central Medical Stores

Central medical store is a generic term used for public or parastatal agencies that combine forecasting, planning, and warehousing functions, as well as procurement and distribution in some cases. The specific agencies may have different names and abbreviations in different countries (for example, Pharmaceutical Fund and Supply Agency or PFSA in Ethiopia, Central Medical Store or CMS in Ghana, Kenya Medical Supplies Agency or KEMSA in Kenya, and National Drug Service or NDS in Liberia). These agencies serve primarily or exclusively the public sector and usually exist only in low- and middle-income countries with publicly run health systems. The category includes regional subsidiaries, which might be called regional medical stores or depots. These subsidiaries might be managed by the CMS, or they might be managed by a regional administration but logistically connected with the CMS.

Most CMSs serve a range of upstream clients, which include the national government (usually the MOH); bilateral donors that sponsor treatment programs; the Global Fund to Fight AIDS, Tuberculosis, and Malaria; the United Nations Children's Fund (UNICEF); the Global Alliance for Vaccines and Immunization; and other donors and agencies that need a place to store drugs and infrastructure to distribute them to health service providers. The resources available to the people working at a CMS often do not match the complexity of tasks and processes for which they are responsible. Restrictive public sector human resource policies may limit the ability to hire, retain, and motivate highly qualified staff. Lack of accountability within the public sector supply chain can lead to low payment discipline and consequent low service quality. A combination of lack of resources and the systematic weaknesses of the CMS management model leads to frequent stock-outs of essential drugs in many countries. As a result, there is widespread dissatisfaction with the traditional CMS model. A recent study by the World Bank in a number of countries that tried to introduce some private sector management principles into their public supply chain found that significant improvements in performance are possible if CMS management gets more autonomy, can control its own resources, becomes exposed to competition, and is held accountable for results (World Bank forthcoming a).

Unfortunately, CMSs have been associated with corruption and political favoritism in some countries, which also sometimes limits options or political will to address obvious performance problems.

Retail Pharmacists and Drug Sellers

At the retail level, drugs are dispensed to patients, usually as an over-the-counter (OTC) transaction in which money changes hands or with indirect payment from a third-party payer (health insurance) against a documented prescription and sales receipt. Depending on legislation and enforcement in a given country, drugs can be obtained from retail pharmacy shops or chain pharmacy outlets, licensed drug sellers, dispensaries in hospitals and clinics, dispensing physicians or nurse practitioners, or informal drug sellers. Nonpharmacist drug sellers, even if licensed, are usually not allowed to sell prescription drugs, with some exemptions that are justified by public health priorities. Pharmacists in most countries can legally dispense prescription drugs only when a prescription from a physician or licensed nurse practitioner (depending on the country) is presented. However, in most low- and middle-income countries, this rule cannot be enforced effectively, and prescription drugs (with the likely exception of controlled drugs such as narcotics and psychotropics) are routinely available over the counter for cash. Given the shortage of qualified physicians and nurses providing primary care, pharmacists are de facto primary care providers for patients who are not able or willing to make the trip to the health center or doctor's office. This situation raises the question whether such a role could be more formally recognized and backed up by specific training. In the United States, for example, discussions are ongoing to define a category of "behind-the-counter" drugs that can be dispensed by a pharmacist without prescription on the basis of a simple diagnostic protocol. Whether such a category makes sense in other countries depends on the regulations for OTC drugs: in the United States, these drugs are displayed openly on the shelves of drugstores and supermarkets, whereas in many other countries, their sale is already restricted to licensed pharmacies.

Pharmacists make money by selling drugs, usually on the basis of a percentage margin that is regulated. The margin sometimes is structured regressively, allowing a higher percentage for low-price drugs than for higher-price drugs. In some developed markets, flat compensation for pharmacists per prescription or dispensed drug has replaced the margin system, neutralizing any incentive to dispense expensive drugs (for prescription drugs only—OTC drugs are still sold with a margin).

In the presence of a prescription, the pharmacist can, in some countries, decide which brand of several equivalent products is dispensed to the patient (*substitution right*). In other countries, he or she has to dispense the brand prescribed by the physician. Giving pharmacists substitution rights is an element in a generic drug policy, particularly if the profit for the pharmacist is not linked to the drug price.

Prescribers

Prescribers are usually physicians; in some countries, nurse practitioners or other health workers are also licensed to issue prescriptions for drugs that cannot be legally obtained without prescription. Prescribers, because of their exclusive role in the selection of drugs that are then purchased by the patient or paid for by a reimbursement system, are a key target for all interventions aimed at influencing drug use. The individual prescribing decision is based on several possible factors, such as professional education and training, personal experience, perceptions of quality or effectiveness, peer influence, patient wishes, advertising and promotion, knowledge about availability of drugs at the pharmacy where the patient fills the prescription, and affordability considerations. In countries that do not have an established and independent system for continuing medical education, often drug companies are the only provider of such education; therefore, such companies tend to have a strong influence on prescriber knowledge, perceptions, and attitudes.

If physicians are self-dispensing or work for an institution that partially relies on drug sales for financing, their prescription behavior is likely to reflect the financial incentive. Self-dispensing physicians usually cause higher drug expenditure per capita than their peers without dispensing rights (Huang and others 2005); the same is true if doctors' incomes are linked to drug sales, as is still the case in most clinics and hospitals in China (World Bank forthcoming b).

Prescribing physicians are a challenging stakeholder group for policy makers, because such physicians are usually well organized through associations and sometimes vocal in their criticism of all measures that restrict their freedom to prescribe whatever they consider best for the patient or even monitor their prescribing behavior. In some countries, physicians associations have used media campaigns to discredit government efforts to introduce cost-containment measures targeting irrational prescribing habits or restricting reimbursement of certain drugs considered less cost-effective. In some instances, interests of drug manufacturers are aligned with the interests of doctors who benefit from partnerships with such manufacturers (for example, as investigators in clinical trials or speakers at industry-sponsored seminars). Because physicians have higher credibility with politicians and the public than do company spokespersons, industry marketing executives routinely try to win over physicians to promote their corporate interests.

Consumers

Consumers fall into two categories: (a) patients and their relatives, who are confronted with a particular health condition that requires treatment, and (b) healthy citizens who look at the health system as something they hope to not have to use any time soon. For the first group, regaining their own health or the health of a loved one may be the highest priority, and their demands on the system do not respect financial limits. For the second group, spending on health is usually not something they prioritize, meaning they might sympathize more with messages about cost-effectiveness.

Health issues are emotional, and interest groups tend to use heart-breaking stories of individuals with severe conditions to create public support for their goals. For example, take the case where a neutral scientific body assesses a new, extremely expensive treatment for a rare form of kidney cancer as too costly to be included in a basic treatment package provided free under an existing health insurance scheme. The manufacturer may nevertheless try to garner support from the specialists treating this condition and from a patients' organization (sometimes even founded specifically for this purpose with support from a drug company). It may launch a public relations campaign that highlights individual cases of people whose hope is pinned on the treatment in question. Public outrage at the cruel logic of health economics then may sweep away the rational decision and ensure that the treatment is covered—even if such coverage means that funding will be insufficient for other treatments, which perhaps could save 10 times as many lives for the same amount of money.

Most education systems fail to provide the general population with basic knowledge about medicines and drug treatment, so in many countries a naive belief in the possibilities of drug treatment persists, along with a "more is better" attitude. Patients may expect a doctor to prescribe three or four drugs per visit. Injections are viewed as more powerful, even if there is no rational basis for this belief, and in fact, the rate of potential complications is much higher than for oral treatment. Such perceptions influence physicians' behavior as well; a physician who resists a patient's irrational expectation may fear losing the patient to another doctor.

The difference in attitudes between patients and healthy citizens has been quite visible in the debate about health reform in the United States in 2009. On one side, some parts of society resist plans to introduce an obligation to buy health insurance as a violation of their individual freedom. On the other side, those who are ill and suffering from crippling out-of-pocket expenses for drugs and medical procedures have a strong interest in broadening the basis for solidarity and ending a practice in which the insured subsidize the costs incurred for emergency room visits of the uninsured. (Emergency rooms in the United States cannot turn away patients even if the patient may not be able to pay for the treatment.)

Traditional consumer groups, advocating for consumer rights and protection as a counterweight to the various industries trying to sell products or services to consumers, usually do not choose the pharmaceutical sector as a primary target. This outcome may be thanks to the agent role of the physician, who is supposed to choose on behalf and in the best interest of the consumer. Given the individual patient-doctor relationship, physicians are usually not targeted for organized consumer advocacy.

Public Policy Makers: Legislative and Executive

On the executive side, the main policy-making entity is usually the MOH. Sometimes, other ministries that are in charge of social security, science and technology, or industrial development have complementary or overlapping responsibilities.

In a parliamentary democracy, legislative proposals are drafted either by one of the ministries or by parliamentarians. On the legislative side, a health commission, usually formed by the parliament, reviews draft legislation, discusses it, and modifies it according to the political balance before the parliament passes the legislation and it becomes effective.

Ministers issue orders, bylaws, or regulations that interpret the law and provide more detailed guidance for enforcement by regulatory agencies. Various departments of the ministries involved are responsible for the different aspects of drug policy and implementation. In many low- and middle-income countries, these departments are relatively small and not very well funded, limiting their effectiveness and contributing to high turnover in leadership positions because drug policy issues regularly come up as hot topics during elections.

The political significance of drug policy leads in some cases to an elevation of policy dilemmas to the level of the head of government or a supraministerial body such as a council of ministers, because the MOH alone may not have a strong enough position to deal with the challenges posed by the sector.

Regulatory and Executive Agencies

Although in some countries all regulatory and executive functions still remain within the MOH, the majority have created separate, independent regulatory agencies for the pharmaceutical sector. The rationale for creating such agencies is the need to ensure consistency, political independence, and technical capacity for the regulatory function in a way that is difficult to achieve within a ministry. Ministers and ministerial department heads come and go with political change. Public sector compensation rules, which may be binding for ministerial bureaucracies, may not be attractive enough to hire and retain the experts needed in a drug regulatory function. A separate technical agency can operate somewhat removed from day-to-day politics and can be granted a status that gives more flexibility in human resource policies. Some drug regulatory agencies remain under the authority of the MOH; others are controlled by an independent board, by a council of ministers, or by a parliamentary oversight body. In a few cases, the agency head reports directly to the president or head of state. The regulatory agency's role is to enforce the law, license drugs for marketing, license clinical trials, monitor the market, and ensure that all market participants respect rules concerning quality, information, advertising, and the like.

Sometimes the central regulatory agency is also in charge of granting business and operational licenses for manufacturers, wholesalers, and retail pharmacies. In federally organized countries, this responsibility may sit with regional authorities. They might also act as enforcers on behalf of the central agency, for example, by performing inspections to monitor adherence to good manufacturing practice guidelines.

Other executive agencies potentially involved in the pharmaceutical sector are, particularly in low-income countries, government procurement agencies and pharmaceutical supply agencies. These agencies are covered in more detail elsewhere in this chapter in the discussion of CMSs and of international agencies and donors.

Expert Commissions and Advisers

Typically staffed by university experts (medical specialists, pharmacists, pharmacologists, economists, and so on), expert commissions can have multiple roles in assisting the legislative and executive branches of the government in developing policies, legislation, and regulation and in making regulatory or executive decisions. Expert commissions can come under significant pressure from other stakeholders if they make decisions that define access to funding, for example, on inclusion of new drugs in a formulary for procurement or in a reimbursement list. Because the number of experts in a particular field can be quite limited even in large economies, conflicts of interest are possible—for instance, if the same expert who was involved in clinical tests of a new drug later has a role in reimbursement decisions.

Civil Society Organizations

NGOs and faith-based organizations provide health services in many low- and middle-income countries. Some of these organizations rely on existing national supply chains for their procurement of drugs; others have their own logistics system or operate a hybrid system in which they buy some supplies from a CMS and other supplies through pooled procurement directly from the private sector or through international procurement agencies such as Missionpharma or the IDA Foundation. In the absence of functioning insurance systems, NGO or faith-based clinics and hospitals sell drugs to patients for cash like all other clinics. Income from drug sales is one part of the revenue stream for these providers, but the limited data available on retail drug prices in developing markets suggest that the margins applied by these providers are usually lower than those in the private sector.[9] Given their humanitarian agenda and the ethical or religious framework under which they operate, NGOs and faith-based organizations that operate as service providers in developing countries usually keep a low political profile.

In contrast, international NGOs and advocacy groups play a significant role in shaping the debate on global pharmaceutical policies. Focus areas are drug prices (for example, advocacy groups significantly influenced the massive drop in prices for antiretroviral drugs in Sub-Saharan Africa); access to medicines; intellectual property; innovation for neglected diseases; and other aspects of global policy. International and national NGOs interact with WHO, the World Bank, and other development banks as well as with various United Nations (UN) agencies to make their voices heard.

Although some of the international NGOs also operate in direct service delivery in deprived regions of the globe or provide disaster relief, no unifying platform exists for civil society groups that operate globally and those that engage mainly in service delivery within countries. Hence, the different organizations hold diverse views on the various policy issues.

International Agencies and Donors

Most low-income and several middle-income countries rely on some form of external assistance in the pharmaceutical sector. At a minimum, the national WHO office provides policy advice and technical support, or the country benefits indirectly from WHO services such as the prequalification of drugs for certain diseases (such as HIV/AIDS, malaria, and tuberculosis). Particularly in low-income countries, donor financing and drug donations cover some of the routine supplies of drugs in the public sector. Specialized UN organizations such as UNICEF assist the government in procurement or run entire campaigns addressing defined health priorities.

When an international organization or bilateral donor commits significant resources to support a country, it will have to document all transactions in its own management system, which creates a significant workload for the officials in the recipient country's ministries or agencies, who have to provide the data in a format requested by the donor. Donor organizations may also require changes in procurement and delivery systems as precondition for their aid and bring in technical advisers to help implement such changes. Such requirements again create transactional costs for the local administration, whose employees may lack training, skills, and productivity-enhancing tools such as functioning computer networks.

If several donor organizations interact with the same government officials in an uncoordinated way, such officials may soon feel overburdened and unable to cope with all the requirements. This situation will have a negative impact on project performance and prevent sustainable capacity building from within institutions. Recent initiatives like the International Health Partnership (see http://www.internationalhealthpartnership.net) aim at creating a joint platform for all donors so that national officials can focus on project work rather than being distracted by multiple competing bureaucratic requirements.

On the policy level, international organizations or bilateral donors assist client country governments by financing work in priority areas defined by the government, such as

- Analytical work to collect the data and information needed to identify weaknesses and set realistic goals
- Development of legislation and regulation for the sector
- Design or reform of institutions, such as the regulatory authority for the sector
- Development of financing systems and payment mechanisms
- Development of procurement, logistics, and delivery systems
- Design and implementation of information technology and management systems

On the global level, international organizations, bilateral donors, private foundations, and companies work together on a diverse range of initiatives aimed at improving access to lifesaving drugs for poor people in developing countries. Such initiatives include the following:

- Product development partnerships to address the gap in pharmaceutical innovation for diseases of the poor
- Provision of free drugs for certain diseases (such as leprosy and river blindness)
- Alternative incentive schemes that encourage innovators to develop drugs for neglected diseases (for example, the Health Impact Fund; see http://www.yale.edu/macmillan/igh/)
- Financing mechanisms for specific drugs, such as the Affordable Medicines Facility–malaria (see http://www.theglobalfund.org/en/amfm/)
- Initiatives to ensure quality of drugs (for example, WHO prequalification) and prevent counterfeiting
- Pooled procurement of drugs for certain diseases to achieve lower prices without compromising quality

Public Purchasers

Institutional buyers of drugs that use public budget funds—for example, procurement offices or CMSs—exist in many low- and middle-income countries with public sector–owned health service delivery systems. Public purchasing is dominant in the inpatient sector; only a few countries have a completely privatized hospital sector. Public procurement laws and regulations typically bind public purchasers. Because public purchasing of drugs involves large sums of money, it has an inherent risk of abuse of institutional power for personal gain. To reduce this risk, commissions usually make the decisions. In some systems, separate units have responsibility for planning, selection, and procurement. A hospital may have a commission that develops a procurement plan. A separate public procurement unit (sometimes located in the ministry of finance) may then organize the tender, which a joint commission awards. A separate financial department may make payments after the hospital confirms receipt of the goods.

From a general government perspective, the public procurement of drugs is frequently seen as a problem area because it requires a significant share of the budget. At the same time, it is very difficult for a minister of finance to judge whether the responsible unit is purchasing efficiently and getting the best value for money. This need to justify spending on drugs to other departments of the government, combined with public pressure on the responsible ministry if facilities are short on important drugs, contributes to the high political relevance of the public drug purchasing function.

Payers

Payers pay for drugs without being involved in the purchasing decision. Either they reimburse the patient or (more often) the provider or pharmacist for all or part of the costs of a particular prescription, or they pay a health service provider a flat fee for a particular service that includes costs for drugs used by the provider while treating the patient. Any third-party payment for certain goods and transactions creates an incentive on the provider side (a) to produce and sell more of these goods and transactions or (b) to simply cheat the system and collect reimbursement without actually delivering the drug or service. Payers such as insurance funds therefore try to set up rules that restrict abuse of services and limit their financial obligations. They may exclude certain drugs from reimbursement on a so-called negative list or define in the form of a positive list which drugs can be reimbursed. They try to introduce co-payments to create a patient incentive against expensive prescriptions and monitor doctors and pharmacists to prevent abuse and fraud. In high-income countries, the trend has moved away from the passive payer role toward a model in which insurance funds take a more active role in negotiating prices and terms of use for drugs, trying to get better cost control along the entire supply chain from manufacturer to patient. In developed markets, insurance funds have increasingly become drivers of pharmaceutical policy, partially taking over some of the traditional roles of MOHs, including regulating drug prices, monitoring rational use, and defining treatment algorithms under cost-effectiveness criteria.

Pharmaceutical Benefit Managers

A more recent spin-off of the private health insurance industry, pharmaceutical benefit managers (PBMs) are specialized service providers for payers (health insurance companies) in countries with a strong private insurance component in health financing. Their main territory is the United States, but they exist in a few other countries as well. PBMs try to optimize the value for money from the payer perspective and can bundle purchasing power from several payers in a fragmented system to get better terms from suppliers. On the demand side, they try to ensure more cost-effective use of medicines by health service providers and patients by adjusting incentives for providers and co-payments for patients within a framework set by the insurance company for which they operate.

PBMs are politically low key. The insurance funds or companies that contract with them do all the lobbying, but benefit managers obviously have significant technical know-how about managing pharmaceutical benefits and could therefore play an important advisory role in reform projects aimed at increasing cost-effectiveness and cost-efficiency in the sector.

Consultants

Although not usually listed as stakeholders on their own, consultants may be worth a second look before simply assuming that they always represent exactly the line of the institutions that contract them. Consultants in the pharmaceutical sector are usually experts with varying backgrounds and professional affiliations, working on a project basis for different stakeholders. The same medical expert may work in a commission that advises the MOH on drug policy, while going on lecture tours for a pharmaceutical company—a case of potential conflict of interest. Generalists with little specific insights into the sector may recruit policy consultants for international organizations, leaving the consultants with a lot of leeway in terms of their recommendations. For example, a consultant who works on a sector analysis in a low-income country but is paid by a development organization in New York; Washington, D.C.; or Geneva may target his or her work toward the expectations of the paying organization. Thus, the consultant may provide a wealth of detail and discussion of options in the analysis, wary of leaving out anything that could later be interpreted as oversight. Unfortunately, such a report aimed at the highest academic standards may be of little use for the clients in the country that was analyzed if it does not recognize their limitations in terms of resources or political economy and fails to break down a few key recommendations into practical steps for implementation. In that sense, policy makers may consider looking at the ubiquitous consultants as a group of stakeholders in their own right who may be more useful if attention is paid to their specific incentive framework.

Notes

1. See, for example, the description of FDA's origins on the FDA Web site (http://www.fda.gov/AboutFDA/WhatWeDo/History/Origin/ucm124403.htm).

2. A *new chemical entity* or *new molecular entity* is a new pharmaceutically active molecule that has not previously been described in the literature, as opposed to a new drug based on a different formulation of an existing drug molecule (such as a slow-release form) or a combination of existing drug molecules.

3. The patent is issued for 20 years, but about 10 years of the patent's lifetime are used for development and licensing of the new drug before it can be marketed. Effective monopoly periods can be longer for biologicals, which are more difficult to copy and register as generics.

4. According to Wikipedia, the annual sales of the Sinopharm group in 2007 were about US$5 billion; official numbers are not available.

5. Dr. Reddy's Laboratories ranks 52nd, with sales of US$1.579 billion (see http://www.scrip100.com).

6. Additional barriers may be in place, such as a data exclusivity rule preventing generics manufacturers from referring to originator data in their registration filing.

7. A pharmaceutical preparation contains one or more active ingredients, such as ibuprofen, ampicillin, or atenolol, together with so-called excipients (such as cornstarch, gelatin, or magnesium stearate), which are needed as fillers, binders, lubricants, preservatives, or other purposes but do not have any pharmaceutical activity.

8. *Multisource drugs* is a term used for generic drugs that are available from different manufacturers under various brand names but equivalent in terms of quality, clinical efficacy, and safety.

9. The data are from drug pricing studies performed by WHO and Health Action International in several countries; see http://www.haiweb.org/medicineprices.

References

Bogdanich, Walt, and Jake Hooker. 2007. "From China to Panama, a Trail of Poisoned Medicine." *New York Times*, May 6.

Bumpas, Janet, and Ekkehard Betsch. 2009. "Exploratory Study on Active Pharmaceutical Ingredient Manufacturing for Essential Medicines." HNP Discussion Paper, Health, Nutrition, and Population Sector, World Bank, Washington, DC.

Forzley, Michele. 2008. "Study to Identify Typical Roadblocks for Bank-Financed Procurement of Pharmaceuticals and Medical Supplies." World Bank, Washington, DC.

Huang, Nicole, Yiing-Jenq Chou, Hong-Jen Chang, Monto Ho, and Laura Morlock. 2005. "Antibiotic Prescribing by Ambulatory Care Physicians for Adults with Nasopharyngitis, URIs, and Acute Bronchitis in Taiwan: A Multi-level Modeling Approach." *Family Practice* 22 (2): 160–67.

Masia, Neal. 2006. "The Cost of Developing a New Drug." In *Focus on Intellectual Property Rights*, 82–83. Bureau of International Information Programs, U.S. Department of State. http://www.america.gov/media/pdf/books/iprbook .pdf#popup.

United Nations Foundation. 2001. "Drug Companies Drop Lawsuit against South Africa." U.N. Wire, Washington, DC, April 19. http://www.unwire.org/unwire/ 20010419/14324_story.asp.

WHO (World Health Organization). 2007. *A Model Quality Assurance System for Procurement Agencies: Recommendations for Quality Assurance Systems Focusing on Prequalification of Products and Manufacturers, Purchasing, Storage, and Distribution of Pharmaceutical Products.* WHO/PSM/PAR/2007.3. Geneva: WHO. http://www.who.int/medicines/publications/ModelQuality Assurance.pdf.

World Bank. Forthcoming a. "Impact of the Marketization of Public Sector Pharmaceutical Supply in Burkina Faso, Cameroon, and Senegal: Review and Analysis of the Evidence on Service Quality, Product Quality, and Access." World Bank, Washington, DC.

———. Forthcoming b. "Pharmaceutical Policy Reform in China." World Bank, Washington, DC.

CHAPTER 3

Patterns of Dysfunction

Typical Problems in the Pharmaceutical Sector

Problems in the pharmaceutical sector that alert policy makers and force them to act are usually not isolated system dysfunctions with simple, straightforward causality. They tend to be complex, lead to different symptoms on various levels of the system, and have multicausal relationships. However, pharmaceutical sector problems do tend to occur in certain typical patterns. Identifying one or two symptoms typical for such patterns can lead to the discovery of the other symptoms as well, even if those symptoms initially are not as obvious. As an example, stock-outs at facility level are a highly visible symptom, frequently linked to less visible planning and capacity problems in the supply chain, which are sometimes associated with high levels of indebtedness that make public suppliers refuse delivery of drugs even if they are available at the central medical store. Other potential parts of such a pattern of dysfunction can be theft and diversion of drugs that were originally meant for the public sector but that instead are sold in the private sector, with profits enriching corrupt officials somewhere along the supply chain.

Another example of such a pattern of dysfunction could start with complaints about affordability problems and high drug prices, despite a government policy of administrative price caps for certain essential generic drugs aimed at improving access to affordable medicines. Joint efforts of industry, doctors, and pharmacists, who all benefit from sales of expensive drugs as long as profit is defined as a percentage margin and manufacturers offer incentives to prescribers, may have created a perception that cheap generics are less effective and unsafe and that therefore branded, imported products are preferable. The price-controlled, cheap generics may not even be available in clinics and pharmacies, thus forcing patients to buy the more expensive brands.

The idea of looking at patterns rather than individual symptoms of dysfunction is of particular relevance when policy makers plan systemic changes to improve overall system performance, with the general objective of facilitating access to quality medicines appropriate for a given country based on public health priorities and economic situation. *Access* has been defined in various ways. One widely used definition was provided by Management Sciences for Health (MSH) in 2000, breaking down access to medicines into four dimensions:

1. *Accessibility.* This dimension refers to a person's ability to physically reach a health center or other outlet where drugs can be prescribed and sold. Determinants of accessibility are not only density of health facilities, road access, and transportation, but also the absence of other barriers such as discrimination, long waiting times, or unresponsive and unfriendly staff members who might discourage poor people from seeking help even if the facility is close by.
2. *Availability.* This parameter refers to the availability of the adequate medicines at the place of service or the attached or contracted pharmacy shop.
3. *Affordability.* This parameter refers to the costs to the individual for the treatment and includes not only the price to be paid for the medicine but also transportation costs, user fees, bribes that need to be paid in some places to see a doctor and get a prescription, and the loss of income because of absence from work.
4. *Acceptability.* This parameter means that both the prescriber and the patient perceive the selected medicine as adequate, safe, and effective. Patients may have certain views, influenced by family members, friends, or traditional healers, but may not have the courage or time to bring them up in the consultation. As a result, they may not fill the prescription or may not take a prescribed medicine.

Access to medicines as defined by these four dimensions is not sufficient to ensure health outcomes. Pharmaceutical policy should also try to ensure that medicines are prescribed properly and used properly by patients. Looking at the multiple parameters for access and their links, one can see clearly that pharmaceutical policy itself has to be multidimensional (because it must try to address various parameters at the same time) and dynamic (so that it can respond to changes in the pattern in a timely way).

To facilitate the analysis that precedes every policy reform, this chapter takes a closer look at various functional segments of the overall pharmaceutical sector and tries to characterize them in terms of typical failures or problems.

Inadequate Regulation of Core Pharmaceutical Sector Functions

Effective regulation of the pharmaceutical sector with regard to market access and quality of the products available in a given country is characterized by several process-related parameters, such as the following:

- All pharmaceutical businesses are registered and certified on the basis of legally defined criteria for space, storage conditions, equipment, staffing, training, record keeping, manufacturing process, quality assurance, and so on.
- Predictable and transparent pathways exist for registering a pharmaceutical business and licensing a pharmaceutical product.
- Effective processes are in place for detecting side effects and quality problems and for recalling products from the market.
- Prescription is enforced—pharmacists refuse to sell prescription drugs over the counter.
- Adequate, complete, and understandable information is provided for and with every pharmaceutical product for health professionals and patients.
- Advertising and promotion for pharmaceuticals are truthful and in line with the international marketing code.
- All clinical drug trials are registered and adhere to internationally accepted procedural and ethics standards.

The following measurable outputs are achieved by applying the preceding processes:

- High and consistent quality of drugs in circulation
- Absence of an informal drug market with unlicensed sellers and drug peddlers

- Absence of counterfeit, nonregistered, and substandard drugs from the market
- Presence of a competitive pharmaceutical sector with adequate product choices for treating the majority of conditions relevant for public and private health (may be limited by affordability, which is addressed in other chapters)
- Documented ability to track side effects and recall unsafe drugs

Although most high-income countries are able to fulfill these criteria to a large extent, many low- and middle-income countries lack the resources to control their markets and enforce their laws, even though the drug law may cover all the mentioned areas. The consequence is regulatory failure in varying degrees, characterized by any of the following symptoms or a combination of them:

- Inconsistent enforcement of good manufacturing practices (GMPs), good distribution practices, and so on, leading to potential quality problems with drugs that are legally in circulation
- Presence of nonregistered, counterfeit, or substandard drugs in the market
- Presence of substandard manufacturing, wholesale, or retail businesses (drug peddlers) in the pharmaceutical sector
- Delays in licensing of pharmaceutical businesses or drugs, nontransparent processes, and potential for corruption (for example, officials may ask for a bribe to provide a license)
- Nonexistent or insufficient reporting mechanisms for side effects and quality problems, creating an inability to recall a faulty product through the distribution system
- Easy purchase of prescription drugs even without prescription
- No easily accessible source for validated information on drugs for professionals, no translation of prescribing information for imported drugs into local languages, and no package leaflet distributed with drugs dispensed to patients
- No monitoring or sanctions for unethical marketing practices or advertisements with exaggerated claims
- Clinical trials performed in violation of standards (for example, without obtaining informed consent from patients)

Most likely, a thorough analysis of pharmaceutical regulation and enforcement would find some degree of deficiency in one or more of the preceding parameters in almost all developing markets—and in at least some developed markets as well. The question for policy makers is, given that resources will always be too limited to address all problems at the same time, which aspects of regulation should they prioritize with an eye on the overall public health effect. Table 3.1 shows links between regulatory weaknesses and factors that influence access to medicines.

Certain regulatory functions have far more relevance for general drug policy than others. For example, if providers and patients, as is the case in many countries, do not trust low-price generic drugs because of reports or rumors of quality problems and lack of regulatory stringency, then a policy that favors the use of generics for cost reasons can be easily rejected or undermined. Alternatively, if the regulatory agency in a low-income country has a two-year backlog of unprocessed registration files, certain manufacturers may turn away from the country, thereby limiting options for public procurement. Procurement law in many cases allows companies to

Table 3.1   Links between Enforcement of Drug Regulation and Access to Medicines

Area of regulatory weakness	Potential systemic effect
Circulation of low-quality drugs and inconsistent enforcement of manufacturing standards	Lack of confidence in drug quality and preference for more expensive branded or imported drugs
Weak licensing process for businesses and products	Fewer products on the market, potential procurement delays, and possible delays in the launch of new drugs
Inadequate reporting of adverse events and inadequate recall mechanism	Reliance on adverse event data from developed countries, with possibly disastrous health impacts
Sale of prescription drugs over the counter	Risk of irrational use of a drug or use in cases where the drug is contraindicated, with negative impacts on individuals' health; drug resistance; and a potential benefit for a pharmacy shop if it is the only place where people can, for example, obtain malaria drugs because a clinic is too far away
Inadequate information provided with drugs	Risk of irrational use or use in cases where a drug is contraindicated, with negative impacts on individuals' health
Unethical marketing practices	Overuse and inappropriate use of certain drugs and skewed advice to committees that develop drug lists for institutions or health insurance
Lack of oversight for clinical trials	Reduction of in-country clinical trials by drug companies and trial data that is unacceptable to authorities in other countries

Source: Author's compilation.

bid even if their product is not yet registered in a country. However, if a winning bidder faces major hurdles in registering, the procurement may fall through and stock-outs at the facility level may occur. In contrast, regulatory weakness in areas such as oversight of advertising and marketing or control of the sale of prescription drugs may have only a limited effect on the scale of irrational use of drugs. Compared to using alternative strategies for tackling irrational drug use, such as modifications of the provider payment system, the effort required to correct such weaknesses on the regulatory side may be higher and the results less impressive.

Lack or Misuse of Funds

Access to medicines requires someone to pay for these medicines. In reality, for the majority of people in low- and middle-income countries and for some in high-income countries (such as the United States), people have to pay out of pocket for drugs if they become ill. The issue of availability of funds for this group of people is linked to general economic development and the generation of employment and incomes that cover an individual's basic health needs. Even for earners of average incomes, the cost burden of treatment for a disease such as cancer or a chronic condition such as diabetes can mean financial ruin, leaving people in poverty or with high debt. Inability to pay for treatment can lead to disease progression, which will eventually require expensive inpatient care, loss of income because of the individual's inability to work, and overall low societal welfare.

Major advances for life expectancy and health status of the poor depend on access to essential drugs that are inexpensive and easily available on the global market. Many governments try to provide these drugs through a public health system with full or (more commonly) partial funding from the government budget. In low-income countries, public funds are usually not sufficient to cover demand even for the minimum essential drug benefit package. Money from donors may be available to close the gap between the available budget and needed funding. However, availability of donor funds for certain specific purposes may lead to a reallocation of the government budget from the items that receive donor support to other programs that lack financing. As an example, a country may have budgeted for buying malaria drugs but can only cover 40 percent of need. If the country then gets a grant that pays for the remaining 60 percent, the budgeting authorities may move the funds that were initially budgeted for malaria to another underfunded line item, such as making hospital upgrades or hiring more community nurses.

In countries with weak public governance, funds provided for purchasing drugs may be diverted for private gain or used in inefficient ways. For example, they may be spent on overpriced drugs because of rigged procurement processes.

The World Health Organization (WHO) estimates that about US$5 per capita a year is required to meet the most basic needs for essential drugs in developing countries (WHO 2004). This figure is higher in countries with a high HIV/AIDS burden. With the establishment of the Global Fund to Fight AIDS, Tuberculosis, and Malaria, availability of financing for drugs to treat these three diseases has significantly improved, lessening the burden on poor countries and improving access to medicines covered by the fund. However, chronic shortages of funding for other, equally important drugs are one of the causes of stock-outs in health facilities.

Ineffective or Inefficient Procurement

If governments directly provide health services to their population, the drugs are usually procured and delivered through a public supply chain. At the top of this supply chain is the procurement function, either located in the drug supply agency (see the discussion of central medical stores in chapter 2) or in a separate department. Written to ensure adequate and efficient use of public funds and to reduce the risk of corruption, public procurement guidelines and procedures tend to be very bureaucratic. Successful and efficient procurement depends on flawless execution of a complex process, from planning and budgeting to assessing the market, drafting specifications, publishing tenders, evaluating bids, verifying documents, contracting suppliers, monitoring performance and quality, paying on time, and ensuring optimal scheduling of deliveries (figure 3.1).

Although companies are usually eager to grow their business, some pharmaceutical companies, even though they make the products that are tendered, hesitate to submit bids on public tenders if they are not sure the selection process is fair and payments will be made according to schedule. Preparing a bid is substantial work and makes sense for a company only if it stands a reasonable chance of making a profit. Brokers that submit bids on behalf of smaller manufacturers are not necessarily reliable business partners and may take advantage of the weaknesses of the procurement process in a low-income country (see the discussion of brokers in chapter 2).

Figure 3.1   Example of a Pharmaceutical Procurement Cycle

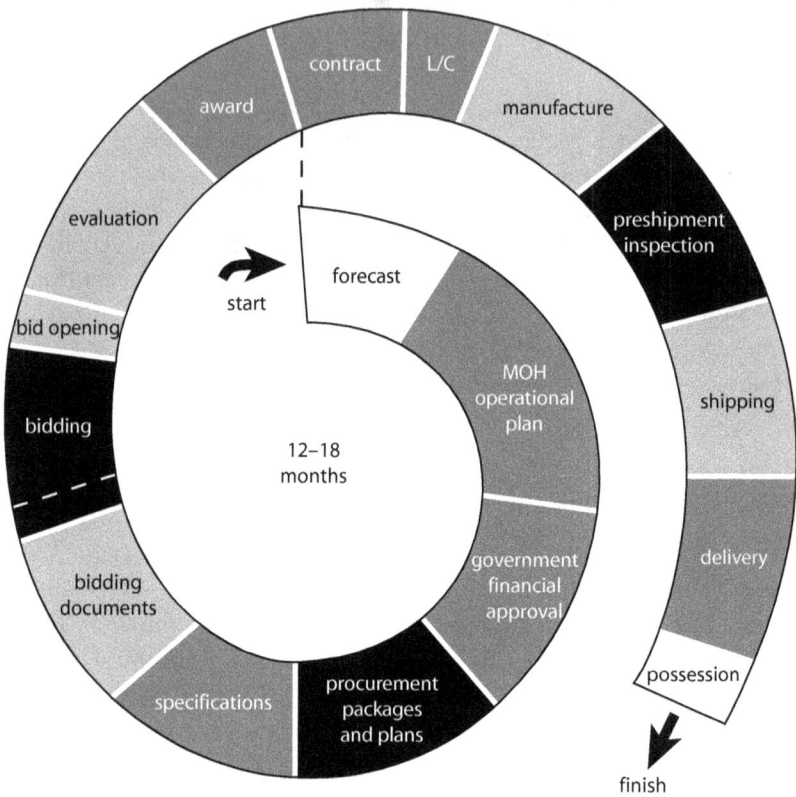

Source: Courtesy of PATH and WHO 2009, Module 5, http://www.path.org/files/RH_proc_cap_toolkit_v2_mod5.pdf.
Note: L/C = letter of credit; MOH = ministry of health.

Flawless execution of complicated processes is difficult for the bureaucracies in most developing (and many developed) countries. Therefore, the procurement process is frequently a source of major headaches for government officials or donors who provide funding. Some typical problems and their likely consequences are listed in table 3.2.

Procurement is only one element of a functioning supply chain, which should be judged by its ability to deliver drugs to patients when and where they are needed. The following section looks at the entire chain and the typical problems encountered in a public sector model that tends to separate procurement from the rest of the chain and thereby interrupts the essential flow of information from clients to suppliers.

Table 3.2   Typical Problems in Pharmaceutical Procurement and Their Consequences

Problem or dysfunction	Potential consequences
Corrupt officials try to leverage their decision-making power for personal gain.	More drug shortages occur. Quality problems are possible if procurement is rigged. Performance problems go unsanctioned.
Employees in critical functions lack training, motivation, or the necessary tools to do their work.	The process is delayed. Errors lead to performance problems.
Planning of amounts to be procured is based on past consumption only or on low-quality data in general.	Amounts procured are not adequate for real demand. Stock-outs of certain items and overstocking of others occur.
Long cycle times are common, caused by lack of capacity or indecision at higher levels.	Stock-outs occur, with the concomitant need for expensive emergency procurements to fill the most important gaps.
Specifications are too broad.	Too many bidders with varying product specifications make selection difficult. The procuring entity risks complaints or lawsuits from losing bidders.
Specifications are too narrow.	Tender could be rigged in favor of a specific company. The procuring entity risks higher prices or procurement failure if not enough bids come in.
Information on market or prices is lacking.	The budget may not be sufficient. Inadequate specifications lead to lack of bidders or to higher prices.
Political pressure may exist to buy from local suppliers.	Suppliers may have potential quality issues or charge higher prices.
Capacity is lacking to assess bidders and verify certification documents that are provided with bids.	Procurement of substandard or counterfeit drugs may result.
Contract-related issues may cause problems, such as failure to keep to a delivery schedule or lack of sanctions for performance problems.	Deficiencies in supplier performance may go unchecked, causing delays and stock-outs.
Funds for payment are not available in time.	Suppliers may stop delivering. Stock-outs may result. Consecutive tenders may result in lack of participation or be for higher prices.
Lack of coordination exists between procurement and the customs and receiving unit.	Goods may be stuck at the border for a long time. Drugs expire before reaching the patients. Supply interruptions occur.

Source: Author's compilation.

Dysfunctional Supply Chains

The role of the supply chain is to bring the product from the manufacturer to the end user. In the private sector, supply chains usually function well as long as a market exists for a product. Frequently used prescription drugs are widely available for cash even in very poor postconflict regions, although availability might be limited to urban areas where the wealthier part of the population lives. Private sector actors such as importers, wholesalers, and retail drug sellers are free to contract with each other at terms that are profitable for both sides. The result is an effective supply chain, but not necessarily an efficient one. Retail prices may be relatively high in markets with a small customer base because new competitors to an established business may not have market space, and intermediaries charge high margins to compensate for small volumes and high transportation costs. The supply chain may also fail with regard to essential, but rarely used drugs that do not carry a high profit. If an essential drug is very cheap but more "modern" and expensive alternatives are available, suppliers may choose to carry only the more expensive alternatives because they are more profitable. Lack of regulatory supervision increases the risk that, instead of good-quality drugs, private suppliers buy and sell substandard and counterfeit drugs that are cheaper to obtain.

In more developed markets, private supply chains tend to become more efficient because of competition between various suppliers, investment in better infrastructure, and better information flow. Higher incomes and availability of funds for drug purchases also increase the number of drugs that can be sold profitably, so the risk of unavailability of rarely used drugs is reduced. In developed markets, contractual arrangements between payers and private sector suppliers ensure availability of all drugs; logistics systems allow twice-daily deliveries to pharmacies, and even rarely used drugs can be shipped quickly so that stock-outs are practically unheard of.

In low-income and some middle-income countries, public supply chains try to complement a private sector that is financially out of range for many and not necessarily reliable as a provider of quality essential drugs. However, public supply chains usually lack the well-aligned profit incentive that makes goods flow in the private sector. Low public salaries do not attract the most capable professionals, and centralized decision making on human resource issues decreases accountability. Investments in infrastructure and information technology tend to be based on budget availability and political convenience rather than on efficiency considerations alone.

Lack of coordination between budget cycles and procurement can lead to supply interruptions at the top of the supply chain. Lack of payment discipline on the buyer side (usually underfinanced public clinics and hospitals) decapitalizes the public supplier and leads to a vicious cycle of stock-outs and cash shortages.

One important financing model in public drug supply chains is the so-called revolving drug fund. The idea is that the institutions along the supply chain that buy and sell drugs are capitalized once to stock up on supplies. From then on, they refinance purchases from the revenues they make from selling the drugs to the next lower levels of the chain or to patients. Prices or margins are regulated based on assumptions about the costs and losses at each level. The more centralized parts of the supply chain usually fare better in this regulation, giving them higher margins than the peripheral retail level.

Although such a refinancing model sounds good in theory, it may, for many reasons, fail in reality. Entities that manage revolving drug funds may not have adequate accounting expertise or discipline. For example, the managers of institutions may tap into the drug funds to address other financial emergencies, which tend to be frequent in poor countries. Losses caused by overstocking of drugs that do not sell well, by damage, or from theft may be bigger than anticipated. If drugs are imported, currency risks are an issue. As a result, the drug fund shrinks and is insufficient to pay the bill from the following order. A particular feature of public supply chains is that they are linked to long and slow procurement cycles, so sometimes orders can be placed only once or twice a year. If the shipment then arrives, it contains a huge volume of drugs and is accompanied by a hefty bill. With depletion of their drug funds, peripheral units owe more and more money to the central medical store or to intermediate distributors. After a while, the suppliers stop delivering, and the whole system breaks down unless it receives a bailout from the government or a donor.

Private sector firms try to keep their logistics costs low by applying "just-in-time" principles. Through close collaboration with suppliers (pharmaceutical manufacturers), they are able to keep stock levels and capital costs within the supply chain low and can transmit consumption data directly to suppliers. Suppliers are responsible for restocking the warehouses as soon as stocks fall below defined levels, and they manage their own inventory and production cycles accordingly. In the public sector, such agreements with providers are largely unknown. Rigid procurement guidelines focus on the price of the goods based on FOB (free on board) or CIF (paid customs, insurance, and freight) Incoterms[1] but ignore the substantial costs incurred further down the supply chain to maintain stock levels needed for continuous supply. These costs may correlate more with the predictability of shipments than with the variations of costs of goods between suppliers. Less frequent and predictable shipments mean that higher buffer stocks are needed to maintain a defined service level. Box 3.1 gives an example of a specific country case in which cost drivers in the supply chain were analyzed on the basis of available historic data.

Box 3.1

Major Cost Drivers for Ensuring Drug Availability in Health Centers in Lesotho

Using data obtained from the inventory management system at the National Drug Service Organization (NDSO) of Lesotho, a group of logistics consultants ran simulations for the purpose of optimizing inventory. The question they wanted to answer was "How much buffer stock does NDSO need to achieve a target of 80 percent, 95 percent, and 99 percent of drug availability at health centers?" Buffer stock is needed to balance fluctuations in demand and in supplier lead time. Demand fluctuations depend on disease outbreaks and drug use patterns and cannot be influenced by those in charge of managing the supply chain. Therefore, the focus was on supplier lead times. Supplier lead times in Lesotho turned out to vary between 30 and 150 days and showed high variability even for different shipments from the same suppliers. This variability, more than the long lead times as such, put the biggest strain on the supply chain and was the major factor for stock-outs.

The simulation showed that moving from 80 percent to 95 percent availability without changing lead-time variability would require the inventory to be doubled. Another increase of 41 percent would be necessary to move from 95 percent to 99 percent. The investment needed to pay for this additional inventory would have been out of reach for NDSO. Alternatively, if lead-time variability could be reduced by 50 percent, availability could be brought up to 95 percent without major investment in additional inventory. These findings illustrate the importance of a holistic assessment of supply chains. Procuring the cheapest drugs alone is not the most cost-effective strategy; other factors, such as supplier lead-time variability, can be major cost drivers for achieving defined availability goals and need to be considered in procurement decisions and contracting.

Source: World Bank 2009.

Corruption, Abuse of Public Funds, and Unethical Business Practices

In all countries, the pharmaceutical sector is vulnerable to nontransparent dealings by special interest groups and individuals who put their own wealth above the public interest. In general, problems can occur in countries where public officials are in positions of power to make decisions affecting income generation for individuals or firms; rules are ambiguous; and transparency, enforcement capacity, and public oversight are lacking. Structural weak points are individuals or commissions that make decisions on registration, licensing, pricing, procurement, and inclusion of drugs in reimbursement lists.

Bribery can have many forms and variations, from cash payments or gift certificates to free use of company cars or apartments, memberships in exclusive clubs, free trips, payment for domestic services or home improvement work, school fees for children, jobs for relatives, or consulting contracts. Sometimes consulting firms are created specifically to make bribes look like legitimate business transactions. Low salaries in the public sector may increase vulnerability, but no data show that increasing salaries alone would affect corruption: some highly paid medical specialists also accept bribes or personal benefits.

Accepting bribes makes officials or experts vulnerable to blackmail, thereby creating a vicious circle. Honest public servants witnessing corruption may become frustrated and leave—or become cynical and join the ranks of the corrupt.

Most large international pharmaceutical companies have explicit policies against corruption and unethical business practices, based on one of the international codes for ethical marketing. From a corporate perspective, corrupt practices not only are a cost factor but also come with a significant risk of major legal and financial consequences, should an insider at some point go public with such information. Of course, corporate policies are not always fully enforced, particularly in countries with weak overall governance. Individual salespersons and managers have some discretion over their actions and deal with a daily conflict between meeting their targets and following the rules. Smaller local or regional companies— particularly privately held companies—are usually less exposed to corporate oversight and therefore may be more likely to resort to unethical practices as a means of achieving business goals.

Another potential entry point for questionable business practices is the supply chain. In competitive markets, manufacturers may offer significant bonuses to wholesalers by topping up orders with free drugs, sometimes by as much as 50 to 100 percent of order volume. The intention is to crowd out competitors and avoid direct price competition. This model is most prevalent in markets with regulated maximum prices or reimbursement ceilings. Wholesalers then pass on some of the bonus to retail pharmacies. Pharmacists stock and recommend the drugs that are promoted and charge the full price to the patient or health insurer. This form of volume competition in the supply chain, although legal in many countries, increases the profit margins in the distribution chain significantly. The increase of profits in the segment of the overall pharmaceutical value chain adding least value comes at the expense of manufacturers, who have to lower their margins by giving away free drugs, and of the payer or consumer, who pays the full price nevertheless.

All forms of corruption that require manufacturers or distributors to pay bribes or to offer steep discounts to remain in business have a potentially negative impact on the quality of the products delivered. To preserve the minimum profit margin needed to sustain their business, manufacturers may try to trim their costs, applying measures that will not be visible to the customer. These measures may include using cheaper, lower-quality raw materials; eliminating labor-intensive in-process controls; switching off electricity-consuming air-handling systems; and reducing other activities that are part of GMP requirements.

A common form of fraud in insurance systems with insufficient control of prescribing and consumption patterns is based on a conspiring physician and pharmacist: the physician prescribes an expensive product that the pharmacist "forgets" to dispense. As an example, a physician may prescribe four different drugs on one prescription form, and the pharmacist may dispense only three, assuming that the patient will not pay attention. In insurance systems, the pharmacist usually keeps the prescription form, so the patient has no way of checking the correctness of the transaction after the fact. The undispensed drug is later charged to the insurance, and the payment split between pharmacist and doctor. Box 3.2 describes another example of fraud.

Pharmaceutical companies are effective in influencing physicians' prescribing behavior in various ways, from high-end education programs for doctors to blunt forms of bribery such as cash payment for prescriptions. In health insurance systems that require a patient co-payment, prescriptions of expensive drugs are sometimes facilitated by the use of patient vouchers to cover the co-payment. Vouchers eliminate the barrier effect such co-payments have against prescriptions of expensive drugs and lead

Box 3.2

Fraudulent Abuse of Health Insurance Funds in Germany

In a case that, some years ago, was picked up by the national media in Germany, the sickness fund's control system had identified a physician-pharmacist pair who had significantly higher turnover than average for certain expensive drugs. The investigation found that this particular pair had conspired with patients to use their insurance cards to request reimbursement for the expensive drugs. The patients received free cosmetic products from the pharmacist, while the doctor and pharmacist split the insurance payment for drugs that were never dispensed. Both the doctor and the pharmacist were sentenced to jail terms.

Source: M. Damolin 2007.

to a cost increase for the health insurance fund. Another effect of such vouchers is that they allow the pharmaceutical representative to monitor and potentially "reward" the prescribing pattern of individual doctors.

Another (usually illegal, but rarely prosecuted) way that companies influence doctors' habits and lower the threshold against expensive prescriptions is by sending expensive drugs directly to the physicians. The doctor hands out the drug to the patient and writes a prescription that is delivered directly to a nearby pharmacy. The pharmacist then charges the insurance fund for the prescription.

Medical experts in university hospitals depend on drug makers to support their research and academic publishing through funding for clinical trials and trips to professional conferences. These same experts may be hired by drug companies on company-funded expert advisory boards and by ministries of health in advisory roles that affect drug policy. Conflicts of interest are ubiquitous and not always declared. As a result, any country in which decision making on drug policy is left to medical experts alone, without adequate checks and balances, tends to enjoy high acceptance of new technologies with little consideration of cost-benefit relations and overall public health effects.

Inadequate Incentives for Providers and Policy Makers

Pharmaceutical policy makers expect health service providers to use medicines in a cost-conscious way, based on clinical evidence and with the patient's interest in mind. In the real world, provider behavior tends to deviate from this ideal and follow economic incentives more than idealistic principles, reflecting the fact that providers' self-interest may not necessarily be aligned with the public interest. The discussion of incentives is not meant to imply that professional behavior is defined by external incentives only. One can fairly assume that most human beings generally have an intrinsic desire to be useful to society and to do their job well, and those who chose to work in health care and public service may rank even higher than average on the scale of intrinsic motivation. Nevertheless, as a rule, one can fairly say that factors such as convenience, material advantage, status benefits, and avoidance of unpleasant experiences influence day-to-day choices. Incentives are equivalent to a vector resulting from a mix of such factors, pointing in the direction of the more likely action. In many specific decisions, professionals may choose to follow their sense of duty and integrity, doing "the right thing" even if the incentive vector points in the other direction. Over time and a larger number of cases, however, the attraction of the incentive will be visible and will influence summary outcomes such as cost-efficiency. Aligning individual incentives with politically preferred choices is therefore a key strategy in politics in general.

Figure 3.2 shows the conflicting incentives that can influence a physician's prescribing behavior. In this example, the physician can choose between generic omeprazole or branded, patented esomeprazole for treatment of a duodenal ulcer. Omeprazole is assumed to be cheap, is established as effective, and is well tolerated. Esomeprazole (Nexium) would be significantly more expensive, leading to a higher patient co-payment, and,

Figure 3.2   Incentives Influencing a Physician's Prescribing Behavior

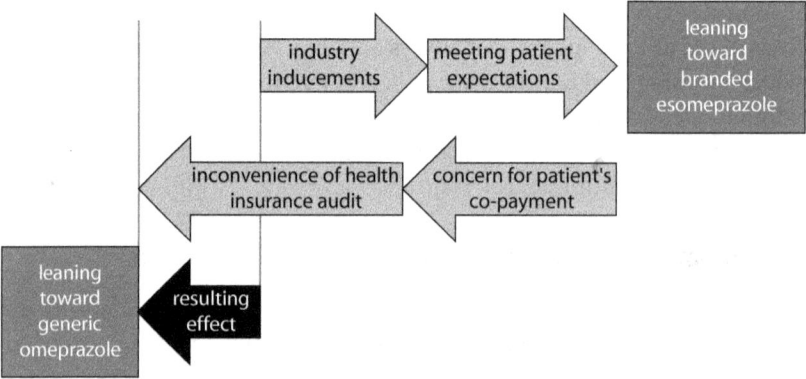

Source: Author's representation.

as the figure shows, increase the likelihood of an audit by the health insurance fund.

At the manufacturer level, economic incentives direct the research and development (R&D) process toward treatments that have large potential markets in high-income countries and away from the diseases that affect mainly the poor. This book does not discuss this aspect in more depth because it is a matter of international rather than national policy and has already attracted the attention of leading academics, politicians, donors, and advocacy groups.

At the national level, manufacturers seek to maximize their profits from sales of existing drugs. Because total profit depends on the margin over costs manufacturers can charge and the volume they can sell, buyers such as procurement agencies or large insurance funds can get lower prices from manufacturers in competitive markets (generic drugs) if they can, in exchange, offer a higher market share for a manufacturer. Innovator companies that sell unique drugs have to think differently because their markets are globally connected through reference pricing systems (in which governments set prices on the basis of those observed in other countries). Such companies will be rigid in defending a high price for their drugs even if this position means lower volume sold in a given country. However, they may be flexible in negotiating solutions that protect the official price but include an access program targeting the poor[2] or in entering risk-sharing agreements that limit the exposure of the payer (insurance fund) to a preset budget ceiling. If the ceiling is met, the manufacturer has to cover treatment costs for additional patients. Other, more recent models include agreements between manufacturers and payers requiring refunds of payments for a drug if certain measurable treatment outcomes (for example, in highly specific cancer treatments) are not achieved in a given patient.

At the wholesale level, because many countries regulate profit margins, incentives are usually linearly linked to sales. Costs are the same for storing and transporting cheap drugs or expensive drugs (except for costs of capital), but profits are higher for expensive drugs. Wholesalers may therefore decide not to carry cheap drugs if capacity is limited and more expensive alternatives are available. If profit margins are set regressively, meaning relatively higher margins are granted for cheap drugs than for expensive ones, the availability of cheap drugs may improve. As mentioned in the previous section, the linear or regressive margin incentive can be undermined by manufacturers' campaigns trying to crowd out competitors with free "bonus" drugs.

Retail pharmacists' incentives are similar to those of wholesalers. If margins are a fixed percentage of the price, retail pharmacists make more money by selling expensive drugs. Their storage capacity is limited, so they have to decide which brands to stock. In most cases, they stock only a fraction of all brands available in a given market. In some countries, pharmacists are allowed, for a given prescription, to switch brands within a group of equivalent drugs with the same ingredients and formulation. Even if they are not legally allowed to do so, they may find a way to condition physicians to prescribe certain brands by making sure these brands are in stock while others are not.

Physicians who are allowed to sell drugs (self-dispensing physicians) and clinics or hospitals that sell drugs to patients for profit have the same incentives as pharmacists to sell more—and more expensive—goods, but they have the added advantage of being able to drive volume and influence selection by issuing prescriptions. In China, this situation is a major problem. Drug expenditures have been rising dramatically in recent years in a system that relies on drug sales to finance hospital expenditures and physician salaries (Hu forthcoming).

Hospital managers' financial incentives are linked to the payment system. In a fee-for-service system in which drugs are paid out of pocket or reimbursed as dispensed to patients, hospital managers' incentives basically follow the incentives for retail pharmacists and for physicians. Drugs are a cost that can be passed on to a third-party payer (or patient). In some countries, hospitals make money by selling drugs. This situation creates one similar to that described for self-dispensing physicians and is likely to lead to overuse of drugs and preference for more expensive (high-margin) drugs. If hospitals are paid on a case basis (for example, through diagnosis-related groups), drug costs are typically borne by the hospital, and the incentive is to manage drug budgets tightly and prescribe the most cost-effective drugs. The hospital is an important entry point for drug companies that want to promote their products, because patients released from the hospital usually have a follow-up prescription or recommendation for ongoing treatment. In some highly competitive product categories (for example, cardiovascular drugs such as beta-blockers and angiotensin-converting enzyme inhibitors), drug companies sometimes provide hospitals with free drugs to get as many patients started on a treatment as possible. Such marketing practices can distort the incentives for hospital managers and physicians and lead to follow-up costs in the outpatient market if the family physician is reluctant to switch to a more cost-effective product or a generic instead of the originator brand that was given to the patient in the hospital because it was free.

Patients generally want the best medicine for their condition and in many countries are willing to pay a significant share of their income for what they perceive is best for them. In desperate cases, they may even sell property that secures their existence or take on large debts to save the life of a loved one. Expert providers heavily influence patient choices, and they are vulnerable to manipulation. For example, patients can be made to believe that expensive originator products are always better than cheaper generics. In some high-income countries with full insurance coverage, patients are conditioned to expect free treatment and react with political pressure to any attempt to erode their benefits. In such environments, patient co-payments can be used to steer patients toward accepting generics or otherwise economically rational choices of treatment. Without insurance and reimbursement systems, possibilities of using patient incentives for influencing drug use patterns are quite limited.

Although incentives throughout the supply chain are relatively easy to understand, the incentives that drive policy makers, members of international organizations with policy influence, employees of regulatory agencies, and various academic advisers are usually less transparent. Potential conflicts of interest have been discussed in previous sections. Factors such as upcoming elections or budget discussions can influence how politicians seek or avoid exposure to topics that resonate with public emotions: access to medicines and drug prices are examples of such topics and have played a role in many elections. Technically sound and reasonable policy decisions may not be politically viable in such periods of vulnerability to public sentiment, because opponents can easily transform the pragmatic debate into an emotional one (see the discussion of consumers in chapter 2 for an example).

Representatives of donor organizations and countries have their own world of conflicting incentives. Their institutional environment is influenced by expectations of far-away stakeholders in donor countries, who usually have little understanding of developmental policy and look for rapid success in areas with mass appeal and high political visibility (AIDS, malaria, child welfare). As taxpayers, citizens of high-income countries expect that their politicians can tell them exactly what happened to their tax dollars, euros, yen, or pounds that were given to development organizations or spent directly in developing countries. A massive control bureaucracy is therefore necessary for international organizations to secure the steady stream of aid that is needed to finance sustainable projects. People working in these organizations suffer from the internal bureaucracy and may well be influenced in their decisions by considerations of "bureaucracy avoidance." The same is true for the recipients of aid, who realize that the transaction costs of a project can become unreasonably high if they must fulfill certain monitoring and reporting schemes that duplicate work done for national systems or other donors using different formats. Another factor influencing donor decisions is budget cycles and fiscal years. If funds are available for only a limited period, decisions may be driven toward the end of that period by the need to spend large amounts of money in a short time. Financing drug procurement is one of the easier options available in such situations. It may solve the bureaucratic problem of otherwise lost funds (which would also lead to bad performance ratings for the project manager), but it may impose an additional burden on a weak distribution system and antagonize efforts for rational planning and good supply-chain management.

Public purchasers of pharmaceuticals or payers such as insurance funds also face conflicting incentives. To maintain political support (and for senior executives to keep their jobs), payers should be generous and cover a wide range of possible treatments seen as desirable by the medical community and the patients. However, given public purchasers' limited budget and general resistance to increasing contributions or raising taxes, payers are supposed to spend money only on treatments that are effective and cost-efficient. Finding a balance between the two competing objectives is usually the mandate of a special commission. The commission may exist within the purchasing organization, if that organization is a service provider (for example, a large hospital), and decide for its own ambit only. In the case of national insurance funds or a national health service, such difficult decisions may be delegated to specific bodies outside the implementing organization, representing a wider range of stakeholders (discussed later in this chapter). This system protects the management of the payer organization against unbearable political pressures, given that decision outcomes will always meet opposition, sometimes from both sides of the "innovation versus cost-effectiveness" dilemma. In developed countries, increasingly elaborate and standardized academic assessment methods for new treatment options have been developed to prepare such decisions and shield them against advocacy campaigns and legal challenges.

Medicine Prices Perceived as Too High

Medicine prices are frequently the prime target for policy makers, given the populist appeal of measures to lower prices. The general public in low- and middle-income countries has little sympathy for drug companies and distributors, except maybe in the few countries where the domestic pharmaceutical industry is a major economic force and a source of national pride. Consumers usually have no clear reference framework for medicine prices in a given country. Anecdotal evidence of a particular purchase of an expensive drug may be generalized into a perception that drugs are "too expensive." The same consumer, however, may choose a more expensive originator drug over an available generic and pay the difference out of pocket because of vague perceptions of higher strength or better quality. Nevertheless, "making drugs cheaper" is a political promise that mobilizes votes in many countries.

Political analysis of drug prices and options for intervention needs to be well thought through. Following are important questions to ask:

• Which segment of the market needs to be analyzed (drugs in the public sector, reimbursed drugs, drugs for chronic conditions)?
• Whose costs are to be analyzed (costs to the end consumer, to a public payer, or both)? Prices for different buyers may be quite different; drug manufacturers may offer significant institutional discounts and charge the over-the-counter buyer much higher prices.
• Which elements of the price should be assessed (ex-factory price; import, wholesale, and distribution margins; retail margins; taxes and regulatory costs)?
• Which benchmark for prices is considered adequate (global procurement prices, wholesale or retail prices in countries with comparable economic conditions, lowest available price in the market, and so on)?

Large variations exist in the allocation of price among factors; retail and distribution can absorb over 90 percent in some cases (figure 3.3). Discounts or rebates can be applied at any level. Manufacturers' cost components are raw materials, manufacturing, R&D, regulatory costs, administration, marketing, bonus goods, financing, shipping, quality assurance and testing, and profit margins for all levels. Costs for kickbacks or bribes are factored in by sellers and add to the overall cost burden in environments that encourage such practices.

Figure 3.3   Components of the Retail Drug Price

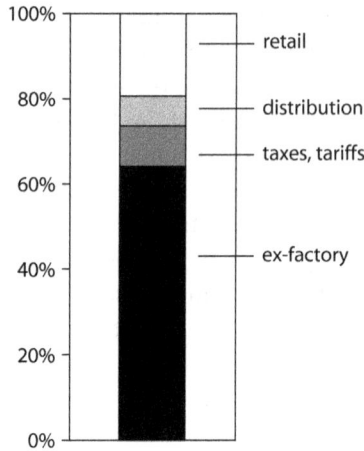

Source: Author's representation.

Various global and regional initiatives try to make drug prices more transparent. WHO and Health Action International developed a standard price and availability survey tool and publish results on a regular basis (Cameron and others 2009). Their approach is to compare prices for a range of essential drugs in public and private sector pharmacies to international procurement prices (such as those published by MSH in its annual *International Drug Price Indicator Guide*[3]) and to the lowest public sector salary. This comparison allows affordability to be evaluated, but it assumes at the same time that drug prices should somehow be linked to the average income—a notion that other stakeholders do not unanimously support.

A European initiative hosted at the Austrian Health Institute collects price data from all European Union (EU) countries and some others that joined the project on a voluntary basis.[4] Prices in the EU, however, may not always be useful as guidance for low-income countries in Africa and Asia, for example.

The market research and consulting company IMS Health collects price and consumption data in most industrial countries and many emerging markets with significance for its main customers—the pharmaceutical industry.[5] IMS Health focuses on providing information for competitive assessment of markets and pricing decisions by manufacturers in these markets. The information is available only to paying customers, and most public policy makers or insurance fund managers are not yet using IMS Health data (which include many other data sets, such as consumption patterns and sales trends, broken down by region, prescriber, and so on) on a regular basis. IMS does make its information available to public health authorities in a way that does not affect its business model. Recently, it provided extensive data on the impact of the 2008–09 recession on drug consumption to WHO.[6]

Manufacturers, wholesalers, and retail pharmacists primarily set prices on the basis of profitability considerations. In many countries, regulators interfere with this process, impose limits on ex-factory prices, and define how the wholesale and retail price is calculated according to the ex-factory price of a given drug. Where market participants have pricing freedom, the sellers usually try to maximize profits by finding the point on the price-volume curve that provides the highest total earnings. Price elasticity of individual demand is low for pharmaceuticals, so even poor people are willing to pay relatively high prices if their health depends on a particular medicine. Compared to other purchasing decisions, the consumer's bargaining power is limited by lack of expert knowledge on the quality and effectiveness of drugs. In many cases, urgency to make a purchase quickly to prevent the worsening of a threatening health condition makes shopping around for a better deal an unrealistic option. These factors explain why many governments feel the need to intervene in the pharmaceutical market and regulate prices.

Pricing regulation needs a reference framework against which prices for a new treatment are set. Some countries use a computation of manufacturing costs, provided by the manufacturer, plus a defined profit margin; this method is called *cost-plus pricing*. Others use price data for similar drugs in the domestic market (known as *internal reference pricing*) or in neighboring markets or a defined basket of countries (known as *external reference pricing*). For pricing of generic drugs, the price of the originator can serve as a reference. In this case, the generic price is discounted to a defined percentage of the originator price. This discount usually increases for the second, third, and subsequent generics to enter the market.

The type of price regulation described in box 3.3 is typical for countries in Europe and the Mediterranean region. Most of these countries have some form of health insurance for their citizens with coverage for drug expenditures. They also have sufficient regulatory and enforcement capacity to make sure that violations of the policy are prosecuted. In low-income

Box 3.3

Example of Price Regulation in Practice

Country A, located in Eastern Europe, uses a basket of 10 other countries to define the reference prices for originator drugs. Countries include three neighboring countries and seven EU countries, most of them toward the lower end of the spectrum of economic strength within the EU. Prices for the drug in question in these reference countries are obtained from industry sources and through direct contacts with authorities in the countries. The regulator then sets the price for the drug in Country A at a level equal to the average of the three lowest prices obtained from the reference countries in which the drug is marketed. To ensure comparability across different pack sizes, the regulator calculates the price on the basis of a defined dose for each dosage form and strength.

When a drug comes off patent, generics entering the market are priced at 30 percent below the price of the originator (first generic), 10 percent below the first generic (second generic), and so on, until a level of 40 percent of the origina- tor price is reached. All additional generics are set at that same price of 40 percent of the originator. Prices are defined as ceilings, meaning that manufacturers are free to charge less than the regulated maximum.

The preceding prices are defined as ex-factory prices. The wholesale and retail prices are calculated by adding a 15 percent margin for wholesalers and a 25 per- cent margin for retailers. On top of the retail price, a value added tax (VAT) of 15 percent is added. Hence, if the ex-factory price is set at 100, the calculations are as follows:

$$100 + 15\% = 115 \text{ (wholesale price)}$$
$$115 + 25\% = 143.75 \text{ (retail price before VAT)}$$
$$143.75 + 15\% = 165.31 \text{ (retail price including VAT)}$$

Source: Author.

countries with weak authorities and insufficient collaboration between reg- ulators, the police, and the judiciary, wholesalers and retailers may just ignore the official price limits and charge whatever they like, knowing the risk of prosecution is limited.

Setting prices in reference to price information from other countries requires objective sources for this price information and comparability between countries. In some countries, list prices of drugs do not mean much because most buyers receive significant institutional discounts and rebates. Referring to the list price as a measure for setting prices in another country may lead to unnecessarily high prices. Conversely, if a government gets a very low price from a manufacturer in exchange for exclusivity in a defined market segment, using the discounted price to set prices in other countries would be seen as unfair by the manufacturer, who would be reluctant to make similar concessions in future negotiations.

External reference pricing, as previously described, is coming to the end of its useful life cycle. Manufacturers of patented originator products are trying more and more to maintain narrow price bands across different markets, knowing that concessions in one country may lead to regulatory price adjustments in other countries. Simple price regulation by comparison should no longer be a primary tool for controlling such drug expenditures.

A general problem with regulating prices by using comparison data from other markets is that the method may be too static. Once prices are set, regulators usually give the manufacturer the burden of reporting price changes in other countries, because regulators do not have the capacity to monitor market moves in all reference countries. If manufacturers "forget" or are not required to report price decreases caused by regulatory intervention or competitive pressure in other markets, patients and insurance funds may be paying more than necessary. In some countries, prices of originator products remain high even after the patent has expired and the prices in other markets have come down drastically. In such cases, regulation could be seen as protecting the interests of the manufacturer by endorsing a high price that the market might not accept otherwise.

The model of setting generic prices as a percentage of the originator price causes similar distortions. For most medicines, manufacturing costs account for only a small share of the originator price. Therefore, a generics manufacturer that gets a price of 40 percent of the originator price may still have very high profit margins. Markets respond to such regulation in different ways. In a system based on out-of-pocket purchases, some manufacturers may decide to lower their price well below the ceiling set by regulation to capture market share among cost-conscious consumers. The originator and the early entrants with higher prices may try to maintain a brand image of higher quality or effectiveness and capture the segment of buyers who are willing to pay more for perceived higher value, but these manufacturers may still feel exposed to price competition—at least in markets with many alternative products. Consequently, regulated prices might be higher than those effectively charged in the marketplace, making regulation redundant.

In markets with third-party payment of a large share of drug costs, the level of reimbursement is frequently set at the lower end of generic prices in the market. In the example of Country A in box 3.3, the health insurance fund might reimburse 40 percent of the originator price, which is the lowest regulated level of generic prices, assuming that some products in this price category are on the market. This method creates an incentive for all manufacturers competing in this specific product category to lower their price to the reimbursement level, unless they have such a strong image that consumers are willing to pay a significant share of the costs out of pocket. Lowering their price further than the 40 percent mark confers no benefit as long as reimbursement is equal for all competitors. With price competition effectively eliminated, manufacturers will not try to increase volume by crowding out competitors in the supply chain. Wholesalers and, in particular, retail pharmacies can carry only a limited variety of brands of the same drug. An effective way to incentivize them is to give them free "bonus" drugs whenever they make a purchase. For example, a manufacturer may offer 100 free packs for every 100 packs that a wholesaler purchases. The wholesaler will then pass on half of that bonus to the pharmacists, who will stock and recommend that brand over the ones from competitors that are not offering such bonuses. Effectively, the manufacturer gets only half the revenue for each pack sold, but given the low manufacturing costs of many drugs, it may still make a profit and will gain market share at competitors' expense. Buyers and reimbursing insurance funds are not involved in the transaction and usually pay or reimburse the full price, creating significant incremental profits for wholesalers and retailers. A similar practice, called *bundling*, involves providing other, potentially unwanted medicines on a "buy 10 and get 5 other medicines free" basis. This approach makes calculating actual medicine costs very difficult and can create incentives for irrational medicine use.

Prices for large institutional buyers are usually set by a formal procurement process. In the case of generic drugs, the contract will go to the lowest bidder or bidders that fulfill the specifications. Most procurement agencies make decisions on the basis of prices quoted for delivery to a port or central warehouse. Unfortunately, such prices do not represent the true costs of providing access to the drug at the point of service. Depending on the delivery schedule, the reliability of the supplier, and the warehouse capacity at different levels of the supply chain, significant downstream costs can be incurred to ensure availability of essential drugs at defined levels (see the previous discussion of dysfunctional supply chains). Public service agencies should therefore manage for total "landed" costs instead of focusing on procurement prices only, but legislation and fragmentation of government functions in many countries make such an integrated approach difficult or impossible. In addition, awarding a tender to a single bidder is potentially dangerous because the winning bidder may fail to deliver. Split awards provide insurance against default and keep multiple suppliers in the market to bid in the next round of tenders.

Competitive procurement does not work well in the case of innovative drugs, for which the patent holder has a temporary monopoly. Institutional buyers usually develop negotiation strategies, based on information sharing with other buyers, evaluation of prices of similar medicines from other manufacturers, and models for quantification of the value of an innovation. The last aspect is highly complex and has led to the development of scientific institutions that provide detailed assessments of new therapies. The best known example is the National Institute of Clinical Excellence (NICE), which acts as an advisory body for decisions on inclusion of new therapies in the formulary used by the U.K. National Health Service (NHS) and provides it with the tools for price negotiations with industry. (NICE itself is not involved in price negotiations.) In contrast, in the Australian Pharmaceutical Benefits Scheme (PBS), assessment and price negotiations are done under one roof. PBS undertakes extensive cost-effectiveness analysis to arrive at a price that rewards innovation while paying what the medicine is worth to the health system.

Many countries with small markets cannot afford such sophisticated assessment tools, nor do they have bargaining power over major international companies. However, in response to the heated public debate in the early 2000s over the price of AIDS treatments, many companies now offer a range of patented, lifesaving drugs such as antiretrovirals and malaria medicines at deeply discounted prices to low-income countries. The situation can be more difficult for middle-income countries with significant high-income market segments, because pharmaceutical companies may not be willing to forgo the profits they make from the wealthy part of the population by offering one low price for the entire market. The Trade-Related Aspects of Intellectual Property Rights (TRIPs) agreement provides an option for governments to issue compulsory licenses for drugs in cases of national need, but its application so far has been limited and would most likely lead to trade disputes with the EU and the United States if countries routinely used TRIPs flexibilities to circumvent originator patents. Even if not applied in a given case, however, the TRIPs options could give government agencies a stronger bargaining position and encourage the development of more sophisticated tools for market segmentation and price differentiation within countries with high inequality of incomes. Manufacturers are reluctant to make price concessions for low-income or government-subsidized market segments in middle-income countries mainly because they fear they would be forced to lower their prices in the wealthy segments as well. If governments adjust their negotiation strategies and provide reassurance against such unwanted spillover effects, companies may be willing to consider differential pricing or voluntary licensing options that benefit the low-income groups without eroding profits.

Conflicts between Innovation and Cost Containment

Pharmaceutical innovation has been a major factor in increasing life expectancy in the industrial economies and parts of the developing world over the past century. It created a profitable industry that has contributed to economic development in many countries, sustains many well-paid jobs, and provides a funding stream for ongoing research in universities and private research institutes. However, every new treatment has also raised the bar for subsequent innovations in terms of effectiveness and safety. Regulators have become wary of potential toxicity and unwanted effects that materialize only after large populations have been exposed to new treatments, leading to very stringent requirements for developing and manufacturing drugs. Medical need for innovation in developed markets is shifting from conditions that affect masses in relatively homogeneous ways (such as hypertension or high cholesterol levels as risk factors for heart attack and stroke) to diseases that affect smaller populations and require more individualized treatment options. Because of all these factors, costs for R&D go up, and the number of patients who can be targeted with a new drug tends to come down. Logically, the cost burden that manufacturers have to place on every single patient goes up in such a scenario, so new drugs tend to become more expensive. Even in some high-income countries, new treatments for cancer or other severe chronic illnesses are already unaffordable for average earners or require major sacrifices in spending on other aspects of life. Fortunately, most high-income countries offer universal coverage with health insurance that pays for innovative drugs. In this case, the financial pressure is on insurance funds or companies that are confronted with increasing demands for reimbursement of new, expensive drugs. Overall, higher consumption of health services and products by an aging population adds to the financial pressures. Longer-term observations show that drug expenditure has been growing at an annual rate of 5.7 percent over the past 20 years—faster than overall health expenditure and faster than gross domestic product (OECD 2009).

Sometimes, new drugs lead to a change in treatment patterns that offsets higher drugs costs with savings elsewhere; the introduction of H_2-receptor antagonists, for example, drastically reduced the need for surgery in patients with gastrointestinal ulcers. In other cases, a new therapy may add to total health care costs by keeping patients alive and in treatment for a long time. All newly introduced drugs lack long-term data showing their true health and economic effects under realistic treatment conditions. Manufacturers naturally tend to interpret the existing data in the most positive way, try to get the broadest possible indications and highest possible prices approved, and make large marketing investments to generate sales. Insurance funds have a duty to their constituencies to be more conservative, to request independent scientific evidence for claimed benefits, and to challenge prices by using measures of comparative value (how much more is the new treatment worth compared to the old one?) and allocative efficiency (how much welfare gain could be achieved if funds were used in ways other than paying for this new drug?).

Innovation is not the only driver of pharmaceutical expenditure at insurance funds. Price increases for drugs contribute as well, although in recent years the price trend has been partially reversed, thanks to patent expiry of many high-volume drugs and application of more sophisticated purchasing strategies. Another major driver is volume expansion following better diagnosis of patients in need of treatment and improvements in targeting groups that did not have good access to treatment previously. Although discovering all patients who have latent diabetes before they develop complications that bring them in contact with the medical profession is a valuable public health objective, success in doing so will increase consumption of insulin and oral antidiabetics. Manufacturers of such products are aware of this outcome and effectively support public health efforts directed at identifying patients. This strategy may translate into longer-term savings by reducing complication and hospitalization rates, but it will lead to an immediate increase in treatment costs.

The conflict between, on the one side, these two cost drivers—innovation and better targeting of patients who require treatment—and, on the other side, limited drug budgets is a constant source of political tension. Although denying treatment to newly discovered diabetics is not an acceptable option in most countries, insurance funds have varying degrees of discretion about which new drugs they include in their reimbursement schemes. In practice, these decisions tend to be highly politicized. The commissions in charge of such decisions are under pressure from manufacturers, who need reimbursement status to sell meaningful amounts of the product, and from patients and physicians, who see innovation through an individual lens rather than from a public health and cost-efficiency perspective.

Heads of insurance funds can lose their jobs over an emotional public dispute about reimbursement for a new cancer drug. In several high-income countries, insurers or public payers, therefore, have established independent scientific bodies that analyze new technologies and provide recommendations for their use in the country context, for example, by defining for which subpopulation of patients a new treatment should be reserved and what criteria should be satisfied to initiate treatment in an individual case. They also try to quantify the value of an innovation, expressed, for example, in costs for a quality-adjusted life year (QALY). The QALY method allows comparisons across different disease areas and facilitates negotiations with manufacturers about price and potential risk-sharing agreements. Box 3.4 describes NICE, an institution that was established to address the dilemma between innovation and cost and to create a consensus-building process protected from lobbying pressure and political posturing.

Several other countries have set up similar institutions. In some cases, they have slightly different governance structures and roles. (For example, PBS in Australia, unlike NICE, is directly involved in price negotiations with industry.)

If choices regarding coverage for innovative drugs are hard for high-income countries with drug budgets in the annual range of US$300 to more than US$500 per capita, they are much harder for a middle-income country providing drug coverage for a large population with a budget that may be in the range of US$30 to US$70 per capita a year. As pointed out in previous sections, the industry is not generally willing to make major price concessions on the basis of affordability or purchasing power. Thus, decision makers have few choices:

1. Rejection of new treatments except for the few that, according to budget impact assessment, have a potential for short-term savings

Box 3.4

NICE: Example of an Institution Set Up to Manage the Conflict between Innovation and Cost Containment in Health Care

The National Institute for Health and Clinical Excellence is the independent organization responsible for providing guidance on the promotion of good health and the prevention and treatment of ill health in the United Kingdom. NICE produces guidance in three areas of health:

- *Public health.* Guidance on the promotion of good health and the prevention of ill health for those working in the NHS, local authorities, and the wider public and voluntary sector
- *Health technologies.* Guidance on the use of new and existing medicines, treatments, and procedures within the NHS
- *Clinical practice.* Guidance on the appropriate treatment and care of people with specific diseases and conditions within the NHS

   NICE develops its guidance using the expertise of the NHS and the wider health care community, including NHS staff, health care professionals, patients and caregivers, industry, and academia.

Source: http://www.nice.org.uk/aboutnice/.

compared to existing treatment practices (for example, a treatment that can be applied in outpatient care whereas the previous treatment required hospitalization)

2. Acceptance of some new treatments based on pharmacoeconomic and public health needs assessment, combined with an explicit or implicit rationing mechanism (requiring preapproval for individual patients, wait-listing, limiting availability to a few university centers)

3. Use of the TRIPs agreement, which allows a country to issue a compulsory license for a drug in the case of a public health crisis (see box 3.5)

4. Significant budget increases or tolerance for overspending to absorb costs for new treatments in the absence of a stringent selection process and rationing

5. Reallocation of funds from other budget positions to cover costs for new treatments, which may mean cuts for programs that are more cost-effective than the new treatment but have less political visibility

Box 3.5

Access to Medicines and the TRIPs Agreement in Brazil

The TRIPs agreement defines minimum standards for trade-related intellectual property protection for World Trade Organization member states. Under this agreement, World Trade Organization members (except for the least developed countries, which benefit from a waiver until 2016) have to honor patents for pharmaceuticals. However, the TRIPs agreement allows the possibility of issuing compulsory licenses in the case of a public health crisis, for example. Since the terms of this exception were clarified in the Doha Declaration, only a few countries have made use of it. Many practical difficulties as well as a need to adapt national legislation still remain. In addition, several bilateral free trade agreements further limit the options countries have under the agreement.

Brazil is one of the countries that have used the TRIPs agreement's flexibilities systematically, mostly as a bargaining tool to get lower prices for antiretrovirals for the treatment of HIV/AIDS. Brazil's treatment program is widely recognized as one of the most comprehensive of its kind; access to affordable antiretrovirals is key to its success and financial sustainability. The Brazilian pharmaceutical industry has a credible capacity to reverse-engineer drug substances and produce copies of patented drugs. Under these circumstances, the threat of issuing a compulsory license and manufacturing a generic copy of a patented antiretroviral drug was credible and induced the originator companies to make significant price concessions.

Overall, the complexities of intellectual property rights and international trade agreements go beyond the scope of this book. Although using the TRIPs agreement can be a consideration for specific countries in specific situations, one could not realistically classify this option as a standard tool for cost containment.

Source: Cohen 2004.

Although some of these choices appear better than others, none is easy and convenient. The more sophisticated second option requires strong political backing, as well as capacity for making assessments and defining usage criteria under significant public and lobby pressure. In reality, most countries find themselves caught letting things drift passively toward options 4 and 5 while trying to get the upper hand with more proactive policies modeled after option 2.

Conflicts between Industrial Policy and Public Health Objectives

Policy makers in countries that have a substantial domestic pharmaceutical industry have to balance pressures from the public health side to ensure low-cost supplies of high-quality drugs against the industry side, which wants to ensure profitable growth. Companies want to keep prices high and generally resist regulation that increases their costs, unless it protects them against competition. As an example, many low- and middle-income countries struggle to enforce manufacturing standards in line with current good manufacturing practices (cGMPs) in their industry. However, some companies cannot finance the enhancements required to achieve cGMP standards. These companies, often supported by local politicians who are concerned about the effect on the local economy, lobby against stricter rules or for delays in enforcement. In contrast, stronger companies that may already operate under cGMPs for export purposes may favor stricter rules, because they see such rules as an opportunity to squeeze out smaller competitors and grow their own market share.

Under the influence of local manufacturers (and representatives of foreign firms as well), procurement or pricing authorities sometimes allow higher prices for locally produced drugs than for imports. Alternatively, they may design price control mechanisms in ways that lead to higher prices relative to countries with similar economic conditions. The argument in favor of such permissive pricing policies is that they support the local economy. Because the drugs are purchased either from a limited health budget or out of the pockets of people who are sick, such policies could amount to a cross-subsidy from the sick to an industry that might otherwise not be competitive—unless the higher drug expenditure is compensated by additional public revenue from duties and taxes from local industrial activity.

Countries with an export-oriented drug industry sometimes allow higher domestic drug prices because pricing decisions in countries receiving the exports are potentially influenced by the price in the country of origin. In this case, the economic argument may be more convincing, particularly if the industry is a good taxpayer, because some of the export revenues will find their way back into the budget and compensate for the higher cost burden on the domestic health system.

On a global scale, the general public interest in future pharmaceutical innovation conflicts with the increasing hurdles faced by innovator companies when they want to develop and market new products. The scope of this book does not include discussion of the merits and limitations of intellectual property–based innovation systems. However, such systems clearly tend to fail if innovations do not have a major commercial market, because they are mainly for people in poor countries who are not able to pay for them. Alternative reward systems have been discussed, such as the Health Impact Fund promoted by a group of experts from Yale University (Hollis and Pogge 2008). The problem is that such initiatives face huge political and administrative hurdles and could be realized only if a group of major donor countries is willing to make significant long-term funding commitments. In the meantime, a limited number of R&D partnerships receive funding from large private donations, donor countries, and international organizations for their work in disease areas that have major public health impact in developing countries. A number of pharmaceutical companies also provide financial and in-kind support to not-for-profit R&D projects as part of their "good corporate citizenship" agenda.

Disease patterns in many middle-income countries are increasingly converging with those in high-income countries. Noncommunicable diseases are on the rise because of aging populations and economic development that reduces the morbidity associated with poverty. The more similar the disease patterns become, the more those countries will be able to benefit from innovations stimulated by large markets in high-income countries. However, because of the price barriers described in previous sections, significant delays may occur before wide adoption of new technologies. In the worst case, new technologies will become widely available only after they are off patent and can be manufactured at low costs, meaning at least 10 years after their introduction in high-income countries. No global agreement exists yet about how the costs of innovation could be shared across countries of different income levels. Nor do good models exist suggesting how poor patients in countries that as a whole are economically strong enough to constitute relevant markets could get earlier access to new drugs that are priced far beyond their purchasing power. Some companies have pursued individual solutions to this problem, for example, through access programs that provide certain lifesaving drugs free if patients cannot afford them. Another alternative is voluntary licenses to local generics companies that are limited to supplying certain market segments. Companies may be reluctant to share details of such arrangements because they could create a precedent for future decisions. Furthermore, antitrust regulations bar companies from jointly developing guidelines for providing access to new drugs through differential pricing.

Irrational or Inappropriate Use of Drugs

In an ideal world, prescription drugs are selected by a physician (or a licensed professional such as a nurse practitioner) on the basis of clinical evidence, ease of use, and considerations of economic efficiency. A pharmacist then dispenses the drug and may double-check that the prescriber did not overlook potential risk factors or drug interactions and advise the patient on how to take the drug correctly. The patient is expected to follow the expert advice and complete the treatment.

Most regulators and clinical pharmacologists look at drugs from a purely rational standpoint, seeing only the scientifically documented evidence. In the transaction between doctor and patient, however, the rational, scientifically objectified element is only one side. Drugs are also mediators of an act of transactional healing that happens between doctor and patient. The evidence for this role lies in the placebo effect, which is a measurable clinical effect of inert medicines that contain only filling materials and no active substance. In some indications, this effect is so strong that drug companies are challenged to demonstrate the effectiveness of their active drugs in clinical trials. The placebo effect has its roots in how the brain processes pain and stress and how it interprets causality between external events and internal perceptions. Experiments have shown that placebo pain medication can stimulate release of endogenous opioids, which are natural painkillers (PhysOrg.com 2007). When the interference of psychological factors with the physiological effects of medicines under real-world conditions is taken into account, it should be no surprise that medicine use in practice differs from the evidence-based approach endorsed by policy makers.

In most cultures, patients expect a prescription when they visit a doctor. In many cases, the more drugs the doctor prescribes, the more the patient feels valued by the physician. The physician has limited time per patient and in most cases access to only a limited range of diagnostic tools, so the initial diagnosis often is uncertain. In such a situation, doctors tend to overprescribe to fulfill patient expectations and to be on the safe side—for example, if what appears to be a viral infection later turns out to be caused by bacteria with potentially more harmful consequences. Economic incentives are another potential reason for overprescribing if, for example, doctors are allowed to dispense medicines and thereby can increase their income.

Patients, although initially expecting a prescription, may change their attitude when they confront the pharmacist and have to pay for the drugs. Patients may decide to skip one that appears too expensive without knowing how this decision will affect the treatment outcome. Depending on the severity of symptoms, they may lower or increase the dosage without consulting with the expert. Treatments that have delayed onset of effects may be dropped after a few days unless the physician has made sure to manage the patient's expectations. After symptoms improve, the patient may stop treatment. If the patient develops similar symptoms in the future, he or she may try to self-medicate with leftover medication from the last episode. Lack of adherence to treatment protocols is of particular concern in chronic diseases such as hypertension and diabetes, where symptoms may be absent over long periods of time, or in infectious diseases that require long-term treatment (such as tuberculosis). On the patient side, therefore, irrational drug use is a problem of both over- and underuse, whereas on the provider side, the dominant issue is overuse.

Prescribers' choices of drugs for their patients are influenced by several factors in addition to the considerations already described, such as the following:

- *Professional training and upbringing.* A doctor who has been trained in the field in Bangladesh may have different prescription preferences than one who has been trained in a university hospital in Paris.
- *Personal experience with various treatments.* The availability of these treatments in the place where the physician practices influences this experience.
- *Knowledge about availability.* The doctor may know certain drugs can be found in the pharmacies that are accessible for the patient.
- *Perceptions about quality of drugs in the market.* Such perceptions may be influenced by anecdotal experience, hearsay, or targeted campaigning by companies that represent the higher-price segment.
- *Formularies and prescription guides.* Doctors are guided by the formularies and guides issued by the institution where they work.
- *Professional training received on continuing basis.* Such training is frequently sponsored by the industry.
- *Individual counseling by drug representatives.* Drug companies have counseling programs to educate physicians about their products.
- *Incentives offered by drug companies.* Such incentives come in various forms.
- *Self-dispensing doctors.* These practitioners benefit economically from selling medicines.

Drug companies spend large sums of money to educate doctors about their products and promote them in various ways within—but often also outside—the ethics code[7] published by international industry associations (IFPMA 2006) and by WHO (1988). These marketing efforts are without doubt effective; otherwise, the industry would not continue to invest in them. In contrast, policy makers in charge of defining rules for rational use of drugs frequently do not have the budget or expertise to develop adequate information and training tools to make sure that prescribers know what is expected of them and where to turn for information.

In summary, irrational use of drugs is a multifactorial problem with economic, scientific, psychological, and educational dimensions (some of which appear perfectly rational from the doctor's or patient's viewpoint), interacting in various ways and leading to a range of relatively predictable patterns (table 3.3). Irrational use of drugs leads to suboptimal health outcomes (in particular because of undertreatment of chronic conditions and side effects of drug overuse) and to inefficient allocation of limited resources.

A Tool to Assess the Sector and Diagnose Dysfunctions

As shown in earlier sections, an apparent problem in one segment of the pharmaceutical sector may be a symptom of dysfunction in other segments. For example, if prices are perceived as too high, the underlying issues may be related to governance problems (regulatory capture), perceptions favoring more expensive treatments, payment systems, incentives in the supply chain, or a mix of these factors. Hence, an assessment tool used to inform pharmaceutical policy decisions should be neutral in its diagnostic approach and not preempt conclusions by limiting the scope of questions to one problem area. Such a tool needs to verify, describe, and—as much as possible—quantify the problem. The data generated by the assessment then provide a basis for the analysis of potential causalities. The analytical process is one that requires expert knowledge in interpreting data and dialogue with insightful stakeholders to reach useful conclusions. In many cases, data will be incomplete and opinions between stakeholders divergent, so aspects of political acceptance, experiences from other countries, and the general "do no harm" principle will guide the final recommendations.

Table 3.3 Common Patterns of Irrational Drug Use and Their Likely Causes

Irrational use parameter	Prescriber-side factors	Patient-side factors
General overprescribing (measured in number of items per prescription)	Being "on the safe side" in unclear cases, meeting patient expectations, and obtaining financial incentives	Having naive perceptions that "more is better" and limited opportunity to see doctor for follow-up
Overuse of antibiotics	Having difficulty diagnosing causal agents of infections	Expecting quick relief
Overuse of injections	Controlling application (the patient may not be compliant with the treatment) and receiving a higher fee	Experiencing a stronger placebo effect and believing that injections are more powerful and provide faster relief
Use of expensive, newer drugs despite lack of objective data on superiority	Obtaining industry-led training, promotion, and incentives	Believing that new, expensive drugs work better
Use of expensive brands instead of cheap generics with the same ingredient	Perceiving that cheaper generics may be of lower quality and efficacy (may be a rational perception if regulatory system is weak)	Perceiving that cheaper generics may be of lower quality and efficacy
Underuse of treatments for chronic diseases	Dealing with access barriers for certain groups based on distance, social status, income, and ethnicity	Stopping use because of an absence of symptoms, affordability problems, perceptional barriers, and side effects

Source: Author's compilation.

The tool presented here is a structured checklist covering the relevant aspects of the pharmaceutical sector, defining which data should be collected, and offering potential data sources at international level and within countries. The main areas covered are

- Pharmaceutical market
- Pharmaceutical policy and regulation
- Public and private drug expenditure
- Drug pricing
- Purchasing, procurement, and reimbursement
- Service delivery and logistics
- Industry and trade
- Rational use of drugs

The generic tool (provided in appendix A) needs to be customized by the expert doing the assessment to match the situation in a given country and the requested scope of the work. Appendix B shows an example for the customized version of the tool as it was used for a pharmaceutical sector assessment in Turkey (Çelik and Seiter 2008).

Data and information collected from available sources are then reviewed and assessed against the background of the expert's individual framework of knowledge and experience in similar situations. This part of the analytical process can best be described as a "pattern recognition" process that leads to an initial hypothesis on the causes for the identified problems. This hypothesis can be refined through the political process or hardened with additional, more specific research.

Additional tools for assessing the pharmaceutical sector in a given country are available from other sources and include the Pharmaceutical Sector Scan Framework of the Medicines Transparency Alliance (MeTA).[8] This tool comes with more detailed explanations and can be used directly to collect data.

Notes

1. For an explanation of Incoterms used in international trade, see http://www .iccwbo.org/incoterms/.

2. The Glivec International Patient Assistance Program is an example; see http://www.themaxfoundation.org/GIPAP/

3. An interactive version of the guide can be accessed at http://erc.msh.org/ mainpage.cfm?file=1.0.htm&module=DMP&language=English. It is also available in print.

4. For more information about the initiative, Pharmaceutical Pricing and Reimbursement Information (PPRI), visit the PPRI Web site at http://ppri .oebig.at.

5. See the company's Web site, http://www.imshealth.com/portal/site/imshealth, for more information.

6. The reports to WHO are available online at http://www.who.int/medicines/ areas/policy/imsreport/en/.

7. Multinational company headquarters can be subjected to the "name and shame" approach to accountability for ethics code violations, even if they happen in countries with limited oversight. Many smaller generics companies, however, do not sign up to any ethics code or reside in countries that have no platform for exposing ethically questionable promotional practices.

8. The tool was developed by the World Health Organization Collaborating Center on Pharmaceutical Policy on behalf of MeTA (see Vialle-Valentin and Ross-Degnan 2009).

References

Cameron, Alexandra, Margaret Ewen, Dennis Ross-Degnan, Douglas Ball, and Richard Laing. 2009. "Medicine Prices, Availability, and Affordability in 36 Developing and Middle-Income Countries: A Secondary Analysis." *Lancet* 373 (9659): 240–49.

Çelik, Yusuf, and Andreas Seiter. 2008. "Turkey: Pharmaceutical Sector Analysis." World Bank, Ankara.

Cohen, Jillian Clare. 2004. "Canada and Brazil Dealing with Tension between Ensuring Access to Medicines and Complying with Pharmaceutical Patent Standards: Is the Story the Same?" Comparative Program on Health and Society, Working Paper Series 2003/2004, University of Toronto, Toronto, ON.

Damolin, Mario. 2007. Bauchweh, Migräne, Fußpilz; Frankfurter Allgemeine Zeitung, April 14, No. 87, p. 3.

Hollis, Aidan, and Thomas Pogge. 2008. *The Health Impact Fund: Making New Medicines Accessible for All.* New Haven, CT: Incentives for Global Health. http://www.yale.edu/macmillan/igh/.

Hu, Shanlian. Forthcoming. "Review of Financing, Pricing, and Utilization of Pharmaceuticals in China." School of Public Health, Fudan University, Shanghai, November 2008.

IFPMA (International Federation of Pharmaceutical Manufacturers and Associations). 2006. "IFPMA Code of Pharmaceutical Marketing Practices." IFPMA, Geneva. http://www.ifpma.org/EthicalPromotion.

OECD (Organisation for Economic Co-operation and Development). 2009. *OECD Health Policy Studies: Achieving Better Value for Money in Health Care.* Paris: OECD.

PATH (Program for Appropriate Technology in Health) and WHO (World Health Organization). 2009. *Procurement Capacity Toolkit: Tools and Resources for Procurement of Reproductive Health Supplies, Version 2.* Seattle, WA: PATH. http://www.path.org/publications/details.php?i=1652.

PhysOrg.com. 2007. "Researchers Demonstrate How Placebo Effect Works in the Brain." PhysOrg.com, July 30. http://www.physorg.com/news105029324.html.

Vialle-Valentin, Catherine, and Dennis Ross-Degnan. 2009. "Assessing the Baseline Pharmaceutical Sector Situation in MeTA Pilot Countries." Medicines Transparency Alliance, East Sussex, U.K. http://www.medicinestransparency .org/news-events/article/view/assessing-the-baseline-pharmaceutical-sector-situation-in-meta-pilot-countries/549/.

WHO (World Health Organization). 1988. "Ethical Criteria for Medicinal Drug Promotion." Essential Drugs Monitor 017, WHO, Geneva.

———. 2004. *WHO Medicines Strategy: Countries at the Core, 2004–2007.* Geneva: WHO.

WHO-MSH (World Health Organization-Management Sciences for Health). 2000. "Essential Drugs, Vaccines, and Health Commodities." Report of the Consultative Meeting, Ferney-Voltaire, France, December 11.

World Bank. 2009. "Strategic Analysis of Supply Chains for Informed Decision Making: World Bank Experience from Two Countries—Kenya and Lesotho." World Bank, Washington, DC.

CHAPTER 4

Key Elements of a Successful Pharmaceutical Policy

Chapter 3 explored the various performance problems in the pharmaceutical sector that trigger calls for reform. It also provided an instrument for a quick sector assessment. The outcome of the assessment should highlight the key issues and likely causes that policy changes can then target. Sometimes the underlying problem cannot be addressed directly—for example, if it falls into the responsibility of another authority than the one in charge of reform. However, the multifactorial nature of sector outcomes (such as drug availability and prices) usually provides other options to influence outcome parameters. If, for example, the issue is weak regulatory oversight and questionable quality of drugs in circulation, finding the resources necessary to strengthen regulatory oversight to the point that the problem is eliminated may be difficult. Alternatively, the quality issue could perhaps be addressed, at least for a segment of the market, through pooled procurement among a group of clinics, hospitals, or even countries, so that quality standards can be enforced through contractual terms.

This chapter introduces a range of policy options that various countries have applied to address systemic sector dysfunctions in an attempt to lower access barriers and increase efficiencies in the sector. Where necessary, the options are broken down for different economic or political contexts.

Where current approaches in most countries have not led to satisfactory outcomes, alternative strategies are suggested on the basis of models from other sectors. Overlaps between different policy options are inevitable and are reviewed in chapter 5, which talks about the integrated policy planning process in a given country.

Ensuring Access to Safe and Effective Drugs through Well-Designed Supply Chains

For the purposes of this chapter, the supply chain includes all administrative transactions, financial transactions, physical movements, and information flows that are needed to get drugs from the manufacturer's finished goods warehouse to the outlets where drugs are dispensed to the patient.

In high-income and some middle-income countries, the supply chain is completely in private hands. Goods move from manufacturers to wholesalers and on to retail pharmacies, while money, as well as information on stock levels and sales, moves in the opposite direction. The *service level*, defined as the percentage of orders that can be fulfilled within a set time frame, is nearly 100 percent in places with high population density and sufficient purchasing power. Instead of a central authority collecting consumption data and creating forecasts, information systems at the retail level record transactions and pass the information on to the wholesaler and, in aggregated form, back to manufacturers. Using this information, manufacturers plan their production and deliver the next batch to the wholesaler when inventory falls below a preagreed level. Wholesalers do the same with retailers, and the drugs on the shelves of retailers remain in the manufacturer's or wholesaler's possession until they are sold. An inventory management agreement between the involved parties regulates these transactions. If the demand for a drug unexpectedly drops so that the drug takes more shelf space than it should, the retail pharmacist can return it to the wholesaler. Similarly, wholesalers can return overstocked drugs to the manufacturer without penalty. All parties involved in such a system have a financial incentive to ensure availability of drugs at the retail level. The risk of overstocking is shifted back to the manufacturer, who is in the best position to absorb it by redirecting supplies and lowering future production volumes.

Such an integrated supply chain functions as a closed-loop control system, ensuring that demand is fulfilled within a wide range of variations. Of course, every system has a breaking point. A system will fail, for example, if an epidemic outbreak depletes stocks at the manufacturer's level, and production cannot keep up with demand. Successfully introducing a closed-loop control system requires that several conditions be fulfilled:

- Adequate purchasing power or reimbursement from a central fund at the retail level and payment discipline at all levels are required so that money flows always match the flows of goods. Otherwise, parties will be reluctant to position goods forward without payment.

- Transparent and competitive markets are necessary, in which all players are interested in efficiency to increase profits. Corruption in the relationship between sellers and buyers of medicines undermines competition; prices are likely to be higher to compensate for the kickback to the buyer.

- Private sector capacity must be sufficient to develop, install, and maintain the information system that an integrated supply chain needs and to manage the logistics chain on a permanent basis. This requirement can lead to a "chicken-and-egg" problem: one could argue that many low-income countries do not have a private sector sufficiently developed for such advanced integrated systems. In reality, however, such a system grows in small steps, starting with sufficiently attractive opportunities for the private sector that then attract investment in capacity building. For example, a public payer could contract with private providers for a few high-volume items in a limited area with good accessibility, allowing them to make a profit without major start-up investments. Such a system can be scaled up over time as capacity and familiarity grow on both sides.

- A transport network must allow movement of goods in a predictable way. This condition is relative: in remote areas with seasonal accessibility problems, the system can still function if supported by a regional distribution center, if service levels are defined realistically, and if prices are set high enough or higher logistics costs can be cross-subsidized.

- Regulatory oversight must ensure quality of goods in the market and adherence to good professional practice standards by market participants. Lack of regulatory oversight may not interfere with the availability of drugs in the system, but it creates a high risk that patient will receive substandard or counterfeit drugs. As an alternative to a system with regulatory oversight, a single payer (for example, an insurance fund) or group of payers who contract with suppliers selected through a prequalification process can manage quality. In this situation, rather than being controlled by a regulatory body, suppliers are controlled by an agent hired by the payer. Pharmacists are reimbursed only for drugs that are purchased from the contracted suppliers.

Figure 4.1 illustrates the principles of an integrated pharmaceutical supply chain as described here for a system with a third-party payer.

Such advanced supply-chain models are common in the private sector across all types of goods traded at the retail level on a daily basis; however, most low-income countries maintain public sector supply chains that function in a very different way. The most common model is one in which governments provide the financing for all inputs that go into the

Figure 4.1   Example of an Integrated Pharmaceutical Supply Chain

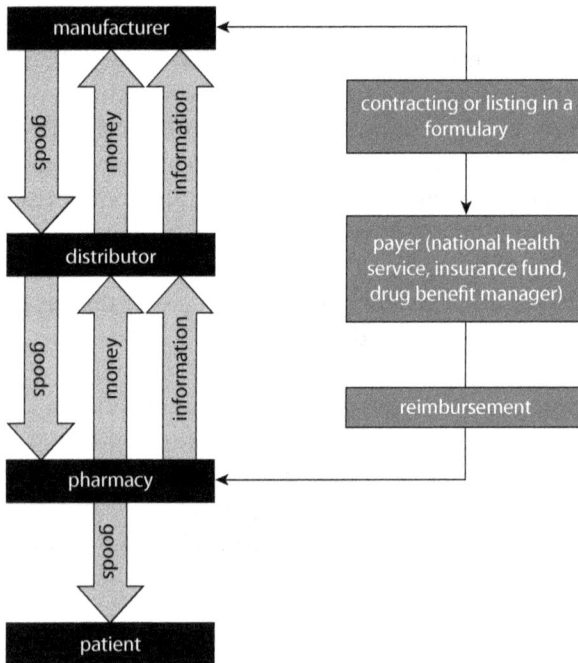

Source: Author's representation.
Note: An integrated supply chain is characterized by a steady flow of information on sales transactions and inventory levels, allowing manufacturers to anticipate orders and schedule production so that they can deliver on time. The parties contractually agree on the flow of funds. Institutional payers typically reimburse pharmacists and provide market access to manufacturers through either contracting or listing in a formulary.

delivery of health services to the population, including drugs, consumables, equipment, buildings, salaries, and operating costs. The use of government money combined with limited administrative capacity usually leads to a centralized, top-down management approach.

At the top of the public supply chain sits the procurement function. Significant purchasing power is concentrated at this level, raising concerns about potential inefficiencies and corruption, which usually lead to a rigid set of rules to guide this function. The public procurement process, described in detail in a number of technical publications and toolkits (for example, MSH 1997), is characterized by significant bureaucratic requirements causing long lead times between the initial demand signal and the arrival of the goods at the retail level. Procurement in yearly cycles is not unusual, which makes the information that provided the basis for the procurement plan long outdated by the time the goods arrive at the facility. At the facility level, long-term forecasting is required to ensure future drug supplies. Because disease patterns can vary and drug consumption is influenced by additional factors such as purchasing power, changing preferences of prescribers, and fluctuation of patient numbers, long-term forecasts are notoriously unreliable. Furthermore, the aggregation of forecasts from facilities by the central level is only one input for the procurement plan. Depending on the budget, the actual order volume might be reduced below the numbers required by the forecast. Facilities, having experienced shortages of certain drugs caused by previous rationing, may adjust their forecasts to compensate for the likely reductions made at central level, which further weakens the quality of data in the system. In many cases, the data flow is based on written tables and order forms and fragmented into several steps—for example, from facility to district depot, from there to a regional warehouse, and finally to the central purchasing authority. At each level, data can potentially be adjusted and lower-level inputs overruled.

The core procurement process is usually a tender process in which suppliers are invited to submit bids. Predefined criteria mandate how the winning bidder is selected. Usually, price is the main or only parameter for selection. Quality criteria, such as adherence to current good manufacturing practices (cGMPs), are applied either prior to the tender process during prequalification of bidders or after the bid evaluation during postqualification of the winning bidder. The contract for the bidder is issued only if the qualification criteria are fulfilled. This process, together with pre- or postshipment testing of the actual products, is supposed to ensure the quality of the drugs procured with public funds. The contract between the procurement office and the bidder defines not only the volumes and prices but also the delivery schedule and timelines, as well as the procedure for handling complaints, potential penalties, and so on. In most cases, the contract defines a one-off business relationship, ending when the defined amount has been delivered and paid for. Then the next procurement cycle starts, and the supplier has to bid again, without any assurance of ongoing business. Physical delivery of goods is usually made to a central warehouse. Sometimes deliveries are scheduled in several separate shipments. In other cases, all goods for a year arrive at once. Few public procurement systems contract with suppliers for delivery directly to regional warehouses. In most cases, the suppliers have no involvement with the part of the supply chain that reaches from the receiving warehouses to the patient.

Connected with the first part only through a periodic planning exercise and bulk shipments of drugs arriving at one or more central warehouses, this second part of the supply chain has to ensure that the supplies arriving at the top are distributed to the facility level in a timely manner and in adequate amounts, so that facilities do not run out of important drugs. It can use a "push" system: through a central allocation method, drugs are distributed to facilities (usually through one or two intermediary warehouses) or made available for pickup by a truck hired by the facility. An alternative is a "pull" system, in which facilities order and receive or pick up only the amounts they order (assuming that stock levels are sufficient).

In most countries, the flow of goods initiates a flow of funds in the opposite direction. Usually, drugs are dispensed in public facilities for cash at a set price. Intermediary warehouses need to recover their costs by adding an agreed margin to the price of the drugs. Financial transactions between public sector entities tend to be more bureaucratic than transactions in the private sector. For example, a hospital that wants to pay its drug bill to the regional medical store may require approval from a local finance officer in the district administration. In some cases, the available funds may not be sufficient to pay for a shipment that was allocated on the basis of an order issued several months ago. Salaries for public servants in the periphery and in the center are usually not linked to financial performance, so they have limited incentive to pay bills on time or to collect receivables. Interinstitutional indebtedness is therefore a common problem in public supply chains.

Figure 4.2 demonstrates the disconnect between upstream and downstream supply chains in many public sector systems. The disconnect

Figure 4.2   Example of a Public Sector Supply System

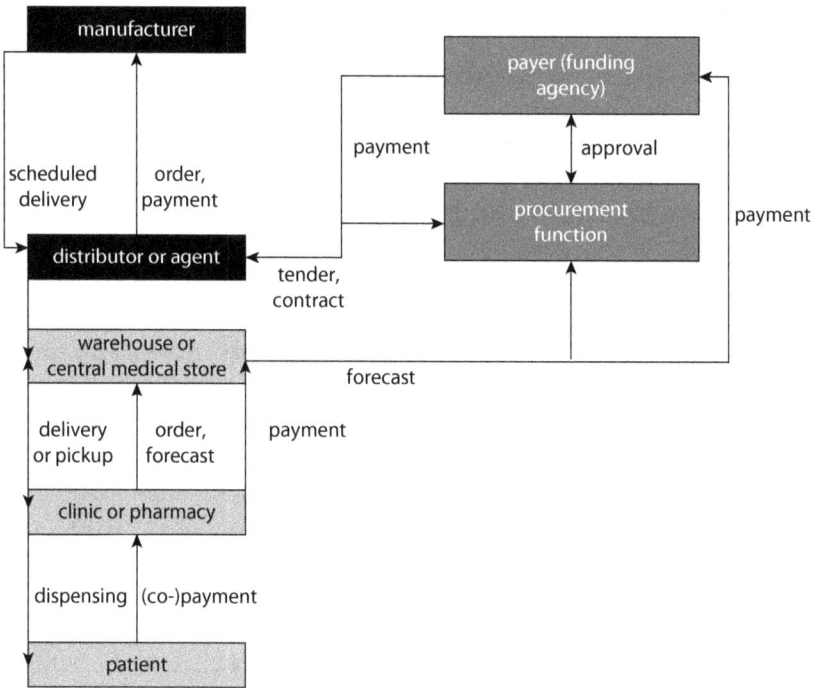

Source: Author's representation.
Note: Instead of a steady flow of goods, information, and money along the supply chain, this model is defined by multilateral interactions among payers, buyers, and suppliers. The main warehouse and its suppliers exchange information only via the procurement function, which usually works on the basis of annual cycles. Two payment pathways exist: (a) the funding agency usually pays the supplier, and (b) along the peripheral supply chain, cash payments flow to the central warehouse for covering distribution costs, in some cases reimbursing the payer for costs of supplied drugs.

between the upstream supply chain from manufacturer to the main warehouse and the downstream part in most public systems is more than a logistics issue that is responsible for frequent mismatches between supply and demand. It can lead to economic inefficiencies that eat up all the savings achieved by lowering ex-factory prices for drugs through a bidding process. If the system is managed for a certain performance or service level (for example, 90 percent availability of certain drugs at the facility level at all times), high investments in buffer stocks and warehouse capacity may be necessary to cope with uncertainties in forecasting and long lead times for deliveries. Unlike the integrated supply chain with constant real-time information flow, the information in the public supply chains described here is transmitted only once in a given period, and data quality is usually low because of counting or transmission errors, manipulation in trying to play the system, or other reasons embedded in human behavior. An analysis done in 2009 in Lesotho showed that, given the parameters obtained from procurement records and supply-chain transactions, achieving a satisfactory service level within the current system would be very costly (World Bank 2009). Capital and logistics costs for buffer stocks would be so high that the actual price paid by the procurement office would be only a minor determinant of total expenditure.

Many other countries would probably find themselves in a similar situation if they did such an analysis: if public procurement and supply-chain management remain two largely unconnected tasks, the investment in buffer stocks needed to reduce stock-outs to a defined and tolerable minimum might be prohibitively high. Moreover, under the agreements with their major donors, countries may not be permitted to use donor funds to buy buffer stocks. This situation leaves two major policy options: (a) lowering expectations and accepting supply interruptions or (b) redesigning the supply chain so that the upstream and downstream parts are better integrated and information can flow freely.

The first option is the status quo and is therefore not discussed further here. The major challenge in redesigning the supply chain is the existing law in most countries, which assumes that procurement and supply-chain management are two different and separate activities. Although technically one could create a publicly owned entity that has a public health mandate to ensure access to essential drugs, operates according to private sector principles, and covers the entire supply chain from the manufacturer's exit gate to the patient, doing so would require a change of the law and an exception from or an amendment to public procurement rules in many countries. Where such a change in legislation is politically feasible, additional hurdles need to be overcome to make a public sector supply system work:

- A sustainable and predictable source of funding must be available, adequate for the expected types and amounts of medicines passed through the system. Ideally, the supply-chain redesign is linked to a redesign of the financing mechanism that puts purchasing power into the hands of patients (such as health insurance) or peripheral institutions (earmarked budgets for drug purchases) rather than paying for drugs out of central budgets.

- Human resource policies, information systems, and operational policies (such as purchasing, contracting, client service, and return policies) should be derived from successful private sector logistics systems to ensure that incentives are aligned with desired outcomes and goods and that money and information can flow as required. This realignment requires institutional autonomy and a strong governance structure with an independent board and auditing function. Enforcement of sanctions internally and against business partners in breach of contract must be ensured.

Few countries have tried to radically redesign their public sector supply agencies. Ethiopia developed a "Business-Process Re-engineering" plan for its public supply agency in 2008, but implementation is ongoing and financing up to full scale is still a challenge. Step-by-step autonomization of functions that previously were closely controlled combined with increased budget autonomy for health care providers is usually a more viable option. Burkina Faso and Cameroon used such an approach, for example, to pursue the "marketization" of central medical stores, and success varied.

This discussion is closely linked to the debate on centralization versus decentralization in health care. A study done by the Harvard School of Public Health suggests specific criteria for deciding which functions should be managed centrally and which are better decentralized (Bossert and others 2003). The study's findings, in short, suggest that more peripheral decision space in budgeting, forecasting, and procurement increases logistics performance. In contrast, the management information system needs to be centralized and standardized for all levels and units to maximize performance. In extension of this logic, procurement contracts should be negotiated centrally, but preferably in the form of framework agreements that specify at which prices facilities or intermediary distribution points can purchase the contracted items. If the prices agreed in framework contracts with manufacturers include shipment of the product to a subwarehouse or even to the facilities, the manufacturers have an interest in optimizing shipping logistics to ensure availability (which equals higher sales) and to minimize logistics costs. At such a point, the supply-chain operation has effectively been outsourced to the private sector. The public sector can focus on monitoring contract fulfillment and service quality. Box 4.1 describes in more detail how framework contracts with manufacturers can be structured.

Box 4.1

Scope and Purpose of a Framework Contract

A framework contract aims at reducing and standardizing drug prices and ensuring product availability and consistent quality for facilities by negotiating with manufacturers, importers, or first-line distributors. Such contracts apply to all health service providers that belong to the public sector network or to a defined subset. Private or nongovernmental organization providers can also be included if they have a contractual relationship with the public sector.

Procurement Process

Even if no physical delivery of drugs to the procuring unit and no payment from the procuring unit take place, the standard principles of competitive procurement can still be applied. A preferred procurement method for multisource drugs is limited international bidding among prequalified manufacturers. Ability to manage parts of the downstream logistics would be part of the prequalification criteria in this case.

Possible Type of Contract

The contract can define retail price, quality standards, and availability at the facility level as quantifiable criteria and include built-in incentives for the provider to perform according to agreed levels for these criteria. The contract would not necessarily bind the negotiating or purchasing entities to buy certain amounts. However, the group purchaser would provide an estimate for the demand based on historic data or a survey among facilities or reimbursement schemes. The central contracting entity has the authority to advise all providers entitled to purchase drugs under the agreement to use the brands that are subject to the contract as preferred options.

The central contracting unit would neither buy nor pay for any drugs under this contract. As before, health facilities or contracted pharmacies buy drugs (but now under defined conditions and with prenegotiated prices), and patients or reimbursement schemes pay for them when they are dispensed.

Duration

Such framework contracts involve several parties and require a learning and trust-building period before optimal results can be obtained. A contract period of two years is not unusual in such cases.

Number of Preferred Brands for One Molecule

To ensure continuity of supply and avoid monopolies, contracting with two or three alternative manufacturers for drugs with high public health impact and

(continued)

Box 4.1 *(continued)*

turnover may make sense. Such arrangements may require some form of assurance for manufacturers that they get a certain share of the market, for example, by giving each manufacturer "preferred status" for a certain region or institutional level, guaranteeing minimum sales, or rotating the default option in an electronic purchasing system.

Monitoring and Enforcement of the Agreed Service Level

Ensuring availability of the preferred brands at the facility or pharmacy level is important. It can be done by agreeing to certain penalties or price cuts if availability levels are not achieved, for example.

Quality Standards

Quality assurance parameters should be defined in discussions with the regulatory agency to ensure they are enforceable in the local market without requiring major additional resources. The regulatory agency may have records of good manufacturing practice inspections and analysis of samples and might be able to assist in the prequalification of bidders.

Communication and Training

A key parameter for the functioning of such framework contracts is full awareness and understanding among facilities and intermediary distributors, because they are supposed to execute these contracts in daily transactions that are based on the negotiated terms. The contracting agency could develop a training module, easy-to-use instruction materials, and a service hotline for facilities. Facilities also have a role in providing feedback to the contracting agency on availability and provider compliance. In addition, effective communication with the public is important to get patient buy-in and acceptance of the preselection of certain brands based on quality and price.

Source: Author.

A simple way to initiate the transition from a classic public sector supply system with separation of procurement and distribution to a more integrated system relying on private sector capacity is to empower intermediary distribution centers and health facilities to manage their own drug budgets and to buy from the private sector if the conditions are better or if the public sector has supply shortages. If sufficient funding is available, the private sector will quickly establish the supply chain needed to catch the opportunity. Facilities may prefer buying from private suppliers even if the prices are higher, because such suppliers offer more flexible delivery and payment conditions and allow for smaller shipments that better match the cash-flow situation in facilities. Ghana provides an interesting example. In some parts of the country, the private sector provides 80 percent and more of supplies for regional medical stores and facilities (Seiter and Gyansa-Lutterodt 2009). A boost in availability of money to purchase drugs caused by the rollout of the National Health Insurance Scheme created demand spikes, and the central medical stores were unable to respond to the increased demand in time. Private wholesalers stepped in and quickly developed additional capacity to capture the new business. The problem with such a Darwinistic free-market approach is that the benefits of pooled purchasing are lost. Buyers may be exposed to low-quality drugs and pay higher prices than necessary. Moreover, the risk of collusion between buyers and wholesalers is a problem in many countries.[1] Although these arrangements may be beneficial in terms of ensuring availability of drugs, they certainly are not economically efficient because the kickbacks paid to the facility manager need to be earned back through higher prices. However, in the Ghanaian context, the National Health Insurance Authority and the procurement unit of the Ministry of Health could at any time introduce a pooled purchasing model. Such a change would address the potential downside of the de facto privatization of parts of the public supply chain.

Although the suggested reforms, if done well and accompanied by adequate financing and payment system modifications, can overcome many logistics problems in accessible and populated areas, reaching the rural poor in remote areas, such as mountains, deserts, jungles, or islands, will always pose major challenges. A combination of low income, high transportation costs, and small populations makes these remote areas very unattractive for any private sector operation. The public sector needs either to maintain its own delivery systems to reach such populations or to contract with private suppliers offering conditions that compensate for the higher costs and smaller market opportunities. Nevertheless, the principles remain the same: the flow of goods, money, and information needs to be unclogged and synchronized. With increased coverage by cell phone networks, mobile communication technology could increasingly become useful for transmission of logistics data in remote areas, thereby improving the cost-efficiency of expensive shipments and ensuring that the right types and amounts of drugs are shipped at the right time.

Box 4.2 highlights a potential model for the creation of a secure supply chain in countries with weak regulation and market oversight.

Box 4.2

Creating a Secure Supply Chain in Liberia

An interesting approach to improving the availability of good-quality essential medicines to poor people in rural areas is currently under consideration in Liberia.[a] The Liberian National Drug Service (NDS) successfully established three essential drugs stores supplied under a framework agreement by a procurement agency in Europe, which ensures the quality of the medicines through manufacturer prequalification and in-house controls. NDS runs the existing stores on a cost-recovery basis, not for profit. Prices for most drugs are significantly lower than in the (still largely unregulated) private sector. The intention is to scale up this model to the national level by opening additional stores in cities with sufficient population and purchasing power and to pilot a mobile unit that takes the NDS pharmacy to markets, where people from nearby villages come together once a week to trade (see also chapter 7).

Source: Author.
a. Proposal to the Japanese Social Development Fund under preparation by the World Bank.

Using Purchasing Power to Get Value for Money

In contrast to consumer markets such as the market for cell phones, the market for prescription pharmaceuticals is an expert-driven market in which consumers have little bargaining power. Furthermore, at least in the case of acute diseases, consumers may not have much time or energy to shop around for a better deal. Although in urban areas with a high density of pharmacies consumers can sometimes get discounts (unless prices are fixed by regulation), they have few options to assess whether the underlying prices are reasonable according to international benchmarks. In some cases (for example, in Thailand), HIV patients have created "buyer clubs" that enable them to purchase drugs at a discount.

Creating a functioning market requires a better balance between the provider and the consumer, which can be achieved by pooling consumer purchasing power in institutions that have sufficient market information and bargaining power to match the provider side. Public procurement of drugs fulfills these criteria and can frequently achieve lower prices than those available in private pharmacies. However, as pointed out earlier, the problem is on the service delivery side: the cheaply procured drugs may not reach the patient, may not be sufficient to meet demand, or may not be accepted by patients influenced to believe they are not effective. Another issue is the lack of enforcement capacity to ensure that retailers adhere to margin regulations. Managers of health facilities tend to use the proceeds from drug sales to fill other budget holes. If oversight is not effective, they may apply higher margins to the publicly procured drugs than are officially permitted. Surveys of prices for malaria drugs have shown that in many cases the private sector prices are used as benchmarks by public sector facility managers when setting their own prices.[2] For example, an artemisinin-based combination therapy procured with donor funds that should be sold to patients at the facility level for a small handling charge of US$0.60 may in reality be priced at US$4.50, yielding the facility manager a profit of US$3.90 per pack.[3] The private pharmacy across the street charges US$6.00 for a similar drug, so patients will still prefer the public facility as long as the supply lasts.

Purchasing power can be used more effectively to lower prices of drugs *and* secure supplies if a reimbursement mechanism links the provider payment with the actual dispensing of the drug to the patient. This system requires third-party financing, through either health insurance or a publicly funded pool from which individual prescriptions for entitled patients are paid. The patients typically have an insurance card or similar identifier with a unique number. Together with the prescription from a contracted physician, the patient identifier allows the pharmacist to invoice the third-party payer. The third-party payer collects information about all transactions and can use it as an input for management decisions. In low- and middle-income countries, most prescriptions are for generic drugs that are available from many alternative sources. The entity that administers the payments can use a bidding process as described in the previous section, leading to framework contracts with manufacturers that lock in lower prices for all beneficiaries of the funding pool. Box 4.3 describes an example of how this system could look in practice.

Other strategies are used for negotiating prices for innovative, patented drugs that are available from only the originator company while the patent is in effect. For a limited range of lifesaving drugs with high relevance for public health in developing countries, manufacturers offer steep discounts to buyers in low-income countries or provide licenses for local manufacturers to make generic versions for low-income market segments. Many middle-income countries, however, may find obtaining such favorable prices difficult, because their markets are too important commercially for the manufacturers. Nevertheless, manufacturers know that their drugs will have a very limited market if they are not covered by

Box 4.3

Hypothetical Example of the Use of Purchasing Power to Ensure Availability of Low-Price Drugs to Patients with Health Insurance

The health insurance fund in country A provides coverage, including a package of essential medicines, for 10 million people. Patients get an insurance card. When they pick up a prescription, they show their insurance card and can obtain the drugs that are listed by the insurance fund at no cost or for a small co-payment. The insurance has negotiated prices with a number of manufacturers for the 50 most prescribed multisource drugs. Pharmacists are contractually obliged to stock these "preferred" drugs and are generally compensated through a flat dispensing fee rather than a profit margin that would create an incentive to recommend more expensive brands. Standard treatment guidelines for physicians indicate the preferred choices in bold print at the top of the list for each relevant condition. Physicians are instructed to issue prescriptions with the generic name of the drug only. Patients can obtain the preferred drugs without co-payment. If they choose an alternative brand not covered under the framework agreements between insurance fund and suppliers, patients have to pay a significant share of the cost out of pocket. Stock-outs are avoided because when one manufacturer has capacity problems, two or three alternative brands are available for each active ingredient on the list of preferred drugs.

Source: Author.

health insurance or an existing public payment system and are willing to enter into negotiations that can lead to significant concessions. Such concessions may not be visible in the list price of the drug. Manufacturers try to keep published prices within a global price band to avoid negative consequences from price regulation models that use international price comparison as a benchmark. Easier to accept for manufacturers in a situation of budget restrictions are volume limits or volume discounts that take the form of free goods to large institutional buyers. Regional pooled procurement models, as are in place, for example, in Latin America (through the Pan American Health Organization) and in the Gulf Cooperation Council countries, may get better prices than national buyers in smaller countries, but they require regulatory harmonization among the participating countries. Table 4.1 shows various models for negotiated solutions aimed at limiting expenditure for patented drugs.

Table 4.1   Negotiated Solutions to Limit Prices of Patented Drugs

Purpose	Solution	Comments
To improve access to expensive drugs for rare diseases	Voluntary patient assistance programs sponsored by manufacturers	Free or subsidized drugs for individual eligible patients (diagnosis, income level)
To limit financial impact on the drug budget of a positive reimbursement decision for a new drug	Price-volume agreements, with clawback of funds, free goods, or lower prices, triggered if an agreed volume threshold is passed	Reliable sales or consumption data needed, typically gathered at the insurance fund; enforcement of clawbacks can be difficult
To share the risk of wasteful spending for expensive drugs with narrow, specific indications	"Pay for performance" contract, with no payment if defined treatment goals are not reached	Only used in indications with objectively measurable treatment start- and endpoints (enzyme levels, cell counts, broken bones)
To improve access to new treatments with broader indication for the low-income population	Dual-brand or restricted licensing agreement under which the manufacturer gets access to the high-end market with the high-priced original and offers or allows making of a low-price generic version for treatment channels serving the poor	Only possible if markets can be segmented to avoid erosion of profitability in the high-income segment by the low-cost version
To use purchasing power of single payer to get better prices for "me-too" drugs or added services from manufacturer	Establishment of a "preferred brand" with a lower co-payment for patients, based on best price offers from manufacturers of competing, interchangeable brands	System required in which co-payments can be used to differentiate between brands and in which pharmacist incentives are aligned
To allow limited access (within a given budget) to new drugs with narrow indications	Creation of special treatment programs managed by few specific institutions, which are supplied by a central purchaser (pooling the purchases should lead to higher volume discounts)	Form of rationing used to eliminate any risk of overspending the budget
To achieve savings in a portfolio as partial compensation for additional costs for new drug	Manufacturer discounts offered on older products in exchange for the listing of new products ("bundling"); such contracts could include diagnostics and other services for better patient management	Potentially applicable in chronic diseases with stepwise treatment approach and a range of treatment options (for example, hypertension)

Source: Author's compilation.

The strategies for better use of institutional purchasing power explained previously require a high degree of sophistication on the side of the institution (for example, the health insurance fund). Many funds in low- and middle-income countries, originating from public sector entities and governed by public sector regulations, may have difficulty developing the necessary contracting skills, establishing a monitoring system that allows tracking of contract fulfillment, and staying on top of the emerging international experience on successful negotiation strategies. Many national insurance funds are still mostly passive payers and make little use of their bargaining power. However, given the dimension of drug budgets—they can easily make up 30 percent and more of a health insurance fund's total expenditures—investments in the skills and tools required for successful management of drug expenditures are likely to pay off quickly. A fund manager can easily calculate how much could be saved if prices for high-volume drugs were lowered by only 10 percent. Savings, even if based on cautious assumptions regarding the success of measures described here, can potentially reach a multiple of the costs for upgrading systems and recruiting the experts needed to staff an active purchasing function.

An alternative to hosting the function that manages the pharmaceutical benefit component of a health service package at the insurance fund or public entity administrating the pool of funds is outsourcing to specialized service providers, as in the U.S. model. In the United States and a few other countries, specialized companies (called pharmaceutical benefit managers, or PBMs) administer drug reimbursement, negotiate prices on behalf of several insurance funds, and adjust incentives for pharmacists and patients to ensure optimal use of resources. Depending on the legislative environment, such a model may be easier to implement than setting up the function within a public insurance fund.

Managing the Decision Process on Formulary Inclusion

As pointed out earlier, health insurance funds or public reimbursement funds for prescription drugs act as gatekeepers to the market by providing purchasing power that may be lacking if individual patients have to pay for drugs out of pocket. In this function, the managers of these funds are under pressure from drug companies to include their drugs in the list of reimbursed medicines. Twenty years ago, several developed countries still had an open reimbursement policy, paying for almost anything a doctor prescribed. Since then, increases in health care costs and the boost in the number of available treatment options have forced fund managers to apply restrictions to funding. In most cases, they do so through a *formulary*, meaning a list that defines which drugs are reimbursed, for which conditions, and at what price. Being on the list is a condition for getting relevant market share in many countries; therefore, drug companies focus their initial marketing efforts at the institutional level, where inclusion decisions are made. Drug companies today employ entire departments that spend significant resources on preparing an appealing case for every new drug to ensure smooth acceptance into major reimbursement lists. No middle-income country today has the internal financial and institutional resources to do a complete and independent assessment of the comprehensive files submitted by drug companies. The usual approach to making the reimbursement decision is through an evaluation process, in which an expert committee reviews documentation provided by the manufacturer and makes a recommendation to the decision-making authority (in many cases, the minister of health). Insurance fund representatives are part of these commissions, but in many cases, they lack veto power to ensure that budget limits are considered in the commission's recommendations.

The hurdle of formulary inclusion provides the insurance fund or public payer significant leverage over the submitting company, which can be used to negotiate concessions and limit budget risks from adding a new treatment option. To use this leverage, many countries need to revise the process of managing inclusion in the reimbursement list to allow the insurance fund a larger role. They could, for example, create a preliminary list of drugs that merit inclusion in the formulary. Manufacturers would then have to pass to a second step of negotiation with the insurance fund or similar competent authority. Once the negotiations have led to an acceptable result, access to the reimbursement list is granted.

Formal price regulation, which still exists in many countries, can prevent flexible negotiated solutions and should be reviewed in this respect. Note that total costs to the system are the relevant parameter, not price per unit. Drug companies are very effective in generating high sales volumes for drugs that have only limited official indications. If price regulation is the only cost management tool, companies will adjust by driving up volume. To counter such a development, the payer would have to introduce rationing measures, which are hard to achieve and not very popular. In contrast, if an agreement locks in a relatively higher price but limits volume at an agreed level, the manufacturer would have to provide free goods once the volume ceiling is exceeded, making the risk for the payer manageable.

The process of establishing a new drug's "worthiness" to be considered for reimbursement has become very complex. To reduce the pressure on decision-making bodies from lobbying groups and the interested public, developed countries have institutionalized the scientific assessment process and developed detailed sets of rules for conducting this process. This limited individual discretion combined with high transparency at every level increases public trust that the decisions are made in the public's best interests. As pointed out in chapter 3, the conflict potential is high in an area in which individual lives and health outcomes are weighed against monetary values. Although agreement exists on the fringe positions—that any cheap and lifesaving treatment should be reimbursed and that an extremely expensive treatment with only marginal benefits should not—the battle for the middle ground can be bitter. Commercial interests of manufacturers who have invested a great deal of money and want a payback and personal interests of affected patients who are clinging to any straw that offers hope for a desperate condition mix into a powerful political cocktail. One widely known institution that has been set up to manage this conflict is the National Institute for Clinical Excellence (NICE) in the United Kingdom. NICE's role extends beyond assessment of specific drugs or procedures to include assessing entire therapeutic areas and providing guidance for prevention, treatment, and health promotion. NICE provides a quality assurance framework with a set of clear procedural principles based on independence, inclusiveness, and transparency, from which it draws its legitimacy. NICE's methodology is published on its Web site (http://www.nice.org.uk), and recently NICE started offering assistance to other countries interested in building up capacity for health technology assessment. NICE is a relatively small institution that provides the technical and administrative backing for the process and takes public responsibility for its recommendations (which are the basis for treatment coverage decisions at the British National Health Service). Academics from U.K. universities contracted by NICE perform the assessment work following NICE rules and procedures.

Economic assessment of new drugs or devices usually quantifies benefits in quality-adjusted life years (QALYs) or disability-adjusted life years (DALYs). QALYs and DALYs are compounded parameters, and they may differ for different populations: quality of life for a young mother in Africa may mean something different from that for a retired single man in the United Kingdom. The monetary values that are considered acceptable for allocating public resources to a particular treatment also vary greatly, depending on a country's economic situation. Whereas a new cancer treatment at a cost of US$50,000 per QALY may be acceptable in the United Kingdom, it may not be in a middle-income country that already has to ration treatment options that cost only US$500 per QALY.

Not every country needs to set up an institution like NICE to cope with the conflict surrounding reimbursement decisions. NICE and similar institutions publish a large number of assessment reports every year that are available to everyone. Smaller countries with limited resources can use these reports with available national data to value new treatment options by comparing them to existing ones and to create priority lists based on the drug's clinical benefits and the country's disease priorities. Drugs for which the relationship between clinical benefit and public health need appears positive can then be analyzed in terms of likely budget impact before they are considered for inclusion in the formulary. This analysis then serves as a basis for negotiations with the supplier, aiming at a risk-sharing agreement that limits financial exposure to an acceptable level. Box 4.4 provides a hypothetical example for such a mechanism.

Although the example in box 4.4 is hypothetical, several upper-middle-income countries are moving in a direction in which such procedures become routine (as they are already in high-income countries). However, most of these countries are still hanging onto the commission model, in which a group of experts decides which drugs are added to the reimbursement list, usually behind closed doors and without making the criteria very transparent. Frequently, these experts hold senior positions in tertiary institutions, thus making them a prime target for the marketing efforts of drug companies. Such experts may have been involved in clinical trials for the drugs on which they later make decisions, and they may have been paid for speaking assignments or publications on these drugs. Appropriate disclosure of such conflicts of interest is therefore very important if these experts serve on public commissions. Conflicts are inevitable unless one excludes the most knowledgeable experts, but such conflicts must be made known and may lead to situations in which specific experts abstain from votes on drugs for which a conflict of interest is reasonably likely.

To reduce discretion or neutralize external influences on decision making of reimbursement commissions, one can consider a more rules-based approach to decision making—for example, through a semi-quantitative score. Even in the absence of good disease statistics and cost data, system insiders have significant knowledge that, if pooled in a commission, can guide rational decisions. As pointed out, ratings of new drugs in countries

Box 4.4

Hypothetical Example of a Low-Cost Assessment Process for New Drugs

The health insurance fund in country X has a small unit, staffed by a physician, a pharmacist, an economist, and three research assistants. This unit screens applications for inclusion of innovative drugs in the reimbursement list. The staff collects all information on the new drugs from international publications (for example, the Web sites of health technology assessment agencies in Europe, Australia, and Canada). For example, when company N submits an application for a new antiviral agent against hepatitis C, the evaluation team finds consistent reports from agencies in developed countries indicating that this treatment is clinically significantly more effective and better tolerated than the current treatment. Chronic hepatitis C cases are a significant cause of liver cancer in country X at a rate about twice the international average. Therefore, the assessment team recommends including this drug in a priority review list and proceeds with the economic assessment. The reimbursement commission, consisting of clinical experts, pharmacologists, and economic experts as well as representatives from the insurance fund, the ministry of health, the ministry of finance, and consumer groups, reviews the report of the assessment team and endorses its recommendations.

Available statistics show about 5,000 hepatitis C patients each year in the country who might benefit from the new treatment. Currently, about US$1 million is spent each year to treat hepatitis C with existing medication, which is less effective than the new drug. Treatment costs per patient are US$500 per year, meaning about 2,000 patients are receiving treatment. Costs for late-stage treatment of avoidable liver cancer are unknown, but likely significant. The quoted price for the new treatment is US$4,000 per year.

On the basis of these data, the insurance fund decides to enter into negotiations with the manufacturer. The fund is in a decent financial position and, given the clear clinical benefits and public health relevance, willing to double the allocation for hepatitis C treatment to US$2 million. It assumes the new treatment will over time replace the old one. At the quoted price, only 500 patients could be treated with the available budget. Country X recently introduced an amendment to the drug law that specifies that administrative price setting based on external reference prices, which is the standard for all patented drugs, can be waived if companies enter into specific reimbursement agreements with the insurance fund.

(continued)

Box 4.4 *(continued)*

After long negotiations, the following agreement is reached: company N's drug is included in the reimbursement list as a treatment of second choice, to be used if the old treatment has not led to a defined improvement of lab parameters within six months. Country X accepts the list price of US$4,000 but will receive a discount of 20 percent if the number of treated patients exceeds 300 within a year. A volume ceiling of 500 treatments is agreed to. If more patients are enrolled in treatment in the first year, the company provides free treatment for the additional patients. The agreement will be reviewed after nine months with the intention of increasing the financial allocation for the following year if the ceiling of 500 patients is exceeded in the first year.

Source: Author.

with competent health technology assessment institutions can be used as a starting position. A drug that is generally rated as highly effective and superior to other types of treatment will get a high score; one that is seen as not or only marginally superior will get a low score. Additional points are given if the underlying disease is of high, medium, or low relevance from a public health perspective. Aspects of treatment delivery can be rated as well—for example, whether facility standards and diagnostic equipment are sufficient to deliver the treatment effectively and safely. Other parameters can be cost of current versus new treatment, likelihood that the new treatment will be used off-label,[4] and so on.

Box 4.5 shows a hypothetical scoring table that could be used to rank new treatments in terms of priority for inclusion in the reimbursement list. Such scoring systems are easily developed and adjusted to country-specific needs and data availability. A rules-based and structured approach, combined with publication of proceedings and evaluation data, can reduce the public and lobbying pressure on commission members and increase predictability of decision making—an aspect that is valued by the industry also, even if the outcomes are not always in line with the companies' expectations.

Moderated and structured decision-making methods can be used to address group dynamics in decision-making committees and to ensure that all viewpoints get fair consideration. For example, the Croatian Health Insurance Institute is considering use of the Delphi method for the meetings of its reimbursement committee.[5] Another set of principles

Box 4.5

Sample Format for Ranking Drug X for Treatment of Acute Ischemic Stroke within the First 60 Minutes

(Description of the drug, mechanism of action, claims by manufacturer, comparable treatments if any, price per treatment in comparison with current treatment if available)

(Documents used for the neutral assessment)

	Score
• Decisions by other authorities:	
• Netherlands: no reimbursement	0
• United Kingdom: restricted reimbursement, preapproval	1
• Sweden: restricted reimbursement, preapproval	1
• Ontario, Canada: restricted reimbursement, only five hospitals	1
• France: unrestricted reimbursement	2
• Additional parameters:	
• Public health priority: medium	1
• Subjective suffering: medium	1
• Cost compared to current treatment: much higher	0
• Clear clinical advantage for patient: yes in 10 to 20 percent of cases	1
• Delivery of treatment possible in country A: yes	2
• Containment of out-of-label use: medium difficulty	1
Total score:	**11 of 22**

Note: Score values: 2 = positive; 1 = neutral; 0 = negative; maximum score = 22.

for decision making has been laid out by Daniels and Sabin (2002) under the rubric Accountability for Reasonableness (A4R). The four core principles of A4R are

• *Publicity.* Decisions to limit health care and the reasons behind them must be accessible for the public.
• *Relevance.* The discussion leading up to the decision must be based on evidence, reason, and principles that a person with good common sense would affirm.
• *Appeals.* An appeals mechanism for challenging allocation decisions must exist.

- *Regulation.* Such regulation must ensure fulfillment of the first three principles.

Decision-making norms and procedures have to be viewed against the cultural norms and the unwritten rules governing individual behavior. Open societies with strong rule of law and trust in public institutions are usually better at implementing fair procedures based on deliberation, whereas countries with fragile political systems and high endemic corruption may be better off using a structured process supported by a semi-quantitative tool.

Creating Adequate Information Systems

None of the major dysfunction in pharmaceutical systems can be addressed in a sustainable way without access to detailed, timely, and reliable information. Standardized software tools exist for the regulatory function and for the pharmaceutical supply chain. Discussing details of the functionality of these systems goes beyond the scope of this book and is therefore left to the technical agencies specializing in these areas (for example, the World Health Organization, the United Nations Children's Fund, and the U.S. Agency for International Development's DELIVER project). The focus here is on information that can optimize use of drugs under both cost and treatment outcome perspectives.

If left alone, suppliers and health service providers tend to drive up consumption. Drug expenditures in all systems, whether they rely on out-of-pocket payments or third-party payment, tend to grow faster than the overall economy. The two core factors influencing total costs are price and number of units dispensed. Good proxies for these two factors are, respectively, value per prescription and number of items per prescription. These two data points can be obtained easily at the point of transaction in the pharmacy filling the prescription. Although these data can give a rough indication of the extent to which each of the two factors contributes to a cost increase, they may not be sufficient for developing effective instruments to manage costs. Key tools for cost management, as discussed in other chapters, include supply-side measures to lower prices and demand-side measures to ensure rational and cost-effective use of drugs. In both cases, more detailed data about use of specific drugs for specific indications are needed to develop strategies for negotiating with suppliers or identifying focus areas by which to measure improved rational use. Table 4.2 presents a set of data that decision makers on the payer side need to set up an effective management system for drug use.

Table 4.2   Payer-Side Data for Decision Makers

Data type	Method of acquisition
Brand name	Bar code on packaging
Generic name	Bar code on packaging
Dosage form	Bar code on packaging
Dosage	Bar code on packaging
Number of units	Bar code on packaging or manual entry
Price	Retrieved from database
Indication	Code provided by prescriber on prescription form
Patient identifier	Unique number or chip card (insurance card)
Prescriber or provider identifier	Prescription form (unique number or bar code)
Pharmacy identifier	Automatically entered at point of dispensing

Source: Author's compilation.

Figure 4.3   Collection of Prescribing and Drug Use Information at the Pharmacy Level

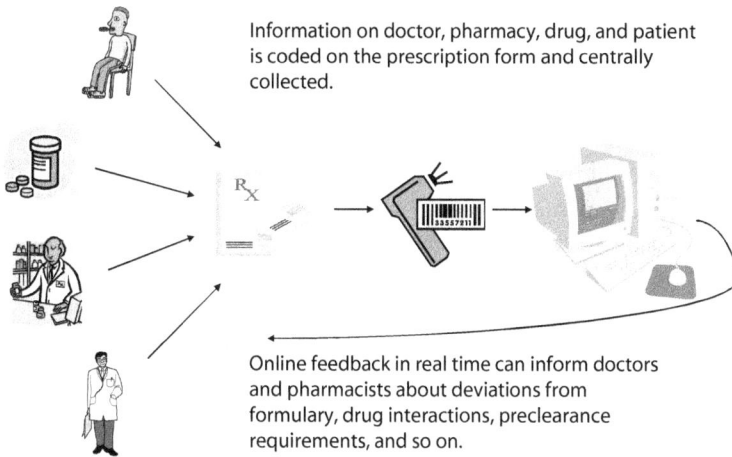

Information on doctor, pharmacy, drug, and patient is coded on the prescription form and centrally collected.

Online feedback in real time can inform doctors and pharmacists about deviations from formulary, drug interactions, preclearance requirements, and so on.

Source: Author's representation.

Figure 4.3 shows a system to collect prescribing and drug use information at the pharmacy level (based on an example from Montenegro). The transactional data are transferred immediately (if the system is online) or at regular intervals to a central database. This database allows data aggregation and generates reports that can be used to inform decision makers.

Following are some queries that can be answered with the help of such a database:

• Average value per prescription, number of items per prescription, trends over time, and regional distribution

- Ranking of drugs in terms of total expenditure (which are the drugs on which the most money is spent?)
- Ranking of physicians in terms of cost per prescription and regional ranking lists
- Rate of adoption of new, more expensive drugs at the expense of older ones
- Rate of generic versus originator product use
- Percentage of patients for which first-line treatment is used (for example, in hypertension), or a ranking list or grouping per physician that, for example, identifies physicians for whom less than 70 percent of patients are on first-line treatment
- Physicians who use more antibiotics than a set target value (for example, 20 percent of all prescriptions) or who make up the top quintile in antibiotic prescription

As the example shows, a prescription database can provide information on all imaginable aspects of drug use, allowing managers to develop strategies for behavior change through targeted feedback, training, or specific incentives for patients, prescribers, and pharmacists. The data can also be used to inform decisions on reimbursement and negotiations with drug companies. Certain forms of risk-sharing agreements with drug companies (see the previous discussion on managing the decision process on formulary inclusion) require the collection of drug-specific use and expenditure data to define the point at which the risk-sharing clause becomes applicable.

Another important aspect is the elimination of fraud, which can be a major problem in systems with third-party payers. Fraud or abuse can happen in various forms, such as the following:

- A pharmacist "forgets" to dispense one of several drugs on a prescription form but still charges the payer for it.
- The physician and pharmacist conspire so that fake prescriptions are reimbursed but never dispensed to the patient.
- Patients with insurance coverage try to get prescriptions for family members without coverage.
- Patients who are exempt from co-payment try to get prescriptions for family members who would have to make a co-payment.
- Patients visit several doctors and pharmacists to get more than one prescription for the same drug, which they then share with family members or sell on the gray market.

- The patient and pharmacist conspire so that the pharmacist charges the payer for an expensive drug, but the patient receives a cheaper version plus some free cosmetics or over-the-counter (OTC) drugs.

A prescription database alone cannot eliminate all forms of fraud, but it can be used to detect outliers, such as unusual patterns of prescribing and dispensing of expensive drugs by certain doctor-pharmacist pairs. Subsequent fraud investigations can focus on these outliers and confirm the suspicion. Patients who try to cheat the system can be discouraged even before the fraud happens, if pharmacies have an online connection to the central server. Transactions can be checked against certain plausibility criteria—for example, whether sex and age of the patient correspond to the medication that is prescribed, or whether the patient has already received a similar prescription in a different pharmacy during the same period. If inconsistencies are found, the pharmacist would receive a warning on the transaction screen, or the system would deny reimbursement instantly. This mechanism can also be used to detect parallel prescriptions of drugs that may interact in undesirable ways or to prevent dispensing of a drug to which a patient is allergic.

On an academic level, data from prescription and use databases can be used not only as a basis for pharmaceutical sector studies but also as a proxy for potentially missing data on health status and disease incidence in a given country. For example, if the country has no good system for recording the number of diabetic patients, the number of patients getting prescriptions for antidiabetic drugs may be a good approximation instead.

Ensuring Rational and Cost-Effective Use of Medicines

As has been pointed out, several factors contribute to inappropriate use and overuse of pharmaceuticals. Such irrational prescribing contributes to suboptimal treatment outcomes, avoidable side effects, and unnecessary expenditures of money that could be used better elsewhere in the system. Therefore, the policy objective to improve rational use has a qualitative and a quantitative aspect. The goal is to ensure that patients receive the drugs that are proven to have the best risk-benefit ratio for their particular condition (evidence-based medicine); in addition, the available funds should be used in the most cost-efficient way, ensuring the "greatest good for the greatest number." Unfortunately, this utilitarian principle is frequently at odds with the politics of resource allocation. Certain conditions and subpopulations tend to get a larger share of public attention or compassion and higher budget allocations per life saved than others. The significant funding available for HIV/AIDS treatment in developing countries compared to the small budgets for most other drugs exemplifies such political preferences.

Influencing patient preferences and provider behavior is among the most difficult tasks for pharmaceutical policy makers. It requires a bundle of measures that tackle the problem from different angles in a sustained effort over a period of years to achieve measurable results. Table 4.3 breaks

Table 4.3   Improving Rational Use of Medicines

What to do	How to do it
Defining what rational use means	• Evidence-based guidelines • National policy on rational use of medicines • Economic assessment
Promoting rational use	• Education and training (continuing medical education) • Manuals and drug lists for prescribers • Formularies (see the discussion in the text of managing the decision process on formulary inclusion) • Electronic databases and defaults in e-prescribing forms • Instant feedback in online pharmacy benefit management systems (see the discussion in the text on creating adequate information systems) • Academic detailing • Physician ranking lists based on rational use parameters • Consumer education
Monitoring rational use	• Electronic prescription or transaction tracking and database (see the discussion in the text on creating adequate information systems) • Regular monitoring, targeted surveys, and institutional audits
Creating incentives for rational use	• Differential co-payments for patients to promote generics • Compulsory training for physicians who show consistently low scores for rational prescribing • Financial incentives (such as a fee bonus) linked to achievement of rational use targets • Physician fund holding or budgeting • Flat dispensing fees for pharmacists
Curbing incentives that work against rational use	• Taxing of certain marketing expenses (for example, free goods given to wholesalers or hospitals to boost market share) • Limiting of access of pharmaceutical representatives or charging of companies through representative's visits to public institutions

Source: Author's compilation.

down the various dimensions of rational and cost-effective use of drugs and links them to specific action items on the policy agenda.

Successful strategies to improve rational use need to be anchored in overall drug policy, be sufficiently funded, and address all four dimensions (definition, promotion, monitoring, and incentives). Otherwise, the forces that undermine rational use (such as commercial and profit interests, inducements for prescribers, prejudice against generic drugs, and drug advertising and promotion) are likely to prevail. For this reason, measures to curb irrational use in cash-and-carry markets without a third-party payer tend to have little or no effect: no effective way exists to incentivize patients, prescribers, or pharmacists to use drugs more rationally if policy makers have no control over the financing and payment part of the transaction.

Given the wide range of potential diagnoses and treatments, most low- and middle-income countries will have resources to focus on only a few therapeutic areas at a time. These areas should be selected in accordance with public health and economic priorities. For example, a country may decide to focus all efforts for two years on reducing the prescribing of antibiotics for common colds and viral fevers. When this objective has been achieved, a subsequent campaign may target cardiovascular diseases and promote the appropriate use of first-line rather than second-line treatments.

Although, in general, rational use should lead to realization of savings in the drug budget (less use of antibiotics, less use of injections, use of generics instead of originator products), in some situations, the reverse occurs. The introduction of artemisinin-based combination therapies as first-line treatment for malaria, replacing cheap but increasingly ineffective chloroquine, has led to a significant increase in expenditures for malaria treatment in endemic countries.

Another aspect of rational use is undertreatment of certain conditions with negative long-term impact on health and economic parameters. Even in developed countries, a significant share of patients with hypertension, diabetes, and other initially asymptomatic conditions go undiagnosed and untreated or do not comply with prescribed treatments. This situation leads to unnecessary deaths, hospitalization, and loss of productivity. Diagnosing and treating these patients would be a perfectly rational goal, but at the same time, it would cause an increase in drug expenditure. Consequently, drug budgets need to be adjusted upward if investments in primary care and disease prevention lower the barrier for patients to access the health care system.

Securing Adequate Financing and Payment Mechanism for Pharmaceuticals

The average country in the Organisation for Economic Co-operation and Development (OECD) spent US$401[6] per capita for pharmaceuticals in 2005 (OECD 2008). This figure compares to a single-digit dollar amount for the poorest countries and a range of US$30 to US$100 for most middle-income countries.[7] Most financing for drugs in OECD countries comes from public budgets, statutory insurance funds, or private health insurance. In contrast, many developing countries can finance only a small share of all drugs consumed in the country from public or solidarity funds; patients purchase most drugs with cash. As pointed out earlier, the cash market is prone to market failure, causing patients to overpay for drugs they may not even need, exposing them to substandard drugs, and offering policy makers few options to improve the situation. Increasing purchasing power in countries with good economic development will attract more actors on the supply side, making the problem potentially worse for patients, who will be exposed to more sophisticated marketing and promotion efforts. In the longer term, every country should therefore consider (a) introducing some form of pooled financing and third-party payment mechanism for medicines (also called a *drug benefit*) as a precondition for ensuring equitable access to essential drugs and (b) applying effective policy measures to steer the market in a direction that aligns with public health goals and makes efficient use of resources.

Financing for essential drugs is usually embedded in a larger health financing program that pays for preventive, diagnostic, and therapeutic services in outpatient and inpatient settings. A broader discussion of health financing is beyond the scope of this book; other World Bank publications cover the area in more detail (see, for example, Gottret, Schieber, and Waters 2008). Two principal models exist. The first, which is prevalent in low-income countries, uses public budget and donor funds to directly fund service providers and buy commodities; services and goods then are supposed to be offered to patients free or for a fee that covers the difference between true costs and the available public budget. The second model, which is prevalent in most high-income and higher-middle-income countries, is based on some form of health fund or insurance financed from contributions or general tax revenue that entitles the individual to obtain health goods and services from a range of contracted providers. The payment is made directly from the fund to the provider. Some benefit schemes do not include any drug benefit or cover only drugs used in inpatient care. However, absence of a comprehensive drug benefit package (including outpatients) likely limits the protective effect of health insurance against catastrophic health expenditure at the household level (Yip and Hsiao 2009) and may lead to a lack of confidence in evolving health insurance systems.

The relative independence of a dedicated health (insurance) fund from political office and budget cycles allows it to focus on its role as an agent for the individual patients, who can benefit from the pooled purchasing power and provider oversight mechanisms such a fund can establish. Whether member contributions, as is typically the case for insurance, or direct or indirect taxation actually finances such a fund is not relevant for its role as a counterweight to correct the market asymmetry typical for the health sector. Donors partially finance emerging health insurance funds in low-income countries experimenting with this model. The Ghanaian National Health Insurance Fund, for example, gets its resources from transfers from the social security fund (which has excess resources because of the country's young population), a levy on value added tax, donor funding, and a small contribution from members.

Introducing third-party financing for drugs is a reliable strategy for improving access to medicines, in particular for low-income populations. However, it always leads to higher drug spending. Initially, the main factor is mobilization of justified and rational demand: people who need treatment but could not afford it get treated as soon as they have the entitlement. However, after a while, the provider side adjusts to the availability of more funding by trying to raise prices and increase volume beyond the limits of what can be considered rational. Applying the tools for drug benefit management, explained in previous sections, from the beginning is therefore essential for the sustainability of a third-party financing scheme that pays for drugs.

Table 4.4 compares direct public service provision and third-party payment mechanisms in terms of possibilities for effective drug benefit management. The table shows that the competition between (a) a publicly owned and financed system of providing drugs and (b) a privately run system with financing through reimbursement from a central entitlement fund has no clear winner. The first option may be the only one available in postconflict countries or those with very little purchasing power, because such countries may lack structures in the private sector that can take over responsibility for service delivery from the public sector. However, that option is vulnerable to various kinds of inefficiencies

Table 4.4   Comparison between Government-Run Health Service and Third-Party Fund

Drug benefit management parameter	Government-run health services	Separate health fund with reimbursement for providers
Ensuring low drug prices	Centralized procurement can ensure good prices.	Framework agreements with suppliers or indirect price controls through reimbursement ceilings control prices.
Ensuring drug availability	Public supply chains are difficult to organize effectively (see the discussion of dysfunctional supply chains in chapter 3); budget limits, inaccurate forecasts, inefficiencies, perverse incentives, and fraud lead to frequent stock-outs.	Private suppliers have strong incentive to ensure that drugs are available on the basis of demand and financing.
Ensuring drug quality in the supply chain	Quality can be effectively controlled at central level, but potential risks exist at the periphery.	A regulatory system and enforcement mechanism are needed; alternatively, a contractual arrangement and control system are possible.
Monitoring drug use	Public service delivery requires up-front investment in systems and human resources that most countries are not able or willing to make.	Monitoring drug use can be part of contract fulfillment by providers; costs are absorbed through reimbursement without the need for up-front public investment.
Managing costs	Crude cost management can be done through budget ceiling and rationing (stock-outs) after the budget has been spent.	Formulary restrictions, volume limits, preapproval, and other priority-based rationing methods can incentivize rational drug use to manage costs.
Ensuring rational use	Guidelines, instructions, and training are helpful, but little room for incentives exists under public sector human resource policies; typically, no good data exist to monitor rational use.	Payers have a strong interest in collecting data and developing incentives for rational use; however, resistance from interest groups can undermine efforts.

Source: Author's compilation.

and governance issues, which result in problems with service quality and availability.

The second option, a system that is based on contracts between a central payer and providers, serviced by a private sector supply chain, requires a solid level of regulatory oversight and enforcement to ensure quality on the supply side. It also needs a degree of sophistication in management that may not yet be available in some low-income countries. However, it is more reliable in delivering drugs to patients, and it offers more "control knobs" to influence patient and provider behavior. Most countries, therefore, make the transition between the two systems at some point in their economic development, usually going through a long period in which both options exist in parallel. Countries in transition may have some form of insurance coverage for public employees and the formal sector, while government-run health centers serve the poor and those employed in the informal sector. Another potential split, observed, for example, in Poland, is to deliver certain expensive medicines through a government-managed program with central procurement (budget based, with strict volume limits), while offering insurance coverage for the bulk of less expensive standard treatments.

A critical observer could say that countries with health insurance generally are in better economic condition and have significantly higher per capita budgets for drugs than those with a publicly run health system. In other words, underfunding may be the main cause of the dysfunctions of many public systems. In practice, the assessment of the system "as is" should provide sufficient information on the efficiency of resource use and management quality. If a public system indeed appears to deliver well within its limited means, it may be worth building on it and providing more funding to close service gaps. The United Kingdom is an example of a high-income country that maintains a public sector system, although drug distribution and retail are in private hands, and pharmacists are contract partners who are reimbursed by the National Health Service. Thus, the system is a hybrid that, from the provider perspective, has more similarities with health insurance systems in continental Europe than with government-run health systems in Africa.

Reconciling Health Policy and Industrial Policy in the Pharmaceutical Sector

As pointed out in chapter 3, an inherent conflict exists between the public health objective of access to affordable, high-quality essential drugs and an industrial policy objective of developing a thriving, profitable pharmaceutical industry. The global pharmaceutical market is quite competitive: for large-scale buyers, good-quality generic drugs are available at prices that many smaller, nationally oriented manufacturers in developing countries cannot match, particularly if they are forced to manufacture to the same quality standards (defined on the basis of cGMPs as applied in developed markets[8]).

An influential publication on the subject of local manufacturing in low- and middle-income countries postulates that, from an economic viewpoint, manufacturing of drugs makes sense only in larger middle-income countries with a significant domestic market, solid regulation, and sufficient technical know-how (Kaplan and Laing 2005). However, in political reality, decision makers find simply exposing their domestic industry to global market forces a difficult proposition. That difficulty leads to a range of direct and indirect measures aimed at protecting the domestic pharmaceutical industry, including the following:

- Direct subsidies, loans, or tax breaks for modernization investments
- Import restrictions or import duties for competitor products
- Export subsidies
- Preferential treatment in public procurement
- Preference in regulatory approvals
- Preferential treatment in pricing decisions
- Reluctance to enforce strict quality standards
- Subsidies for mergers of foreign investors into domestic companies

Some of these measures benefit only companies that are locally owned and have their dominant market within the borders of a country. Others benefit importing companies as well if they have a domestic presence.

Looking at the options provided in the preceding list, one can see that some of them are clearly more problematic in terms of public health than others. Any double standard or low standard in enforcing quality directly affects drug efficacy and safety and therefore health outcomes. Accepting higher prices for drugs than the open market would mean that the sick and vulnerable were cross-subsidizing a business sector that otherwise might not be competitive. A sound industrial policy should therefore focus on policy measures that put the burden on the general taxpayer—for example, by providing temporary funding for measures that help the domestic manufacturers become competitive and market their products successfully outside the country. From a more holistic perspective, some arguments favor domestic manufacturing:

- Advanced, large-scale global manufacturers may not be sufficiently interested in smaller, low-income markets, thereby leaving room for regional players.
- The presence of local manufacturers may encourage regulators to do a better job by challenging them to be up-to-date on good manufacturing practice (GMP) standards and other aspects of quality, therefore potentially benefiting the overall market.
- Similarly, local manufacturers attract local talent and make sure a market exists for educating and training pharmacists, chemists, and lab technicians, which, in turn, can benefit the public sector.
- Local manufacturing can support the economic development of a country by creating jobs and tax revenue, particularly if national manufacturers are able to export.

Some subsegments of the pharmaceutical market are less sensitive to public health outcomes than others, giving additional options to provide room for economic growth in exchange for tougher quality standards and more competitive pressure in the area of essential drugs. For example, one option could be to allow companies to freely set their prices for OTC drugs, nutraceuticals, and other nonessential commodities, if they meet certain standards for the drugs they provide.

In a competitive national market, there is a potential synergy between the more advanced manufacturers and the regulators. Higher regulatory standards create a barrier to entry for low-quality, low-price competition. Although low prices are important to ensure access to medicines, drug policy always tends to prioritize quality over price. Otherwise the risk of negative consequences for health outcomes, declining trust in public health systems (and the responsible politicians), or even disaster in the form of mass casualties is too high.

Table 4.5 lists some standard short- and long-term measures of industrial policy affecting domestic drug companies, along with the time horizon of the measures and their effect on public health parameters.

A pragmatic approach to reconciling public health and industrial policy based on the preceding considerations should always start with an agreement on the long-term objectives. Agreeing on a desired scenario 10 years down the road is usually easier than agreeing on a measure that affects budgets or profits within a year. Companies appreciate predictability of

Table 4.5   Industrial Policy versus Public Health Policy

Industrial policy measure	Time horizon for effect and type of effect	Synergy with public health objectives
Accept higher drug prices from domestic manufacturers.	Short term: increased revenue and reduced competitive pressure on companies	Negative: cross-subsidy from private and public health budgets to the industry
Impose import duties on drugs that compete with products made by domestic manufacturers.	Short term: reduced competitive pressure on companies	Slightly negative: reduced competition in price and quality that could benefit the health sector
Offer direct subsidies or tax breaks to manufacturers for making necessary investments.	Short and long term: increased competitiveness of the industry	Neutral, as long as health budgets are not touched
Allow regulatory tolerance for domestic products from non-GMP production.	Short and long term: companies that otherwise would have to shut down stay alive; reduced competitiveness of industry	Negative: potential impact on drug safety; erosion of patient confidence in domestic drugs
Provide incentives for investments in quality, such as higher prices allowed for drugs from GMP facilities.	Short and long term: improved viability of better companies at the expense of the inferior ones; increased overall competitiveness of industry	Neutral: higher expenditures for drugs, compensated by better quality
Rigidly enforce GMP standards.	Short and long term: many smaller, less profitable companies forced to shut down or sell; increased overall competitiveness of remaining companies	Positive: higher drug quality and confidence in domestically made generics; higher drug price level possible because many low-cost producers unable to survive

Source: Author's compilation.

the political environment and need time to secure financing for invest-ment and to implement technology upgrades. Most countries with a sig-nificant drug industry today would probably want to maintain this industry in the long run but at the same time achieve world standard in drug quality. The latter is essential for having the option to export to an increasing number of markets, which is a necessary part of a long-term business plan for many companies, particularly in countries that do not have sufficiently large domestic markets. Because trade barriers are hard to keep up in the long term, most observers and stakeholders in the process view growing competitive pressure and consolidation of the industry as inevitable. National governments usually combine short-term measures, such as subsidies, price concessions, and regulatory tolerance, with longer-term strategies that include fixed deadlines for achieving regulatory benchmarks spread over a period of several years. This approach gives the more viable companies time to make necessary investments, while those that are not fit for a tougher environment can look for a buyer, refocus their product portfolio toward less regulated market segments (OTC drugs, cosmetic products), or phase out operations in ways that are socially less disruptive than an immediate closure.

Ensuring Good Governance of the Sector

Good governance is a somewhat abstract term that incorporates the rules under which a defined entity or function operates as well as the mechanisms to enforce these rules, for the benefit of the "common good." In the health sector, the multilateral relationship among clients, payers, regulators, and providers adds to the complexity of governance arrangements. If one stakeholder in the pharmaceutical subsector is a profitable industry, which in many cases operates internationally, things may be even more complicated. Governance arrangements in the pharmaceutical sector focus on fair access to markets, quality assurance along the entire supply chain, transparency in the use of public funds for buying drugs, effectiveness and patient safety in the use of drugs, and cost-effective use. Effective governance in the sector is extremely important for the following reasons:

- Patients and health care professionals cannot directly assess the quality, effectiveness, and safety of the product and have to rely on scientific assessments and technical supervision of manufacturing and distribution by authorities.
- Significant amounts of money are spent on drugs, which carry a high value per unit and can easily be transported and stored. This situation creates conditions that make fraud, theft, and abuse possible.
- The high level of regulation creates several interfaces at which public officials make decisions affecting access to profitable markets, thereby creating entry points for potential corruption.

The rules governing the sector are similar in all countries and are based on international technical standards and best practices. Major differences can be observed in implementation and enforcement, based on factors such as

- General rule of law and respect for an independent judiciary
- Standards of accountability for public officials and participation of civil society groups in decision making
- Financial and human resources (including technical expertise) available for monitoring and enforcement activities
- Systems and institutions designed to reduce scope for arbitrary decisions and to align incentives with desired outcomes

Good governance in the pharmaceutical sector is difficult to achieve in a generally lawless environment or in the absence of regulatory enforcement capacity. However, options exist to address some of the core issues, such as drug quality, price, cost-effectiveness, and use, in contractual arrangements between payers, suppliers, and providers of care. When funds are pooled among institutions to ensure sufficient purchasing power, the supplier can be asked to provide independently verified assurance for manufacturing and product quality, or the buyers can pay a consultant to undertake the necessary inspections and tests. In such situations, buyers sometimes apply risk-based strategies that differentiate between expensive drugs for severe illnesses, for which more rigorous prequalification standards are applied, and more ordinary drugs such as simple pain relievers.

Drugs can also be procured for delivery to the dispensing level, leaving it as the suppliers' responsibility to arrange for proper distribution and to absorb losses incurred while the drugs travel to the final destination. Such arrangements are typically used in crisis and postconflict situations. Sometimes they develop into durable institutions that take over key functions on a permanent basis when a country stabilizes politically and economically. Box 4.2 shows an example of a pooled procurement, distribution, and retail system for essential drugs in Liberia that uses contractual arrangements and corporate governance structures within the executing organization (National Drug Service) as a replacement for governance structures lacking at national level.

Consumers are very sensitive to drug quality issues; consumer mobilization can strengthen efforts to improve governance and transparency. However, campaigns against counterfeit or substandard drugs sold in informal markets are useful only if an accessible and affordable alternative is available to people in need of treatment.

Table 4.6 shows some options for dealing with governance problems in low- and middle-income countries, considering resource constraints and political realities. The table makes clear that governance issues can be addressed either by better laws and effective enforcement or by changing management systems and operational parameters that make behavior more transparent and using incentives that align with the public interest. Both strategies are necessary, but the latter may provide more actionable options in the short term, because it does not require major reallocation of public

Table 4.6   Strategies for Dealing with Governance Issues in Low- and Middle-Income Settings

Governance issue	Principal strategy	Alternative or complementary strategy
Unauthorized, potentially substandard drugs in the market	Strengthen regulatory and enforcement capacity. Enact and enforce adequate regulation.	Create a secure, controlled supply chain that will attract clients and marginalize the uncontrolled market. Make this supply chain the default provider for publicly financed programs
Suspected corruption in regulatory procedures and market-access control	Strengthen enforcement capacity, legal system, and internal control functions of public institutions.	Simplify rules by making process rules explicit and reducing discretion of decision makers. Introduce systems that make processes transparent. Have decisions reviewed by panels that include civil society representatives.
Suspected corruption in public or institutional procurement	Strengthen enforcement capacity, legal system, and internal control functions of public institutions. Improve technical capacity to recognize indicators for corruption in procurement.	Introduce electronic procurement platforms that reduce possibilities for manipulation. Broaden stakeholder involvement in procurement decisions.
Institutional abuse of reimbursement systems and prescription fraud	Strengthen monitoring and enforcement capacity. Use contractual or criminal sanctions as deterrents.	Introduce an integrated management system that records all transactions. Use data to prevent or flag abuse and fraud, provide feedback to prescribers, and offer incentives for rational use of drugs.

(continued)

**Table 4.6   Strategies for Dealing with Governance Issues in Low- and
Middle-Income Settings** *(continued)*

Governance issue	Principal strategy	Alternative or complementary strategy
Use of unethical marketing strategies by drug companies such as paying for prescriptions; preloading of supply chains with free "bonus" drugs	Establish and monitor rules for ethical marketing. Enforce rules with "name and shame" and commercial sanctions or fines.	Use a framework contract with preferred suppliers, based on best price and quality Align incentives in the value chain to address market failure (for example, flat dispensing fee and policy under which pharmacists are obliged to offer preferred generic brands to patients). Attain patients' preference through lower co-payments for preferred brands. Negotiate price-volume agreements with manufacturers for innovative, patented drugs. Tax-free goods at the source or at the recipient level. Charge drug companies for representatives' visits to public institutions.

Source: Author's compilation.

budgets and reorganization of public institutions, some of which are out of the reach for health officials. The table also shows that the same options that were described in previous sections for improving sector performance and cost-effectiveness of public funds spent on drugs will affect governance. In summary, although the problem may present as a governance issue, the solution, in many cases, may well be one of better management.

Notes

1. Characteristic for markets with high collusion levels is a large number of small wholesalers, each of whom does business with only a limited number of local or regional customers. In more transparent, better-functioning markets, distributors tend to merge into large national units with highly efficient logistics. Small regional players are not competitive except in some small niche markets.

2. Personal information obtained from Dalberg during work on the Affordable Medicines Facility—malaria (AMFm) and observations during pharmaceutical sector research in Ghana.

3. This example is based on observations from field studies done during preparations for AMFm.

4. For example, a treatment that is meant as a last resort for severe cases may be used in early disease stages, or a medicine for severe pain in cancer patients may be abused as a general pain treatment.

5. In the Delphi method of consensus building, the facilitator asks participants to write their views down and explain them. The facilitator then reads aloud what the different members wrote without disclosing the names. A second round is then started, and rounds continue until the desired level of consensus is achieved.

6. Figures are in purchasing power parities.

7. These data are from World Bank country assessments.

8. Such as the member countries of the International Conference on Harmonisation of Technical Requirements for Registration of Pharmaceuticals for Human Use are required to do.

References

Bossert, Thomas, Diana Bowser, Johnnie Amenyah, and Becky Copeland. 2003. *Guatemala: Decentralization and Integration in the Health Logistics System.* Arlington, VA: John Snow/DELIVER.

Daniels, Norman, and James Sabin. 2002. *Setting Limits Fairly: Can We Learn to Share Medical Resources?* New York: Oxford University Press.

Gottret, Pablo E., George Schieber, and Hugh R. Waters. 2008. *Good Practices in Health Financing: Lessons from Reforms in Low- and Middle-Income Countries.* Washington, DC: World Bank.

Kaplan, Warren, and Richard Laing. 2005. "Local Production of Pharmaceuticals: Industrial Policy and Access to Medicines." HNP Discussion Paper, Health, Nutrition, and Population Unit, World Bank, Washington, DC.

MSH (Management Sciences for Health). 1997. *Managing Drug Supply.* 2nd ed. West Hartford, CT: Kumarian Press.

OECD (Organisation for Economic Co-operation and Development). 2008. *OECD Health Policy Studies: Pharmaceutical Pricing Policies in a Global Market.* Paris: OECD Publishing.

Seiter, Andreas, and Martha Gyansa-Lutterodt. 2009. "Policy Note: The Pharmaceutical Sector in Ghana." World Bank, Washington, DC.

World Bank. 2009. "Strategic Analysis of Supply Chains for Informed Decision Making: World Bank Experience from Two Countries—Kenya and Lesotho." World Bank, Washington, DC.

Yip, Winnie, and William C. Hsiao. 2009. "Non-evidence-Based Policy: How Effective Is China's New Cooperative Medical Scheme in Reducing Medical Impoverishment?" *Social Science and Medicine* 68 (2): 201–9.

CHAPTER 5

Policy Packages to Achieve Strategic Long-Term Goals

Pharmaceutical policy can be discussed and formulated at three main levels. The highest is the long-term strategic level, answering the question "What is the long-term vision for the pharmaceutical sector in our country?" in a way that covers the perspectives of all relevant stakeholders and links to overall health policy goals as pointed out in chapter 1. The second level, so far dominant in this publication, is the tactical, problem-solving level that dominates the agenda of politicians responsible for the sector. It is largely defined by the issues listed in chapter 3. The third level is the technical implementation level, a domain for technical sector experts familiar with details of scientific and economic evaluation methods, good practice standards for manufacturing and distribution, and systems for managing transactions between the key stakeholders of the sector. Figure 5.1 shows the different policy levels.

This chapter deals with the first, strategic level. It tries to lay out how governments can create a vision for the longer-term development of the sector, for example, as part of a five-year planning exercise. The approach is based on three standard policy packages. Countries can apply them in accordance with their strategic objectives and in consideration of a set of key parameters, such as general income level, resources, and existence and nature of a domestic pharmaceutical industry. In reality, many countries

Figure 5.1   Three Levels of Pharmaceutical Policy

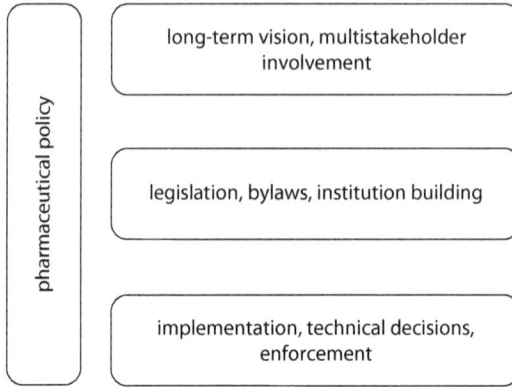

Source: Author's representation.

will mix policies from different templates or use different policies in different market segments.

Essential Medicines Policy

An *essential medicines policy* is a strategic choice that aims at the maximum benefit for public health in a situation of severely restricted funding and similarly strict limits on other resources. Public or solidarity funds are used to pay for essential drugs only.[1] In addition, options should be created for people to buy good-quality essential drugs at affordable prices in the private sector—for example, in franchise drugstores that rely on pooled purchasing and a secure supply chain. An essential medicines policy has been and will be the dominant policy option for low-income countries where a pharmaceutical manufacturing industry has no or only a minor presence. Larger industrial countries may combine such a policy with other policy elements. The term *essential* will have different interpretations in different countries, depending on resources, disease patterns, medical traditions, and the outcome of pharmacoeconomic analysis used to inform drug selection. The policy goal can be formulated as "We want our entire population to have access to affordable, good-quality essential drugs." The policy can be implemented by combining measures to

- Strengthen financing
- Design payment mechanisms so no bias favors nonessential drugs

- Create effective and efficient supply chains
- Strengthen regulatory oversight or set up controlled supply mechanisms for good-quality essential drugs

Core policy options relevant for such a strategy are described in chapter 4 (see figure 5.2). The World Health Organization (WHO) publication *How to Develop and Implement a National Drug Policy* provides detailed guidance for policy makers in low-income countries (see WHO 2001).

An essential medicines policy includes, by default, a generic drugs policy. As pointed out earlier, an efficient supply chain is one that integrates all steps from manufacturing to dispensing and makes sure that availability and total landed costs are managed as core parameters. Because most essential drugs (using the WHO Essential Medicines Lists as the standard) are off patent, the majority of drugs procured under an essential medicines policy will be generics. The following section describes specific requirements for the success of a generic drugs policy.

Figure 5.2   Standard Elements of an Essential Medicines Policy

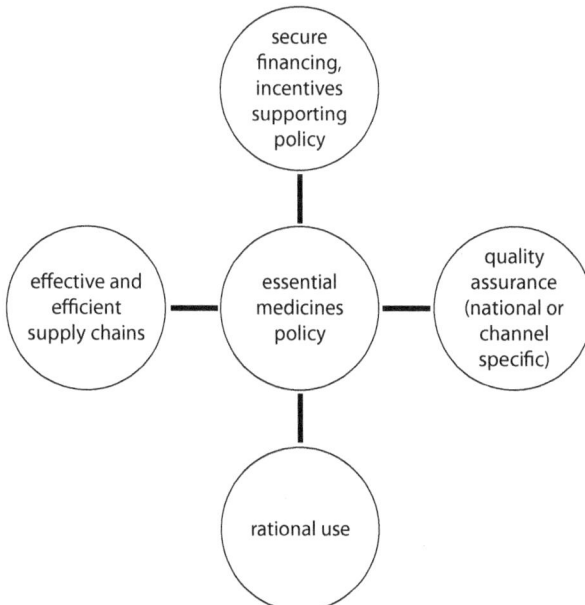

Source: Author's representation.

Generic Drugs Policy

The main goal of a generic drugs policy is to increase efficiency of drug spending by replacing more expensive originator brands with cheaper generics. The scientific justification is that bioequivalent generics, made in factories that operate under current good manufacturing practices, have the same clinical efficacy and safety profile as the originator brand. If a domestic industry exists that makes generic drugs, a secondary policy goal could be to strengthen that industry.

A major factor undermining attempts to broaden the use of generics is the perception, predominantly in low- and middle-income countries, that generics are of lower quality than originator drugs. Investing in the quality of generic drugs (by strengthening legislation and regulatory oversight) as well as in educating and persuading providers and patients that generics are equal in effect and quality (once this objective has been achieved in reality) is therefore an important element of any generic drugs policy (figure 5.3).

Figure 5.3   Standard Elements of a Generic Drugs Policy

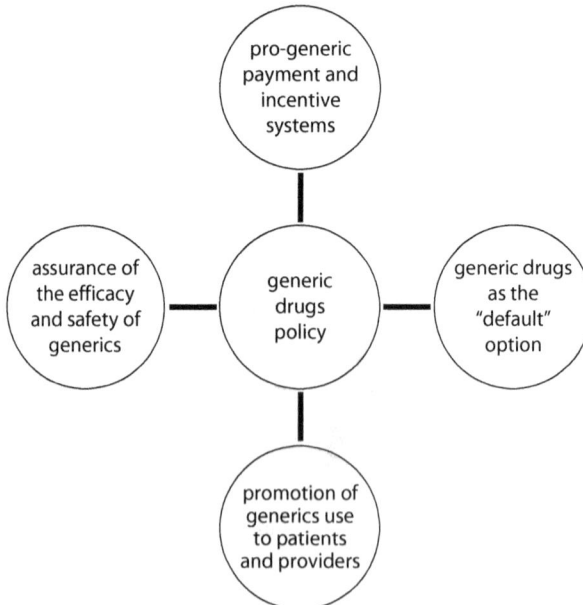

Source: Author's representation.

Other important elements are

- Creating easily accessible information sources for providers on generic drugs
- Facilitating early registration of quality generics, for example, through a Bolar provision,[2] and through mutual recognition of generics licenses between competent drug authorities
- Basing all treatment guidelines and drug lists or formularies on generic drugs
- Neutralizing or reversing financial incentives for doctors, pharmacists, and institutions that reward prescribing and dispensing of more expensive drugs
- Implementing a policy of substitution by pharmacists (substituting a generic for an originator brand unless excluded by the physician on the prescription)
- Limiting reimbursement to generic price levels and introducing differential co-payments for patients under insurance schemes, thus favoring use of generics
- Introducing generics as default options in electronic prescription systems, where such systems exist

Innovation-Friendly Drugs Policy

This version of a pharmaceutical policy framework is applied mainly in developed countries, in particular (but not only) those with a research-based pharmaceutical industry. The underlying assumption is that, in addition to significant public funding for research and development, private investment in developing innovative medicines is necessary to ensure progress in fighting diseases for which current treatments are not satisfactory. A social consensus exists that a high premium for innovation is worth the cost, even if a higher share of total gross national product is used to pay for health care. In most developed countries, the financing burden is shared between the healthy and the sick through some form of health insurance with universal coverage.

Innovation-friendly drug policy is characterized by

- Strong intellectual property protection
- Regulatory pathways that facilitate market access for innovative drugs
- Financing systems that reimburse expensive, innovative drugs

- An industrial policy that favors high-tech industry clusters and close interaction between academia and the private sector
- Financial markets that provide sufficient venture capital for innovators

The last two factors are relevant only for countries that want to support a domestic innovative drug industry. To limit the budget impact of an innovation-friendly drug policy, countries apply a range of cost-containment measures. In most cases, they combine the innovation-friendly policy with elements of a generic drugs policy. In addition, payers use various methods to control market access and use of innovative drugs as described in previous sections. Figure 5.4 shows the elements of an innovation-friendly drug policy.

Combining Several Policy Models within One Country

As pointed out previously, an essential medicines policy should always be based primarily on generic drugs, meaning it will include several elements of a generic drugs policy. For low-income countries, the policy choice will

Figure 5.4   Standard Elements of an Innovation-Friendly Drugs Policy

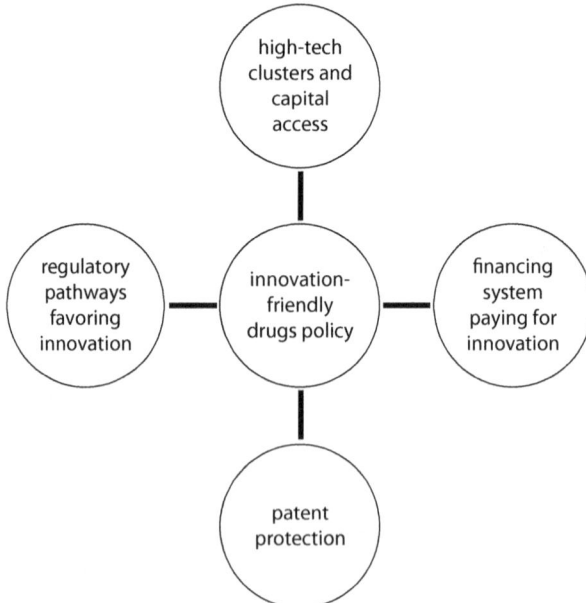

Source: Author's representation.

typically be limited to an attempt to optimize access to essential medicines, leading to a one-tiered policy model. This policy does not mean that there will be no market for innovative drugs, but this market will remain small and not occupy much space in the policy debate.

Middle- and high-income countries typically combine two or all of the preceding three models and apply them to different segments of the market. An industrial middle-income country in Latin America, for example, may decide to focus on a generic drugs policy for the majority of the population that is covered by a third-party payer system, while introducing an essential medicines policy with a much more limited formulary for some low-income groups that depend directly on the state for their health care. At the other end of the spectrum, a regulatory pathway may allow truly innovative drugs to be registered with priority and provide limited financing to patients with pressing medical needs. Private insurance providers may offer broader coverage of innovative drugs to those who can afford their premiums.

Most high-income countries have introduced elements of a generic drugs policy since the 1990s in an attempt to contain the increase in pharmaceutical expenditure. By ensuring a rapid switch to generics after the innovator's patent has expired, the policy saves funds that can be redirected to pay for innovative treatments.

Notes

1. These drugs are usually defined in a national essential drugs list, based on the World Health Organization Model Lists of Essential Medicines (there are now separate lists for adults and children), which are updated every two years.

2. A Bolar provision allows generics manufacturers to apply for a license while the original drug is still patent protected, thereby shortening the lag until the first generic reaches the market after patent expiry.

Reference

WHO (World Health Organization). 2001. *How to Develop and Implement a National Drug Policy.* 2nd ed. Geneva: WHO.

CHAPTER 6

Factors Influencing Policy Implementation

Both a good understanding of the problems of the pharmaceutical sector and a well-crafted plan to address them are needed as a solid basis to start any reform process. However, good preparation and sound arguments are not sufficient to ensure successful execution of reforms. In many cases, attempts to modify dysfunctional systems and processes in the sector have been derailed by antagonistic forces in the political process. Such resistance to change can come from two principal directions:

- Stakeholders benefiting from the status quo mobilize their influence against changes that would hurt their interests.
- Political opponents harness the sensitivity in the general population regarding changes to drug policy and polarize the discussion with emotional arguments (by, for example, talking about rationing, generalizing individual patient anecdotes, or using stereotypes such as "free choice" versus "bureaucrats dictating treatment") to gain a political advantage.

A good example for the first point is the reform of drug dispensing in the Republic of Korea. Self-dispensing physicians and prescribing pharmacists triggered a high level of irrational drug consumption—for example, widespread antibiotic overuse—that made Korea the country with the highest levels of penicillin resistance. Discussion about separating prescribing and dispensing started in 1963. In 1980, a first blueprint for reform was submitted; however, legislation ending the overlapping roles and clearly separating prescribing doctors from dispensing pharmacists was not passed for another 20 years (Kim and Ruger 2008).

The U.S. health reform debate of 2009 and 2010 shows how health reform discussions can become a proxy battle for other political interests.[1] Those who have to defend a reform plan are tied to a specific concept and need to argue rationally. This necessity puts them in a defensive position against targeted attacks of a political opponent who uses stereotypes that tend to trigger negative emotions in the audience.

Politicians in democratic countries want to be reelected and are therefore sensitive to public opinion. In countries with authoritarian regimes, accountability mechanisms tend to play out in the form of a delicate balance between economic prosperity, social safety nets, and acceptance of the ruling elite. Reforms that touch entitlements or negatively affect personal income can lead to social unrest. The ruling elite then typically expel those members who can be blamed for the underlying issue. This mechanism creates a similarly risk-averse behavior, as do elections of politicians and administrators in a democratic country.

Successful implementation of reforms therefore requires a range of measures. Some of these measures are applied behind the scenes, while others aim at steering the public debate to a point at which emotional responses can be contained and acceptance of a reasonable compromise is possible. The following sections explain the most important measures.

Stakeholder Assessment and Involvement

Individuals in different roles and positions make money by participating in the pharmaceutical value chain. Personal income can come from legitimate salaries and profits or from illicit exploitation of positions of power. In any case, stakeholders typically do whatever they can to protect their "franchise" and income. A good assessment and mapping of stakeholder positions helps make their behavior and attitudes toward reform more predictable. The initial mapping exercise can assume that everyone will try to maximize his or her income within the existing legal framework.

Table 6.1 provides an example of a simple stakeholder map, based on an attempt to reinforce compliance with guidelines on rational use of medicines. This table clearly shows that the new policy is likely to face

Table 6.1   Likely Stakeholder Positions toward a Reform That Aims at Greater Compliance with Guidelines for Rational Use of Drugs

Stakeholder	Position	Comment
Physicians	Negative	Stakeholder feels physicians know best, has quality concerns, and may receive material benefits from prescribing expensive drugs.
Pharmacists	Negative	Stakeholder has quality concerns and receives lower profits from cheaper essential drugs.
Patients	Negative	Stakeholder follows expert opinions and favors (perceived) best possible treatment.
Multinational drug companies	Negative or mixed	New policy may have negative impact on short-term sales and profit, but it may create more room in the public budget for innovative drugs.
Generics drug companies	Mixed	Some may lose; some may benefit, depending on product portfolio and market position.
Hospital management	Variable	Stakeholder's position depends on the payment system: if the hospital has to absorb drug costs, management may support reform; otherwise, the stakeholder will probably be in line with physicians and pharmacists.
Payers (public budget, insurance)	Positive	New policy will lower costs and may improve quality of care.
International organizations	Positive	New policy is in line with World Health Organization recommendations; the new policy is more cost-effective, can improve access to drugs, and might improve health outcomes

Source: Author's compilation.

opposition from a coalition of providers, industry, and patients. Even if the government is in a position of power to enact the policy change, a strong enforcement and control apparatus will be required to ensure that providers actually follow the policy in practice—unless it is amended by a number of elements that modify provider incentives and positions.

The next step after the theoretical mapping exercise is stakeholder consultation (see box 6.1 for an example). The purpose of the consultation is

Box 6.1

Example of a Multistakeholder Process to Address Controversial Policy Positions

A good way to organize stakeholder consultations on controversial subjects is to hold forums with a moderator, who tries to break down the complex topic into smaller, distinct elements that allow an expression of consent or dissent. For example, discussion on the goal of "strengthening rational use medicines" could lead to a list of agreed statements, as in the following hypothetical example:

- Scientific evidence based on large-scale trials and rigorous assessment is generally acceptable and preferable as treatment guidance over individual opinion.
- In some specific cases, physicians must retain the possibility of applying their own experience.
- For a majority of routine cases, generic drugs provide adequate and cost-effective treatment options.
- In some cases, innovative drugs provide significant benefits, although at much higher cost per case.
- Quality of generic drugs has to be ensured; otherwise the theoretical benefit may not translate into real treatment outcomes, and patients will lose trust in the system.
- Health professionals have a right to fair compensation. Loss of income caused by a change in policy should be offset by an increase in fees for services or base salaries or a change in profit margins for pharmacies.

This process of breaking down a policy package into single issues and trying to find an agreeable formula among a forum of key stakeholders provides a blueprint for a negotiation solution that may have a better chance of being accepted than the original one-dimensional policy model. The consultation process is complemented by one-on-one meetings with the most skeptical stakeholders and attempts to negotiate a compromise that allows them to give up their resistance.

Source: Author.

to confirm the assumptions on the basis of general knowledge, discover hidden motives, and gauge the options for compromise or compensatory mechanisms that would allow stakeholders to accept the reform and prevent them from undermining its implementation. During the consultation, stakeholders might provide substantive new information that has implications for the reform. For example, providers may produce evidence that a problem, in fact, exists with the quality of many locally procured generic medicines. This evidence could mean that additional changes are necessary in the area of drug regulation and oversight before the use of these drugs can be promoted as the default option.

Strategies to Neutralize Political Opposition

Although stakeholder consultation and negotiated compromise are suitable (but not always successful) tools to lift reform efforts over barriers put up by interest groups, they do very little to discourage or overcome purely political opposition that tries to exploit a vulnerable period of the sitting administration for its own gain.

Two factors are key in winning the political upper hand: timing and communication. The ideal timing for potentially unpopular reform is during a crisis that creates a palpable sense of urgency for corrective action or during a scandal that weakens the opponents of reform. If, for example, the health insurance fund is in danger of running out of money and this fact makes news headlines, public argument against measures to curb drug expenditure will be difficult—whether limiting reimbursement lists, applying tougher economic criteria for the inclusion of new drugs, or putting pressure on providers to cut unnecessary consumption is proposed. Alternatively, if the drug industry is in the public limelight because an investigative journalist uncovered a scheme to bribe doctors, no politician will risk publicly siding with the industry against a measure to strengthen regulatory oversight.

In general, such "golden opportunities" from the perspective of the reform champions are not predictable. When they occur, reform plans may not be ready. However, in some cases, specific reforms that have been postponed because of political antagonism are ready in draft form and can be activated quickly if the opportunity arises and the opponent is weak. In other cases, making certain dysfunctions of the system transparent is sufficient to generate a scandal that then allows enactment of reform. For example, the minister of health in a Middle Eastern country, worried that prices for imported drugs might be too high, had a small (and not scientifically very rigorous) study commissioned to compare prices of five frequently prescribed brand-name drugs with prices for the same drugs in European Union (EU) countries. The results were stunning—for all but one of these drugs, the price in this middle-income country was higher than in any EU country or Switzerland. The results immediately created a public outcry and allowed the ministry to change the pricing rules against the interests of the well-connected importers' lobby.

A variation of the opportunistic timing of reforms is based on the general background noise level in public debate. Pharmaceutical reform is a topic that can stir emotions, but it is not the only topic that can do so. If the public is already emotionally engaged in a heated debate on other controversial topics, the media may not be available as a "sounding board" for attempts to stage the type of emotional campaign that can threaten reform success.

Another important and predictable factor for timing of reforms is electoral cycles. During the 12 to 18 months before an election, politicians tend to focus on reelection as their primary objective. Thus, controversial reforms are more difficult to pass than at the beginning of the cycle, when the next elections are still far off.

The best way to limit the effectiveness of emotional campaigns used to undermine pharmaceutical policy reform is to present the dilemma to the public in a controlled way. Rather than drafting reform within a closed circle and then trying to sell the result to an unprepared public, the actors can put out the key questions and encourage a broad public debate on the underlying dilemma. A neutral institution or individual with high

Figure 6.1   Model Process to Secure Acceptance for a Difficult Reform Project

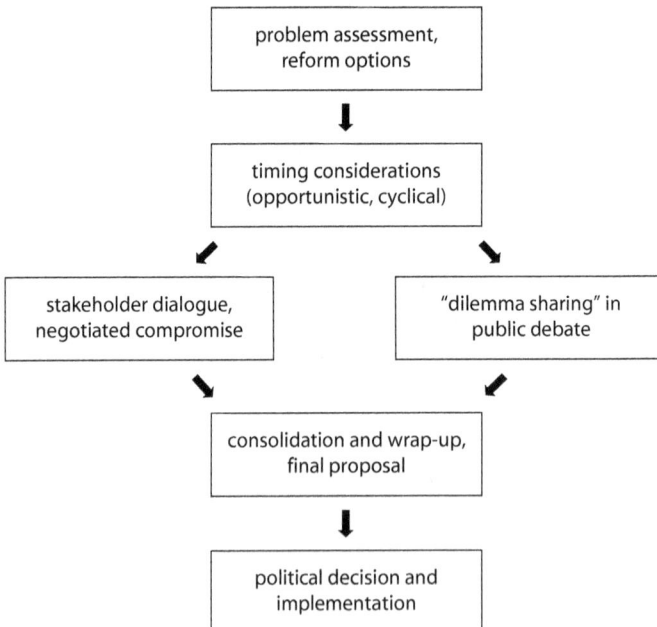

Source: Author's representation.

public credibility, including representatives of various interest groups, could lead the debate. The average citizen is well able to understand the dilemma between offering the best treatment for all without limits and keeping health care costs at a level that is economically sustainable. Sharing the dilemma and allowing people to weigh in with their views creates a degree of protection against campaigns that only show one side so they can stir emotions. Figure 6.1 shows a simplified scheme for a model process to secure acceptance for a difficult reform project among stakeholders and the public.

Note

1. See *New York Times* online coverage of health care reform under "Times Topics" (http://topics.nytimes.com).

Reference

Kim, Hak-Ju, and Jennifer Prah Ruger. 2008. "Pharmaceutical Reform in South Korea and the Lessons It Provides." *Health Affairs* 27 (4): w260–69.

CHAPTER 7

Pharmaceutical Policy Illustrated in Country Examples

Nothing demonstrates the complexity of the pharmaceutical sector, the regulatory challenges, and the various symptoms of market failure better than a glance through some country assessments that were done specifically to assist World Bank client countries in planning policy reforms in the pharmaceutical sector. The following case studies show countries in various stages of development with different kinds of problems and achievements. They focus on the dilemmas faced by each country and provide some thoughts on how the core issues could be tackled in a practical way.

Ghana: National Health Insurance as a "Game Changer"

In Ghana, a West African country with a population of 23 million, about 28 percent of the population lives below poverty levels. Although infant and under-five child mortality is on track for reaching the Millennium Development Goals, maternal mortality is still high, and professional medical assistance for childbirth remains low. Mortality is often avoidable, and causes are primary in nature, such as communicable diseases. Ghana's health system ranges from community health programs to a network of public clinics and hospitals run by the Ghana

Health Service, complemented by faith-based (Christian Health Association of Ghana and the Islamic Ahmadiyya movement) and private providers. See table 7.1 for pharmaceutical sector data.

The public sector procures medicines for public health facilities. The public sector drug supply chain runs between the central medical store, the regional medical stores, and the smaller depots in the districts that sell supplies to the retail-level public hospitals and clinic dispensaries. The Ministry of Health procures essential drugs for public health facilities on the basis of an annual planning cycle.

The current public supply chain does not use a modern logistics management system and is plagued by frequent stock-outs, high levels of indebtedness, and limited flexibility to respond to demand fluctuations. Each entity (warehouse, depot, dispensary) follows a revolving drug fund concept, which means that the system is highly reliant on cash flow from transactions to restock. The system has no contingency allowance for losses caused by shelf-life expiry, accidental damage of stocks, irrecoverable debts, theft, or bad financial management, and these losses hamper the sustainability of the revolving fund.

Given the challenges of the revolving drug fund and the public procurement system, health facility managers are exploring other avenues. One entrepreneurial solution is to allow the public facilities to purchase drugs directly from the private sector, especially in the more populated and accessible areas. This mechanism is expected to help fill the wholesale outlets in big cities, from which distribution will cascade to the smaller towns and villages to supply retail pharmacies, drug sellers, and clinics with needed drugs. Under the law, the public facilities are permitted to procure drugs from the private sector only when stock-outs occur at the public medical stores. At that point, however, the public facilities

Table 7.1   Ghana: Pharmaceutical Sector Data, 2008

Indicator	Amount
Total market for prescription drugs (estimate)	US$210 million
Market share of local manufacturers	30%
Illicit drugs in circulation (estimate)	10% to 20%
Average availability of tracer drugs in public sector institutions	Urban: 80 percent
	Rural: 40 percent
Ministry of Health drug expenditure, including funds from donors	US$31 million
National Health Insurance Scheme drug expenditure	US$57 million
Out-of-pocket drug expenditure (household survey data)	US$160 million

Source: Seiter and Gyansa-Lutterodt 2009.

lack any leverage to negotiate an appropriate price with the private sector because the private sector realizes it is the "last resort" for the public facilities.

In 2005, Ghana took a step toward providing universal access to health care by introducing the National Health Insurance Scheme (NHIS). The NHIS is financed through general taxes (such as value added tax), through employer contributions (Social Security and National Insurance Trust funds), and through premiums from the informal sector. The NHIS entitles its beneficiaries to free health care, including a drug benefit package covering a wide range of treatments. This benefit package was expected to boost demand for drugs; as one indicator, turnover at the level of regional medical stores nearly tripled between 2004 and 2006 (see figure 7.1).

A growing private sector mostly satisfied the increase in demand for drugs. Ghana has six larger and several smaller privately held local manufacturers; some of them also operate import, distribution, and retail businesses. The NHIS contracts with the public provider and some of the private providers, including private pharmacies. In most cases, patients can obtain their medication even if the provider issuing the prescription has run out of a certain drug.

Third-party financing in combination with de facto partial privatization of the supply chain appears to have increased access to medicines for patients in Ghana, although a still significant number of patients (according to latest numbers, 30 to 40 percent[1]) fall outside the insurance system

Figure 7.1   Increase in Turnover of Revolving Drug Funds after Introduction of NHIS in Ghana

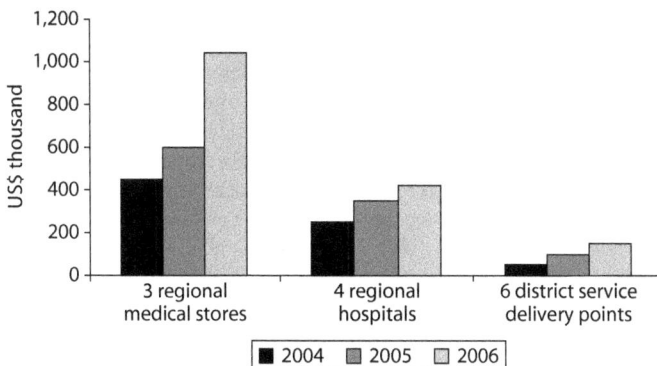

Source: Ministry of Health and Ghana Health Service 2007.

and need to pay cash for their drugs. According to a household survey, only 40 percent of those under the poverty line have access to NHIS cards, which suggests that many of the poor do not have access to free drugs. The downside of the increasing reliance of the public sector on the private sector is that buyers may pay higher prices than if the public sector operated through central procurement.

In addition, drug quality remains a concern. The Ghana Food and Drugs Board is a regulatory authority with a good reputation among peer agencies in the region, but it still does not have the resources to ensure that all drugs in the market are of consistently good quality. The NHIS has its own internal challenges, related mainly to claims management and processing. If providers do not get paid on time, they will stop accepting patients' insurance cards for payment and return to asking patients for cash payments. Cash-flow interruptions also affect the supply chain and lead to stock-outs. Moreover, experience from other countries has shown that a third-party payment mechanism is vulnerable to fraud and abuse of the system by providers and patients. NHIS therefore needs a good information system to track provider behavior and provide the data needed for establishing better expenditure management. Otherwise, the financial sustainability of the insurance scheme is at stake.

Table 7.2 gives a synopsis of the main challenges in Ghana's pharmaceutical sector and the policy options that have been discussed with decision makers in the Ministry of Health and the health insurance organization.

Table 7.2   Pharmaceutical Sector Challenges in Ghana

Main challenges	Preferred policy options
Delayed payment of claims leading to erosion of acceptance of insurance cards, cash-flow problems, and stock-outs	Streamline and reorganize NHIS claims processing.
Silent privatization of public supply chain with potential problems for drug pricing and quality	Consider formal contracting with private sector (framework contracts with quality suppliers at defined prices, allowing public and private providers to purchase within agreed parameters).
Drug overuse and inappropriate use under insurance scheme	Implement an electronic claims management system with built-in controls that flag suspicious transactions and track adherence to rational use. Create incentives to support desired behavior and contractual sanctions for repeat offenders.

Source: Seiter and Gyansa-Lutterodt 2009.

In summary, Ghana is an encouraging example of a low-income country that is addressing the basic problem of lack of access to essential medicines by providing a new financing mechanism and allowing the private sector to step in for procurement and retail sale of drugs where public systems are chronically dysfunctional. As in every major transition, some "teething troubles" and risks for the sustainability of the new approach need to be carefully watched and managed over several years until a new equilibrium is reached and systems are robust enough to survive on their own.

Lithuania: Dealing with the Effects of the Financial Crisis

A member of the European Union since 2004, Lithuania had one of the fastest-growing economies in Europe before the economic crisis hit in 2008. The subsequent sharp economic contraction (the gross domestic product plunged by 15.7 percent in the first nine months of 2009[2]) forced the government to cut back public spending. This cutback affected the 2010 drug budget for the State Patient Fund (SPF, the single-payer health insurance fund for Lithuanian citizens), which was reduced by about 10 percent compared to real 2009 drug expenditure.

As an upper-middle-income country with an educated workforce and significant institutional capacity in the Ministry of Health and the SPF, Lithuania had already introduced several measures to control SPF drug spending. These measures included price controls for reimbursed drugs, reimbursement ceilings for drugs with the same active ingredient (reimbursement limited to the price of the cheapest generic), variable patient co-payments of up to 50 percent of the reimbursement ceiling, and a restrictive policy for adding new drugs to the reimbursement list.

Although these measures may have helped limit expenditure growth, they are not seen as sufficient to achieve the reduction of drug spending required in 2010. In addition, the government is concerned that cutting expenditures for the SPF could lead to higher out-of-pocket payments at a time when individual citizens also feel the hardship of the financial crisis. Lithuanian patients have a high affinity for branded products,[3] even though they have to make significantly higher out-of-pocket payments compared with the cost of cheapest generic in the same category.

Given the situation, Lithuanian policy makers find themselves with limited options:

- Try to increase efficiency of SPF drug spending by "clustering" drugs with therapeutic equivalence but different active ingredients under

one reimbursement ceiling. Thus, for example, the patented, expensive esomeprazole (for treating reflux disease and stomach ulcer) would be reimbursed only at the level of generic omeprazole, which is seen as equally effective and safe.
- Drop some drugs from the reimbursement list that are costly but not important from a public health perspective.
- Try to claw back some of the hidden bonuses (usually in the form of free drugs; see the discussion of corruption in chapter 3) that currently benefit wholesalers and retail pharmacies. For several highly competitive drug classes, the industry is forced to give such bonuses to keep their products moving in the supply chain. In similar situations, some countries (Germany, Turkey) have applied compulsory rebates (to be granted to public buyers or payers) for reimbursed drugs.
- Apply measures to make physicians more accountable for the prescription costs they cause (for example, by introducing drug budgets at physician or institution level).

The first and second options are likely to lead to higher out-of-pocket payments, unless they are paired with the last option (increasing accountability of physicians) and possibly with an adjustment of incentives for pharmacists. Pharmacists who influence patients in their choices tend to recommend the more profitable drugs that inevitably have higher co-payments.

Another measure that may help steer patients away from the expensive branded drugs with high co-payments toward cheaper generics would be to waive all co-payments, including the flat dispensing fee, for the cheapest drug in a given category, while increasing co-payments for other options.

A communication strategy directed at the public and professional audiences and explaining the rationale and benefit of the selected policy measures (see the discussion on ensuring the rational use of medicines in chapter 4) would be necessary to support implementation and cope with the likely political fallout. A united front of industry and health professionals can be expected to use all their influence to prevent or reverse measures that cut deeply into their profits. However, a financial crisis of the magnitude experienced in 2008 and 2009 could create a unique opportunity for Lithuania to introduce measures for curbing drug expenditure growth that otherwise would not find enough political support.

China: Improving Social Protection for the Rural Poor

Most visitors to China are impressed by the world-class infrastructure and apparent wealth displayed in the form of high-end shopping centers in major cities such as Beijing and Shanghai. However, the most populous country in the world has another side. The majority of the Chinese people are still relatively poor, and a large number of people living in rural areas far from the cities are very poor. For them, access to health care is limited. Severe illness can bankrupt even a middle-income household. The Chinese government has made a priority of rapidly increasing the number of people covered by health insurance, particularly in rural areas. China has three different health insurance funds, covering different segments of the population (urban workers, other urban residents, and rural citizens). Largely pooled at city or county level, the insurance funds have disparities in contributions and benefit coverage. Although a central reimbursement list exists, the local administrations can set the reimbursement levels on the basis of available resources. Thus, citizens in poor provinces tend to have higher co-payments than do those in wealthy cities.

Drug expenditure in China makes up an extraordinarily high share of total health expenditure (40 percent). The main reason appears to be that health facilities and physicians rely on income from drug sales to finance a significant share of their budgets and salaries. To counter the trend toward prescribing expensive drugs and the polypharmacy[4] that comes with such a system, the government plans to implement an essential drugs policy, hoping to improve access to affordable essential drugs for everyone, including the rural poor, who are the priority target audience for this policy initiative. The policy faces several hurdles that need to be cleared before it can be successful:

- Agreement on the definition of *essential* may be difficult, given the fragmentation of decision making in the central government, the significant powers of provincial and local authorities, and the influence of economic interests on the decision makers.
- Physicians and hospital managers are likely to resist any policy that reduces their incomes unless it is offset by an increase in service fees (which are currently priced lower than cost) or prepayments (such as case payments for inpatient care and capitation payments for outpatient services) or direct government subsidies.
- The current system makes monitoring drug prescription and dispensing by health facilities or physicians difficult for authorities or insurance funds.

- Wholesalers may try to undermine the policy by not carrying low-cost drugs that are not profitable for them.
- Patients may not accept low-cost generics on grounds of perceived lower quality and performance issues in a country that has a reputation as one of the originators of counterfeit and substandard drugs sold across the globe, despite significant counter-efforts by the Chinese Food and Drug Administration.
- The urban middle class is likely to reject a policy that limits its access to a wider range of treatment options, including newer and more expensive drugs. A tiered insurance system could address this problem and avoid a situation in which out-of-pocket payments become an increasing drag on personal wealth and overall economic development.

The preceding list of challenges demonstrates that major policy initiatives in the pharmaceutical sector require an orchestrated implementation effort that addresses various parameters at the same time and aims at aligning incentives (by changing the provider payment system) of all players in the sector as well as correcting misperceptions about the relationship between drug quality and price. Of course, a core requirement is that decisions be made on a technically sound basis, meaning that (a) a stringent regulatory agency ensures the quality of drugs in circulation and (b) decisions about inclusion on drug lists are based on sound scientific assessment and transparent procedures.

China's essential drugs policy is expected to look very different from a similar policy applied in a low-income country in Africa (see the description of an essential drugs policy in chapter 5). For China, the required set of measures resembles much more a generic drugs policy as described in chapter 5. Very soon, a need may arise to establish institutions that are typical in high-income countries, such as an independent institute that can assess cost-effectiveness of new chemical entities and make recommendations for inclusion on the reimbursement list.

Russian Federation: Affordability and Access to Essential Drugs

In the Russian Federation, patients pay for most medicines out of pocket.[5] Drug expenditure accounts for about 30 percent of total health expenditure, significantly more than in most countries of the Organisation for Economic Co-operation and Development (OECD). Drug prices are rising faster than prices for other goods. After the onset of the financial crisis, retail drug prices rose by 29 percent (from March

2008 to March 2009), whereas the consumer price index increased 15 percent. Interestingly, the prices for already higher-priced brand-name drugs increased significantly more than those for the cheaper generic drugs. High drug prices are a burden for poor households and can force people to postpone or interrupt necessary treatments for economic reasons, leading to a higher disease burden and a potentially negative impact on life expectancy.

One way to address this growing problem would be to introduce a publicly financed essential drug benefit program for outpatients. The World Bank assumes that such a program could be realized at a cost of US$30 to US$60 per capita per year, which would be equivalent to 8 to 14 percent of Russia's total health expenditure (for comparison, the average drug expenditure in OECD countries is about 14 percent of total health expenditure). If the budget situation does not leave room to absorb the incremental costs caused by such a drug benefit program (potential savings would materialize only after years), the introduction or increase of "sin taxes" on tobacco, alcohol, or sugar-containing soft drinks could be considered to raise the required funds.

As pointed out in chapter 3, third-party-financed drug benefit programs are vulnerable to abuse and fraud, unless they are embedded in a framework of provider monitoring and incentives for appropriate and cost-effective prescribing. In the case of Russia, another basic element for the success of a publicly financed essential drugs benefit would be the development of evidence-based treatment guidelines for common conditions, which would become the basis of an effort to ensure quality of outpatient medical care.

Another aspect that needs to be addressed, as in nearly all the other cases described here, is perceptions among professionals and patients regarding the quality and efficacy of low-cost generic drugs. In markets with perceived weak regulatory oversight, it is rational for consumers to prefer branded products and to pay more for them. A combination of strict regulatory enforcement and proactive communication with all relevant audiences over a significant period is required to erode such beliefs and increase the acceptance of generic drugs.

Liberia: Building Up after Conflict

After a protracted civil war, Liberia has recently seen a period of stability and economic recovery, although from a very low level. The public health system is weak. Aid organizations and nongovernmental organizations provide care for many people who do not have access to public health facilities or who cannot afford the private health care providers that are increasingly opening their clinics in urban areas. Public and donor money can buy only limited amounts of essential medicines for free or subsidized treatment programs. The majority of the population has to rely on private pharmacies and drugstores (in urban areas) or informal drug sellers, where payments for drugs are made out of pocket. The quality of drugs in circulation in the private sector is unknown. Liberia does not yet have a functioning regulatory agency for the drug sector;[6] neither does it have a lab equipped for basic drug quality control testing (Finnish Consulting Group International 2007).

To improve access to quality medicines, Liberia's National Drug Service (the central medical store handling the public sector and donor-financed drug programs) set up a small pilot program with three community outreach pharmacies (COPs) in commercial centers with high customer traffic. These COPs sell a defined assortment of essential medicines, procured from an international procurement agency with a quality assurance system in place. Prices are lower than in private pharmacies, and customers receive counseling from a trained nurse, who is the head of the outlet. Customers have to buy the amount needed for an entire treatment: no dispensing of single tablets of, for example, antibiotics or malaria medicines occurs. The COP program has been financially sustainable and well accepted by customers. The success has created a demand for COPs in other areas of the country. Plans for a scale-up project are being developed with donor support, in an effort to reach people in other parts of Liberia. Creation of a mobile COP unit has even been suggested, which could sell drugs at the rotating markets where villagers congregate once a week to sell their crops and buy supplies.

Scaling up the COP program will bring some new challenges in terms of professional management, inventory control and forecasting, logistics and transportation, and involvement of the local communities. However, if successful, it could lead to a significant improvement in access to quality essential medicines. Although the current COP program is still a cash-and-carry system, its franchiselike design with standardized drug selection and prices makes it an ideal partner for any health financing initiative that targets the poor, who still cannot afford to buy drugs even at lower prices. Examples of such tax-, donor- or solidarity-based financing models are voucher programs or community-based mutual insurance schemes.

Notes

1. Information was obtained from Ghana National Health Insurance Association in November 2009.
2. See http://en.wikipedia.org/wiki/Economy_of_Lithuania.
3. Personal information obtained in discussions with the SPF and Ministry of Health in Lithuania.
4. *Polypharmacy* means overuse of drugs, in particular use of several drugs in parallel without clinical evidence that such a combination has any therapeutic justification.
5. Information in this section is based on Marquez and Bonch-Osmolovskiy (2009).
6. A National Medicine Regulatory Committee has been established, but it does not yet have the capacity to provide the basic regulatory functions for the sector.

References

Finnish Consulting Group International. 2007. "Review of the Pharmaceuticals Area and Preparation of a Mid-term Pharmaceuticals Policy and Implementation Plan for the Ministry of Health and Social Welfare, Liberia." Finnish Consulting Group International, Helsinki, for the European Commission, April.

Marquez, Patricio, and Mikhail Bonch-Osmolovskiy. 2009. "Testing Times in Russia: How to Facilitate Access to Essential Drugs and Get More Value out of Pharmaceutical Expenditures?" *Russian Economic Report* 19: 15–21.

Ministry of Health and Ghana Health Service. 2007. "Ghana: Assessment of Medicines Procurement and Supply Management in the Public Health Sector—A Country Report." Ministry of Health and Ghana Health Service, Accra.

Seiter, Andreas, and Martha Gyansa-Lutterodt. 2009. "Policy Note: The Pharmaceutical Sector in Ghana." World Bank, Washington, DC.

CHAPTER 8

Pharmaceutical Policy Outlook

Predicting future developments may appear presumptuous. However, pharmaceutical policy trends over the next years are partially predictable simply by extrapolating from measures currently conceived or debated to address existing problems in the pharmaceutical sector in many countries.

Regulatory Framework

In low-income countries, pressure from donors (worried that health outcomes may be negatively affected by substandard and counterfeit drugs), established industry (eager to keep low-cost competitors out of the market by increasing regulatory hurdles), and civil society (increasingly aware of the dangers of a badly regulated drug market) should lead to continuous effort to strengthen drug regulatory functions. Some regional or bilateral agreements may emerge that free resources for individual agencies by allowing them to recognize licensing decisions made by other agencies or by pooling resources for quality control and enforcement actions. An increasing number of drug control labs (public and private) in low- and middle-income countries will probably become World Health Organization (WHO) prequalified.

Nevertheless, expecting that drug regulatory functions in low-income countries can generally grow to a level needed to effectively suppress the trade in counterfeit and substandard drugs within a 10-year time frame is unrealistic. The required investments in staff and management systems currently appear too big to be politically or economically viable. In addition, many low-income countries are unlikely to be able to achieve, within the given time frame, the independence, capacity, and competence in law enforcement and the judicial system needed for a fully effective regulatory system. High-income countries needed many decades to develop the mature (and still far from perfect) regulatory systems that they rely on today. A similar time frame can be expected for low- and middle-income countries, and strong economic development is a precondition for establishing fully functioning institutions.

In middle-income countries, the current range of regulatory competence and performance between the best and the worst may narrow somewhat over the coming decade. Pressure to improve current systems comes mainly from domestic stakeholders, including pharmaceutical companies seeking more transparency and predictability for licensing and other regulatory decisions. Some countries in the upper-middle-income range and perhaps others with a strong and internationally active domestic pharmaceutical industry may make closing the regulatory gap with developed countries a political priority. They may seek to achieve recognition by the International Conference on Harmonisation of Technical Requirements for Registration of Pharmaceuticals for Human Use. What will be more challenging (and will take more than 10 years) is the elimination of all manufacturing, trading, and selling activity in the substandard segment of the market. This problem will be particularly hard to address in large countries such as China and India that have a huge number of small businesses active in this segment and no realistic chance to meet strict licensing rules or compete with the larger, integrated players on the same level. The problem can be fully addressed only if positive economic development, in combination with constant and increasing regulatory pressure, creates options and incentives for businesses that are engaged in making and selling substandard drugs to give up this business and find other ways of making a living.

Regulatory functions such as pharmacovigilance are likely to benefit from standardization of reporting formats (driven by institutions in developed countries) and better connectivity, which will allow a more regular exchange of data and information between agencies in different countries. WHO's ongoing support for regulatory capacity building, as well as the engagement of technical staff from agencies in developing countries in international exchanges or programs (for example, the WHO prequalification program), should lead to a gradual harmonization of approaches and contribute to the narrowing of the gap between the best and the worst regulatory performers.

Drug Prices

Increasing costs for research and development, licensing, and marketing of innovative medicines mean that prices for these medicines will remain high. However, major pharmaceutical companies have become more responsive to concerns regarding affordability of lifesaving or disease-modifying drugs. Increasingly, such companies are developing access programs targeting patients for whom new drugs are financially out of reach. One model that has been used for antiretrovirals in treating HIV/AIDS is differential pricing: poor countries can get such drugs at massively discounted prices, middle-income countries pay a higher but still discounted price, and patients in high-income countries pay the full innovation premium. For new malaria medicines that do not have a significant market among the wealthy nations, originator companies have accepted no-profit-no-loss pricing or very small profit margins across the board. Differential pricing for medicines that have a significant commercial potential in developed markets has been discouraged in the past because it exposes companies to the risk that pricing authorities use discounted prices offered to poorer countries as a benchmark to regulate prices in rich countries. With a declining role for such external reference pricing systems likely in the future, more potential for market segmentation may exist, hence allowing companies to offer new products to certain channels serving the poor at a lower price than the one officially charged to the more affluent market segment within the same country. Such segmentation strategies may use defined distribution channels, out-licensing and brand differentiation, or "bundling" models (provision of a service package that includes diagnostics, disease management programs, or a range of treatment options at a flat rate) to avoid disclosing the price of a specific input and cannibalization of the profitable core business.

When large purchasers learn to make better use of their bargaining power, prices of generic drugs have the potential to come down in many markets that currently are structured inefficiently. In contrast, regulatory pressure on small manufacturers that can offer cheap drugs because they do not follow good manufacturing practices may lead to industry consolidation and higher floor prices in the market (a trend discussed further later in this chapter).

Financing and Management of Drug Benefits

All health systems that rely mainly on out-of-pocket payments for drugs tend to experience not only inequality in access but also the typical signs of market failure in the pharmaceutical market. These signs are overprescribing and overuse of drugs, preference for expensive originator drugs despite availability of equivalent generics, and other symptoms of irrational use of medicines. Lack of access to drugs and high drug prices are factors ranking high in public awareness. In many cases, politicians have promised to improve access to medicines as part of their election campaigns. Therefore, policy makers will likely try to introduce at least a limited drug benefit in many markets or market segments that are currently relying on out-of-pocket financing. The term *drug benefit* stands for an entitlement to a limited list (formulary) of prescription drugs (free or for a limited co-payment), available to patients covered by a public health plan or a health insurance fund.

Introducing a drug benefit with a limited formulary creates a barrier to market access, at least with respect to the market segment that receives this benefit. Manufacturers need to try to get their drugs on the formulary to make profits in this segment. The decision-making process on formulary inclusion is thus exposed to high pressure; it also has potential for corruption. Decision makers will respond to this pressure by introducing more formal and structured processes, with a tendency to learn from each other and copy models that have gained acceptance from market participants elsewhere. The likely result is convergence to a range of relatively similar approaches that include the following:

- Pharmacoeconomic assessment, whereby assessment methods will become increasingly standardized
- Budget impact assessment combined with a range of tools to control consumption and negotiation strategies to limit the risk of overspending on newly introduced drugs
- Conditional approval of new drugs pending data collection and evidence development during a defined period, after which a final decision is made
- Strict protocols and process rules to shield decision makers against political pressures or unwanted approaches by interest groups

Countries with limited resources probably will use data from other countries or join regional bodies for evaluation of drugs and adapt decisions to local circumstances. The outcome may be a more homogeneous global marketplace, although this development will probably not reach its endpoint for more than 10 years. Differentiation in health insurance offers in countries with growing wealth may partially counteract this trend by creating new market segments in which access barriers differ. However, the different segments are unlikely to use very different sets of tools in making decisions on formulary inclusion. More likely, they will just apply different standards for acceptability and different degrees of rigidity in applying cost control measures.

Effect on Markets and Industry

The use of pharmacoeconomic assessment as a tool to control market access for new drugs has been referred to as the "fourth hurdle" by drug company executives and market analysts (in addition to the three regulatory hurdles of quality, safety, and efficacy that are at the center of every marketing authorization procedure). This fourth hurdle, while already a reality in many markets today, is likely to become more formally established and categorically applied in most markets (although not in the largest market of all, the United States, for the foreseeable future).

The fourth hurdle of pharmacoeconomic assessment as a requirement for access to the purchasing power of major markets makes it less attractive for major drug companies to develop "me-too" drugs without major added benefits over existing treatments. Research today focuses more on areas in which current treatment options are insufficient and on lifestyle indications for which wealthier patients are willing to pay out of pocket. Many new drugs are biologicals with complicated manufacturing processes. Biologicals are not small molecules that can be easily reverse-engineered by generic manufacturers and thus cannot be so easily copied after their patent has expired. "Bio-similars" also face higher regulatory barriers than drugs with traditional chemical active ingredients. Better targeting of patients based on genetic disease profiling can potentially increase treatment success and lower the risk of severe side effects, but it also can reduce market size for a drug, defined by the pool of potential patients available for a manufacturer to recover research and development costs and make a profit. Manufacturers can compensate for this effect only by charging a higher price for such drugs. All these factors combined should lead to a higher number of expensive treatment options and more pressure on payers to decide which patients should get access to new treatments. For multinational research-based drug companies, this situation means a continued high risk that investments in the development of specific drugs may not pay off. Those companies that cannot provide growth based on innovation will become candidates for mergers and acquisitions—a trend that has already been going on for decades and will lead to a less fragmented industry in the future. However, spin-offs of smaller entities may focus on specific markets with defined characteristics. An example is ViiV Healthcare, a new company in which GlaxoSmithKline and Pfizer merged their HIV/AIDS portfolios. Such a company has more flexibility than its large parent organizations in pursuing specific opportunities in its market segment and can better build special relationships with its stakeholders and experiment with new pricing or access strategies without worrying about potential implications for other business lines.

An interesting question is how the various partnerships and financing models aimed at development of treatments for neglected diseases will play out over the next 10 years. Experience so far suggests that smaller, donor-financed drug development partnerships reach a point at which they need access to major financial resources—as well as the know-how of an industrial partner—to put a viable registration dossier together and to ensure successful launch of a new drug in markets with limited marketing and distribution infrastructure. Patent pools, open-source approaches to drug development—as promoted by GlaxoSmithKline (see Witty 2009)—and alternative financing mechanisms such as the Health Impact Fund are currently competing for attention of decision makers on the national and international levels. None of these approaches has a proven track record yet, so predictions at this stage would be speculative.

Although drug companies in Brazil, China, India, the Russian Federation, South Africa, and other major emerging markets are still too small to seriously challenge the leading multinationals in the next 10 years, some of them may be successful in developing new drugs for specific diseases of high relevance for public health in such countries. Of course, one of the bigger players in these emerging markets could become a bidder in a takeover battle for a weakened multinational.

Less clear is the trend in policies that affect pricing and efficiency in the generic drug market. Much inefficiency today, visible in major price differences for the same drugs across different countries in the same income bracket or even within one country, is rooted in lack of political will: those who benefit from inefficient markets become wealthy and can buy political influence or create local cartels that undermine open competition. Sometimes a government change or a major scandal is required to bring irregularities to light. In other cases, budget pressures grow to a level that breaks political alliances. If that happens, effective procurement policies can be introduced or rules against anticompetitive behavior in markets can be issued and implemented. Particularly in light of the current debt crisis in many countries, several opportunities for radical change are likely to occur in the next 10 years. Such change may lead to more widespread use of electronic procurement platforms, more transparent bidding processes and prices for drugs, more experimentation with various ways of creating competition in generic markets, and overall improved efficiency of generic markets. The beneficiaries of such a development would be globally acting generic drug companies or large regional players, whereas some of the currently protected national players would have to seek cover under the roof of a larger conglomerate or would simply go under in a more competitive market.

Similarly, the fragmented wholesale sector typical for many countries with less-than-effective pharmaceutical markets may face massive consolidation pressures if tolerance for anticompetitive behavior fades and deals become more transparent. Many small wholesalers survive today only because they have exclusive or de facto exclusive agreements with buyers or manufacturers, sometimes covering only a small area. Typically, either these agreements are brokered by an official who expects payment for such services or they are based on a kickback for the business generated. In any case, because such expenses need to be recovered, the economic basis for these business practices collapses when markets are liberated. More open and competitive markets can lead to significantly lower prices for generic drugs, as data from developed markets have shown (Kanavos, Costa-Font, and Seeley 2008). Whereas wholesalers in many developing markets need to charge margins of 10 to 15 percent to operate profitably, the large, integrated distributors in developed markets can operate on margins below 5 percent. The potential savings are even greater if the informal rebates and benefits (in the form of free goods and generous payment terms)—common in many countries where distributors control access to certain customers—are considered. The entry of multinational pharmaceutical distributors to developing markets after informal barriers and political hurdles erode will facilitate consolidation in the wholesale sector (as was the case of Laborex in West Africa). In countries with significant public procurement volumes, a potential change in procurement strategy to contracting with manufacturers on the basis of landed costs (that is, making the manufacturer or its primary agent bear distribution costs) would also pressure distributors to become more efficient. In such a scenario, the manufacturers could subcontract with distributors on the basis of a competitive selection.

General Trend: Convergence toward Models That Work

As pointed out previously, problems caused by market failure, lack of resources, and conflicting objectives of various stakeholders in the pharmaceutical sector are persistent and in many countries will not go away even in the midterm. Nevertheless, in several countries, authorities and market participants are becoming increasingly serious in trying to address chronic sector problems. All countries that undertake serious reform efforts look for examples in other countries, thus creating a path toward convergence of policy solutions. A good example from the past 10 years is the widespread introduction of reference pricing models, starting in the European Union and spreading toward Eastern Europe and the Mediterranean region. Although external reference pricing will soon reach the end of its useful life cycle (when almost all countries reference each other and prices converge, the differences between countries diminish), it has been a useful tool in establishing an objective benchmark for pricing policies and responding to the opportunistic, profit-centered pricing policies of international and national drug companies.

Table 8.1 summarizes the likely trends between 2010 and 2020.

Table 8.1   Likely Trends in the Pharmaceutical Sector, 2010–20

Subsector	Likely trends
Regulatory functions	Beginning of regionalization of some functions
	Continued capacity building
	Reaching of international standards by a few middle-income countries
	Increased number of WHO-prequalified drug quality control labs
Financing and payment	Increased experimentation with health insurance or other pooled payment mechanisms in countries that so far rely mainly on out-of-pocket payments
	Increasing reliance on pharmacoeconomic assessment to decide on inclusion of new drugs in reimbursement lists
	Use of a range of contracting tools to share risk of overspending with suppliers

(continued)

Table 8.1   Likely Trends in the Pharmaceutical Sector, 2010–20 *(continued)*

Subsector	Likely trends
Pricing policy	Reduced reliance on reference pricing (with external benchmarking)
	Increased attempts to create price-competitive generics markets, using bargaining power of large buyers and payers
	More price transparency on national and international levels
	Greater range of access programs for innovative drugs essential to public health in low- and middle-income countries, including differential pricing in different channels within one country
Procurement policies	Better understanding of holistic approach to supply chain
	Increased use of framework contracts and landed-costs approach in procurement
Multinational industry	Ongoing consolidation and challenge to develop drugs that can be marketed profitably against a backdrop of increasingly stretched payer budgets
	Continued investment in lifestyle drugs, where markets are less limited by the "fourth hurdle"
	Experimenting with "open source" models, partnerships, and new ways of financing research and development for drugs that have low profit potential but high public health relevance
	More flexibility for accepting differential pricing of new essential medicines, linked to effective segmentation of markets
Multinational generics industry	Continued growth in developed and major developing markets, thanks to the expiration of many patents for top-selling drugs
	Acquisition of national manufacturers in markets that open up to competition
	Potential takeover of a weakened research and development–based manufacturer in a high-income country by a large middle-income country manufacturer
National generics companies	Consolidation pressure if current barriers to market access erode
	Survival for companies that can invest in quality and have a strong franchise in national markets
Drug distributors and wholesalers	Massive consolidation pressure once political and administrative barriers for larger competitors come down
	Stronger national players that will increasingly become subsidiaries of multinational logistics companies

Source: Author's compilation.

References

Kanavos, Panos, Joan Costa-Font, and Elizabeth Seeley. 2008. "Competition in Off-Patent Drug Markets: Issues, Regulation, and Evidence." *Economic Policy* 23 (55): 499–544.

Witty, Andrew. 2009. "Big Pharma as a Catalyst for Change." Speech to Harvard Medical School, February 13.

A Tool to Assess the Pharmaceutical Sector in a Given Country

This tool can be adjusted to the country context and scope of the assessment.

Version: August 2009

Glossary:

EFPIA	European Federation of Pharmaceutical Industries and Associations
EU	European Union
GLP	good laboratory practice
GMP	good manufacturing practice
HIF	health insurance fund
IFPMA	International Federation of Pharmaceutical Manufacturers and Associations
IMS	company that provides pharmaceutical market data in developed and middle-income markets
INN	international nonproprietary name
IT	information technology
MOH	ministry of health
NGO	nongovernmental organization

ÖBIG   Österreichisches Bundesinstitut im Gesundheitswesen
          (Austrian Health Institute)
OECD   Organisation for Economic Co-operation and Development
OTC   over-the-counter
PER   Public Expenditure Review
R&D   research and development
Rx   prescription drugs
TRIPs   Trade-Related Aspects of Intellectual Property Rights
VAT   value added tax
WHO   World Health Organization

Dimension	Sources	Questions, data requests
Pharmaceutical market	IMS, industry associations, MOH, drug agency, HIF	• Total market at retail or ex-factory prices • HIF paid market • Privately paid market (Rx or OTC drugs) • Hospital market • Original brands versus generics • Presence of copies of drugs still patented in OECD countries • Rx share of cheapest generic per substance for some indicator drugs • Locally manufactured versus imported drugs • Existence and size of informal market; circulation of illegal drugs
Pharmaceutical policy and regulation	MOH, drug agency	• Existence of an integrated health strategy with a pharmaceutical component • Existence of a national drug policy • Relevant legislation combined in one drug law • Detailed bylaws governing all regulatory matters • Independent drug agency with adequate resources • Quality control lab with sufficient capacity, certified under GLPs • Enforcement capacity for GMPs, in-market quality surveillance, and pharmacovigilance • Stakeholder representation in relevant commissions and other bodies (including consumers)

(continued)

Dimension	Sources	Questions, data requests
		• Publication of proceedings or minutes by relevant commissions
		• Trade regulation (industry, wholesale and retail level); licensing; and accreditation
		• Implementation of patent rights and use of patents by industry
		• Legal basis for compulsory licensing based on TRIPs exemptions
		• Legal basis for prosecution of counterfeiters
		• Anticounterfeiting strategy
		• Regulatory partnerships or projects with other countries or international bodies (EU, WHO)
Public and private drug expenditure	MOH, HIF, PERs, household surveys, OECD databases, World Bank internal sources	• Drug expenditure by HIF, MOH, and other public payers
		• Other segments, such as special disease programs
		• Top 20 products paid for by HIF
		• Regional pattern of expenditure
		• Expenditure by age group, income level, and type of disease
		• Private out-of-pocket expenditure for co-payments
		• Exemptions from co-payments
		• Household expenditure for cash purchases of Rx and OTC drugs
		• Tracking of public drug expenditure (does central purchasing match what is dispensed at clinic level?)
		• NGO or other nonpublic, donor-financed drug expenditure
		• Private insurance drug expenditure, including corporate employee health plans
		• Total public and private per capita expenditure
		• All data over 3–5 years with trends
Drug pricing	MOH, drug agency, HIF, industry associations, retail pharmacies, WHO, literature, ÖBIG, IMS	• Pricing system, with regulation of patented drugs, generics, and OTC medicines
		• Reference pricing mechanisms
		• VAT and other taxes
		• Wholesale and retail margins
		• Deviations between list prices and actual prices (rebates, free goods, payment terms)
		• Transparency of pricing for patients
		• Price levels compared with other countries

(continued)

Dimension	Sources	Questions, data requests
Purchasing, reimbursement, and procurement	HIF, hospital pharmacies, retail pharmacies, pharmacist associations, MOH, other buyers	• Co-payments and dispensing fees • Special access programs (for example, company-issued patient cards) • Purchasing decisions in public and formal private sector (who defines what is purchased?) • Reimbursement mechanism: direct to pharmacy or patient prepayment • Reimbursement levels • Selection of drugs for reimbursement lists and drug formularies • Pharmacoeconomic assessment of reimbursement decisions • Procurement mechanisms used by different buyers (transparency, effectiveness, efficiency) • Quality controls as part of procurement • Provider incentives related to quality and price (how competitive is the market?) • Preference for local manufacturers • System abuse and corruption risks (in the opinion of different stakeholders)
Service delivery and logistics	MOH, central medical stores, wholesalers, hospitals, pharmacies	• Existence of a public service delivery and distribution mechanism • Planning and management tools and accountability (forecasting, budgeting, transparency) • IT system; logistics software • Performance measurement • Contracting with the private sector: scope, terms, enforcement, data flow, and management
Industry and trade	Industry and professional associations, retail pharmacies	• Number and main role of industry associations • Size and competitive position of national industry (local market, exports) • R&D activities of industry • Local subsidiaries of multinational firms • Manufacturing and licensing agreements between international and national companies • Political influence of industry (national and international) • Manufacturing standards of local industry • Forward integration (industry-wholesale)

(continued)

Dimension	Sources	Questions, data requests
		• Number of wholesalers and market share of top five
		• Number of retail pharmacies, absolute and per capita
		• Rx enforcement in pharmacies
		• Existence of informal sector (manufacturing, wholesale, retail)
		• Capitalization of wholesalers and pharmacies
		• Share of publicly paid Rx business in total pharmacy income
Rational use of drugs	HIF, professional associations, literature, industry, retail pharmacies	• Prescription guidelines for doctors
		• IT system for monitoring and dispensing of Rx, with central data collection in real time and routine analysis of defined parameters for rational use
		• Perceptions among doctors and consumers about drug quality in various market segments
		• Influence of belief systems and traditional medicine on care-seeking behavior
		• Education for professionals and consumers on use of medicines
		• Incentives for doctors, pharmacists, and patients
		• Marketing strategies of industry and whole-salers, with sanctions for unethical marketing practices and application of ethics code (IFPMA, EFPIA, or a similar code)
		• Brand-name or INN-based prescription
		• Co-payments and cheaper options (are doctors required to inform patients?)
		• Substitution rights (do pharmacists have such rights?)

Source: Author's compilation.

Customized Version of the Assessment Tool (Appendix A) for Use in an Assessment of the Pharmaceutical Sector in Turkey

This appendix is an example of a customized tool prepared for a Health Sector Review project in Turkey, realized jointly by the Turkish government, the Organisation for Economic Co-operation and Development, and the World Bank in 2008.

The purpose of the checklist was to give guidance for the collection of data and information that provided the basis for writing the pharmaceutical sector chapter of the review. It is split into two parts: quantitative data requirements and topics that need description and explanation.

Glossary:

AİFD	Araştırmacı İlaç Firmaları Derneği (Association of Research-Based Pharmacies)
ATC	anatomical therapeutic chemical (classification)
copy drugs	drugs that are still patented in OECD countries but sold as generics; introduced prior to the acceptance of patent rights for drugs in Turkey
EU	European Union

GLP	good laboratory practice
GMP	good manufacturing practice
İEİS	İlaç Endüstrisi İşverenler Sendikası (Pharmaceutical Manufacturers Association of Turkey)
IMS	company that provides pharmaceutical market data in developed and middle income markets
INN	international nonproprietary name
MOH	Ministry of Health
ÖBIG	Österreichisches Bundesinstitut im Gesundheitswesen (Austrian Health Institute)
OECD	Organisation for Economic Co-operation and Development
OTC	over-the-counter
PER	Public Expenditure Review
PETS	pharmaceutical expenditure tracking system
R&D	research and development
Rx	prescription drugs
SSI	Social Security Institution
TRIPs	Trade-Related Aspects of Intellectual Property Rights
VAT	value added tax
WHO	World Health Organization

Part 1: Quantitative Data

Dimension	Sources	Data requests
Pharmaceutical market	IMS, AIFD, IEIS, MOH	• Total market at retail prices and units (2003–07) • Per capita consumption by value and units (2003–07) • Hospital market (drugs sold to hospitals, 2003–07) • Total value of drugs that are prescribed for inpatients but dispensed in the outpatient sector (estimate for 2007) • Share of original brands versus generics and copy drugs (Rx only, value and units, 2003–07) • Locally manufactured versus imported drugs (2003–07) • Rx share of cheapest generic per INN for some indicator drugs (use the top 10 in terms of sales of Rx drugs that are available as original and generic in the Turkish market, snapshot 2007 only) • Top 20 list of Rx drugs by value and units (2003–07) • Total number of manufacturers • Number of domestic manufacturers and domestic manufacturing sites of international manufacturers with headquarters outside Turkey • Domestic sales versus export of domestic manufacturers (2003–07) • Top 10 manufacturers by value and units (2003–2007) • Number of wholesalers and market share of top five • Number of retail pharmacies, absolute and per capita (regional breakdown) • Share of publicly paid Rx business in total pharmacy income
Financing of medicines	SSI, MOH, PER data, household survey data	• Public expenditure for medicines (total 2003–07) • Total in units and average cost per unit (2003–07) • Breakdown of outpatient versus inpatient (value only, 2003–07) • Regional breakdown for 2007 (value and units) • Breakdown of original versus generic and domestic versus imported (value and units, 2003–07) • Selective trend analysis on ATC level 4: top 20 by expenditure for 2003–07 • Per capita expenditure for drugs (2003–07), including regional breakdown

(continued)

169

Dimension	Sources	Data requests
		• Out-of-pocket expenditure for Rx and OTC drugs (2003–07), including regional breakdown and breakdown by income quintile
		• Percentage of prescriptions for which patients had to pay a higher co-payment than necessary because the prescribed drug was a more expensive brand than the one defining the reimbursement level (2007 only)
		• Private insurance drug expenditure including corporate employee health plans (if existing)
Use data	SSI	• Number of INNs per prescription (2003–07)
		• Percentage of injections (of all prescriptions or of all outpatient visits, whichever is easier to get, 2003–07)
		• Percentage of antibiotics prescriptions for cold or flu diagnosis or of all prescriptions (2003–07)
		• Other indicators of rational use of drugs, if available
		• Rx filling rate (percentage of drugs that were prescribed but not dispensed; data may not be available unless specific studies were done; breakdown by income quintile, if available)
Medicine price data	MOH, IMS, SSI, ÖBIG, WHO, previous studies	• Unit prices of top 50 drugs (most common form or strength) by value in 2007, compared to a basket of EU countries; if data not available in Turkey, obtain from ÖBIG (will require some funding)
		• Detailed explanation of the retail price for Rx, showing the calculation based on ex-factory price set at 100, adding distribution margins, VAT, and other components
		• Same for SSI reimbursed drugs, demonstrating how rebates are applied

Source: Author's compilation.

Part 2: Descriptive Section

Pharmaceutical Policy and Regulation

- Does Turkey have an integrated health strategy? If so, what is the strategy for the pharmaceutical sector? Does a national drug policy exist, and is it linked to the current legislation and institutional development?
- Describe current legislation and bylaws governing pharmaceuticals, as well as the status of ongoing legislative initiatives (new drug agency).
- Describe the capacity situation at the quality control lab, GLP adherence, and membership in international quality assurance networks.
- Describe enforcement capacity for GMPs, in-market quality surveillance, and pharmacovigilance.
- Does a pharmacovigilance system exist? If so, does it include a system for recall and warning letters?
- Describe trade regulation (industry, wholesale, and retail levels); licensing; and accreditation.
- Describe the implementation of patent rights and use of patents by the industry.
- Does a legal basis exist for compulsory licensing based on TRIPs exemptions?
- What is the legal basis for prosecution of counterfeiters?
- What is the anticounterfeiting strategy?
- Does the country belong to any regulatory partnerships or projects with other countries or international bodies (EU, WHO)?
- Describe the pricing system for and regulation of patented drugs, generics, and OTC drugs.
- Provide a detailed description of any reference pricing mechanisms.
- What VAT and other taxes exist?
- What are the wholesale and retail margins for drugs?
- Describe deviations between list prices and actual prices (rebates, free goods, payment terms).

Governance and Transparency

- Assess political and technical accountability in the sector (quality aspects, access to funding, marketing practices, corruption, and abuse of public funds).
- Describe stakeholder representation in relevant commissions and other bodies (including consumers).
- Assess transparency of decision making and appeals procedures.
- How are conflicts of interest handled?

Purchasing, Reimbursement, and Procurement
- Describe the process of selection of drugs for reimbursement lists and drug formularies.
- What is the pharmacoeconomic assessment capacity?
- Describe the reimbursement levels, co-payments, exemptions (on paper and in reality).
- Describe the procurement mechanisms used by different institutional buyers (transparency, effectiveness, efficiency).
- Are provider incentives related to quality and price? How competitive is the market?
- Is there explicit or implicit preference for local manufacturers?
- Are there system abuses and corruption risks? Consider anecdotal evidence.

Access to Medicines, Financial Protection
- Describe the drug benefit package under insurance, as well as equity aspects.
- Describe the insurance coverage.
- Assess the transparency of drug prices and quality for patients. Is there acceptance of generics?
- Describe the special access programs, such as company-issued patient cards and coupons. Discuss market distortion potential if these programs favor the use of new expensive drugs over older, generic alternatives.
- Describe any physical access barriers, for example, in remote regions.
- Is there supplier-induced demand in the public or private sector? Can public sector physicians recruit patients for their private practice?
- Discuss the catastrophic costs of illness. Does the insurance system protect patients effectively?

Industry and Trade
- Describe the number and main role of industry associations.
- Describe the size and competitive position of national industry (local market, export).
- Describe the R&D activities of industry.
- List the local subsidiaries of multinational firms.
- Describe any manufacturing and licensing agreements between international and national companies.
- Describe any takeover and merger activities in the past five years.

- Describe the strategic initiatives by industry (aimed at increased competitiveness, profitability).
- Describe the manufacturing standards of local industry.
- Is there forward integration (industry-wholesale)?
- Is there Rx enforcement in pharmacies?
- Is there an informal sector?
- What is the capitalization of wholesalers and pharmacies?

Rational Use of Drugs
- Describe the clinical guidelines and prescription guidelines for doctors.
- Describe the information technology system for monitoring of expenditure, prescription, and dispensing (PETS). Are there plans for a data warehouse with the possibility of generating reports on behavior of specific providers?
- What are the perceptions among doctors and consumers about drug quality in various market segments?
- Describe the influence of belief systems and traditional medicine on care-seeking behavior.
- Describe the education for professionals and consumers on use of medicines.
- Describe the incentives for doctors, pharmacists, and patients.
- Describe the influence of marketing strategies. Are there sanctions for unethical marketing practices?
- Is there brand-name or INN-based prescription?
- Are doctors required to inform patients about co-payments and cheaper options?
- Do pharmacists have substitution rights, and how are they using them?

Assessment Tool for Government Procurement Agencies in the Health Sector in India

Ratings: Compliance to Standards
Completely compliant = 3 points
Substantially compliant with minor corrective action required = 2 points
Some compliance and significant corrective action required = 1 point
Noncompliant or unacceptable = 0 points

Name of procurement agency:
Date of assessment:

Standard	Compliance rating	Assessor observations and comments	Instructions for assessor
1.0 General requirements			
1.1 Physical resources			
1.1.1 Premises			
1.1.1.1 Office space is conveniently located for personnel, and storage space is sufficient for documentation records, reports, product samples, and other records relating to all procurement activities.	0 / 1 / 2 / 3		Unencumbered workspace is available for each employee. Records are stored in an orderly and easily retrievable fashion (records and documents should all be filed); a lockable file or container is available for storing vendor bids until bid opening. If drug samples are stored at the agency, storage is secure and temperature controlled.
1.1.1.1.1 Office space is available for arranging prebid meetings, managing receipt of bids, and opening public bids.	0 / 1 / 2 / 3		An office sufficient to seat typical number of bidders (based on review of procurement records for the past 2 years) is available.
1.1.1.2 Computers are available to facilitate procurement procedures.	0 / 3 (mandatory)		Computers and monitors are in good operating condition and available to procurement personnel.
1.1.1.2.1 If computers are available, software is appropriate for the activities performed, the staff is adequately trained in its use, security systems are in place to prevent unauthorized access, backup systems are in place to prevent loss of data, a firewall is installed, and virus protection software is available and updated regularly.	0 / 1 / 2 / 3		Minimally, Microsoft 2000 operating system (or equivalent) with word processing and spreadsheet software is installed, and financial management, purchase order processing, and sales order processing software or systems are available. Observe personnel using computers and software and determine from interviews their familiarity with the software. Document computer security and backup systems. Document whether the organization uses e-tendering or e-procurement, and if so, confirm through interviews that the staff is familiar with those procedures.

Item	Score	Verification
1.1.1.2.2 Computer technical support personnel are available either on site or locally.	0 / 1 / 2 / 3	If support personnel are not on site, does the agency have a contract for technical support or is there a record of support by a local company?
1.1.1.2.3 Computer hardware is sufficient to operate software efficiently; capacity and memory are sufficient for intended use; and printers are available and in proper working order.	0 / 1 / 2 / 3	Interview computer operators, and request information concerning (a) frequency of computer crashes and downtime and (b) operating condition of printers.
1.1.1.2.4 Computer maintenance is performed regularly.	0 / 1 / 2 / 3	Verify existence of computer maintenance records and that personnel are familiar with general computer maintenance programs (that is, Microsoft or equivalent system tools such as defragmenter and antiviral program) and whether those programs are up to date.
1.1.1.3 Telephone and facsimile access is adequate, and if computers are available, e-mail and broadband connectivity to Internet is available 24 hours per day.	0 / 1 / 2 / 3	Personnel with job responsibilities requiring access to phone or e-mail have easy access to equipment.
1.1.1.4 Office equipment (for example, copying machines, scanner, paper shredder); supplies (for example, stationery, computer supplies, printing paper); and office furniture meet the requirements of the procurement office.	0 / 1 / 2 / 3	Verify that routinely needed office equipment, furniture, and supplies are available on site. Such items include copiers, desks, chairs, secured filing cabinets, printers, computer paper, CDs, printer cartridges, computer backup device, forms, paper punch, and staplers.
1.1.1.5 Transportation required for performance of official duties is available, or expenditure is reimbursed.	0 / 1 / 2 / 3	The agency has a policy for travel reimbursement, or the agency provides transportation.
Minimum score for resources	21	
Actual score		

(continued)

Standard	Compliance rating	Assessor observations and comments	Instructions for assessor
1.2 Organization, structure, and functions			
1.2.1 The agency holds legal status (that is, government department, state corporation, registered society) and is accountable to the government.	0 / 3 (mandatory)		The agency has state status.
1.2.2 Written standard operating procedures (SOPs) and policies are available for all procurement-related activities and are reviewed or updated regularly (annually at a minimum).	0 / 1 / 2 / 3		The organization has its own written procurement rules and regulations or follows government-legislated rules and regulations. The policies and associated SOPs enumerated here are available for review. The assessor will comment on policies and SOP availability and document annual review and revision. If no formal written policies or procedures are available, the assessor will evaluate any available documentation related to this area. In addition, interviews with key personnel will be used to determine working knowledge of policies and SOPs. In the rating of compliance to standards for policies and SOPs, only a written SOP together with supporting documentation *and* interviews indicative of adherence to the SOP will be scored as completely compliant ("3"). The maximum score will be 2 points (substantially compliant) when a written SOP is unavailable but other documentation exists to indicate a policy and SOP are in place *and* interviews with key personnel indicate adherence to a less than formalized SOP. These instructions apply to 1.2.2.1–1.2.2.11.

1.2.2.1 Supplier and product prequalification, including facility inspection and product quality (prior to tender or as part of tender process)	0 / 1 / 2 / 3
1.2.2.2 Advertisement of tenders	0 / 1 / 2 / 3
1.2.2.3 Bidder questions or request for clarifications prior to bid opening	0 / 1 / 2 / 3
1.2.2.4 Bid opening	0 / 1 / 2 / 3
1.2.2.5 Tender evaluation and award	0 / 1 / 2 / 3
1.2.2.6 Contract and price negotiation	0 / 1 / 2 / 3
1.2.2.7 Supplier dispute or complaint resolution	0 / 1 / 2 / 3
1.2.2.8 Quality assurance for products procured and operations	0 / 1 / 2 / 3
1.2.2.9 Contract management	0 / 1 / 2 / 3
1.2.2.10 Internal and external audits	0 / 1 / 2 / 3
1.2.2.11 Code of conduct and conflict of interest	0 / 1 / 2 / 3
1.2.3 Agency personnel have experience with health commodity procurement for the following commodity categories (1.2.3.1–1.2.3.4).	
1.2.3.1 Drugs, supplies (including lab and medical supplies), and test kits	0 / 1 / 2 / 3	The standard is met if expenditures exceed US$10,000,000; substantially met if expenditures are between US$500,000 and US$10,000,000; and minimally met if expenditures are between US$250,000 and US$500,000.
1.2.3.2 Medical equipment	0 / 1 / 2 / 3	The standard is met if expenditures exceed US$10,000,000; substantially met if expenditures are between US$500,000 and US$10,000,000; and minimally met if expenditures are between US$250,000 and US$500,000.

(continued)

179

Standard	Compliance rating	Assessor observations and comments	Instructions for assessor
1.2.4 Delegation of thresholds for contracting powers within the organization (invitation and acceptance of bids) is available and regularly updated.	0 / 1 / 2 / 3		If written documentation is not available, the assessor will determine situation from an interview with the managing director or finance director.
1.2.5 Records of all operations are maintained in a secure, easily retrievable manner, and access is limited only to authorized individuals.	0 / 1 / 2 / 3		The assessor verifies that procurement records are filed in an organized fashion and secure (in a locked cabinet); if electronic records are maintained, verify that they are password protected.
1.2.6 The finance staff follows procedures to ensure that available funds are used efficiently and are allocated before tender is issued and released as per the approved purchase contract.	0 / 1 / 2 / 3		Procurement plan and records reflect the availability of funds and payment.
1.2.7 The quality staff ensures that all categories of products procured are of acceptable quality and meet standards required by the funding agency. If no funding agency standards are specified, procurement services agency (PSA) in-house standards are met. For all products procured, testing for quality is carried out in accordance with the principal's (the government of India or the state using the services of the agency) contract terms. If none are specified, the PSA has a quality policy in place, and in the case of health products, if state- or nationally approved testing facilities are available to perform analysis against product specification, such testing is carried out.	0 /1 /2/ 3		For all products procured, quality assurance is carried out in accordance with terms dictated by the principal. If standards are not specified, an internal quality policy for health commodities provides for comprehensive quality assessment, including visual inspection and laboratory analysis where applicable.

1.2.8 A management oversight committee with financial, legal, and program planning experience and expertise reviews adjudicated tenders.	0 / 1 / 2 / 3	Such a committee or its equivalent is in place with written policies and procedures.
Minimum score for resources	39	*Note:* Minimum score per standard for 1.2.3.1 and 1.2.3.2 is 1 point.
Actual score		
Minimum total score for general requirements	60	
Actual total score for general requirements		
2.0 Transparency		
2.1 Detailed records of all procurement proceedings are maintained.	0 / 1 / 2 / 3	Randomly review a minimum of 2 recent procurements (at least 1 for drugs that includes several dozen items and 1 for equipment), and document whether detailed records are available describing the prebid conference (if any), bid opening, pre- or postqualification, tender committee meetings, and contract award proceedings.
2.2 If the agency already handles World Bank–funded procurement, the invitation for bids for international competitive bidding (ICB) is advertised in at least 1 international newspaper or journal and for national competitive bidding (NCB) in at least 1 national newspaper. If the agency does not currently handle World Bank–funded procurement, it is willing to follow the Bank's advertising procedure.	0 / 3 (mandatory for World Bank)	Copies of advertisements are available for inspection, and an advertisement appears in an international newspaper or journal (for example, *United Nations Development Business* and *dgMarket* for ICB). Available records show that tender requests were posted on the agency Web site.
2.3 Bid openings are open to the public (that is, the bidders), and all bidders receive an invitation to bid openings.	0 / 1 / 2 / 3	Randomly review record of at least 2 bid openings to confirm all bidders received an invitation to attend.

(continued)

Standard	Compliance rating	Assessor observations and comments	Instructions for assessor
2.4 The organization does not normally conduct discussions or financial negotiations with bidders after opening of the price bids.	0 / 1 / 2 / 3		A random review of 2 procurement records reveals that price negotiation does not take place on a routine basis.
2.4.1 If discussion or financial negotiations take place after bids are opened, written rules and procedures are strictly adhered to and a record is available to ensure that such negotiation is a fair and transparent process.	0 / 1 / 2 / 3		Written rules and procedures are available, and a random review of 3 procurement records reveals adherence to rules.
2.4.2 The contract award information is disclosed to all companies that have submitted bids following review by an independent competent authority.	0 / 1 / 2 / 3		A review of 2 randomly chosen procurement records confirms adherence to the standard.
2.5 Open competitive bidding is the preferred or default procurement method unless the organization carries out a supplier prequalification process. If manufacturer prequalification is standard, a restricted tender will be the default method.	0 / 1 / 2 / 3		The policy statement is available.
2.5.1 Direct or single-source procurement without a tender process is used in instances in which the product has only 1 prequalified source or in cases of extreme emergency. In such a case, historical "reasonable" pricing is used to negotiate the price with the supplier.	0 / 1 / 2 / 3		Request copies of single-source procurement documents, and verify that the record reveals only 1 prequalified (or not prequalified) source is available and that the price compares favorably with the historical price or current market price.
2.6 Requirements for bid submission and bid and performance securities are required of all bidders.	0 / 3 (mandatory)		Written (preferably) documentation is available. If state law requires an exemption for bid security, the rating is 3 for procurement funded by the government of India or a state, but there is no exemption under World Bank procurement.

Item	Score	Notes
2.7 If the agency does not carry out prequalification of bidders, all suppliers are eligible to bid.	0 / 3 (mandatory)	The policy should state that all tenders are open.
2.8 The process of bid examination and evaluation is rational and fair.	0 / 3 (mandatory)	Bid examination procedures that do not provide an opportunity for bidder discrimination are available, and a random review of tender evaluation committee minutes reveals adherence to procedures.
2.9 There are rules or procedures for bidder suspension and debarment (that is, blacklisting).	0 / 1 / 2 / 3	Rules should also be specified in the procurement contract and the bid document.
2.10 Public disclosure of the complete procurement process is freely available.	0 / 1 / 2 / 3	Public disclosure is available as prescribed by the Right to Information Act, state law or policy, or agency policy.
2.11 Regular meetings are held with the business community or are available to the business community to discuss procurement issues. A record of such meetings is maintained and includes follow-up actions, if any.	0 / 1 / 2 / 3	Verify the record of meetings.
Minimum score for transparency	29 (32 for World Bank)	
Actual score		
3.0 Procurement cycle management		
3.1 Procurement planning		
3.1.1 The hierarchy of sources for procurement rules is well established (that is, laws, government regulations and procedures, organization's own rules and procedures).	0 / 1 / 2 / 3	State the hierarchy.
3.1.1.1 The agency is or can be allowed by its mandate to act as the procurement agent and follow the procurement procedures of the principal (that is, World Bank, government of India, or other states).	0 / 3 (mandatory)	The mandate to act as the procurement agent is evident from the business rules or articles of association.

(continued)

Standard	Compliance rating	Assessor observations and comments	Instructions for assessor
3.1.2 The agency has a procurement plan template that is closely adhered to after a procurement request is received; the plan should include, at a minimum, a schedule for advertising the tender, receipt of bids, bid opening, bid evaluation, and contract award.	0 / 1 / 2 / 3		The agency follows a predetermined procurement plan, and examples are available for inspection.
3.1.2.1 An employee or team is designated to prepare the procurement plan, which includes scheduling of activities at a minimum.	0 / 3 (mandatory)		An employee is in place, and an interview reveals his or her understanding of procurement planning.
3.1.3. An employee is assigned to approve each stage of the procurement cycle, and an overall director is responsible for managing the complete process.	0 / 1 / 2 / 3		Personnel are in place.
3.1.4 There is general adherence to the procurement plan.	0 / 1 / 2 / 3		At least 2 procurement plans should be selected at random and reviewed for adherence to the plan.
Minimum score for procurement planning	13		
Actual score			
3.2 Bidding documents			
3.2.1 Standard bidding documents are used for procurement of health sector goods.	0 / 1 / 2 / 3		Bidding documents are available.
3.2.1.1 Bidding documents are readily adaptable to specific contract situations (that is, modifications made through a bid data sheet, special conditions of contract, or similar).	0 / 1 / 2 / 3		Examples are available.
3.2.2 The procurement staff is knowledgeable in preparation and modification of bidding documents.	0 / 1 / 2 / 3		Interviews with the procurement staff reveal familiarity with preparation and modification of standard bidding documents.

3.2.2.1 The procurement staff is familiar with World Bank procurement policies, guidelines, and standard bidding documents (or the guidelines of the principal, if applicable) and has demonstrated experience with correctly completing the bid data sheet and drafting special conditions of a contract.	0 / 3 (mandatory for World Bank)	Interview the procurement staff about World Bank documents. Check the correspondence with the World Bank, if the agency is already handling Bank-funded procurement.
3.2.3 Technical specifications for health commodity products are clear, neutral, and accurate.	0 / 1 / 2 / 3	Perform a random review of specifications for drugs, medical supplies and kits, equipment, and consumables.
3.2.3.1 Technical specifications are prepared by a committee that includes expert knowledge concerning products to be procured.	0 / 1 / 2 / 3	Technical specifications are provided by the principal, internal staff members, or an outside committee or combination of internal and external experts.
3.2.3.2 Technical specifications for drugs are issued by the principal and are included in bid documents; pharmacy expertise is available for specification review and to request clarifications of specifications issued by the principal; and when specifications are not provided, specifications are prepared with input from staff members or consultants with pharmacy expertise.	0 / 3 (mandatory)	Specifications include the Indian Pharmacopeia, British Pharmacopoeia, United States Pharmacopeia standards. Document whether pharmacy expertise is available in house or from an outside source.
3.2.3.2.1 Shelf-life consideration is included in technical specifications for drugs or other supplies where applicable.	0 / 3 (mandatory)	Shelf life is included among contract terms.
3.2.3.3 Technical specifications for medical equipment and supplies or test kits are provided by the principal and are included in the bid document. Equipment or supply expertise is available for specification review and to request clarifications for specifications issued by the principal.	0 / 3 (mandatory)	A review of tenders includes technical specifications. Document whether medical equipment or supply expertise is available in house or from an outside source.

(continued)

185

Standard	Compliance rating	Assessor observations and comments	Instructions for assessor
3.2.4 Instructions to bidders contain all information necessary to prepare responsive bids (provide clear understanding of eligibility requirements and how evaluation criteria will be applied).	0 / 1 / 2 / 3		Bidder instructions are complete for equipment and supplies and for pharmaceutical contracts.
3.2.4.1 Bid security required in bidding instructions as a condition of responsiveness is an appropriate amount (for example, sliding scale but no more than 3% of total value).	0 / 1 / 2 / 3		Review the bidding instructions.
Minimum score for bidding documents	23 (26 for World Bank)		
Actual score			
3.3 Pre- or postqualification of suppliers			
3.3.1 Supplier and product prequalification or postqualification is carried out prior to award of any health sector contract.	0 / 1 / 2 / 3		Written pre- or postqualification supplier policies and procedures are available. Review of 3 randomly selected procurements reveals documentation that pre- or postqualification was carried out in accordance with policies and procedures.
3.3.1.1 Prequalification or postqualification requirements are clear and completely describe all requisites for submitting a responsive application and qualification requirements.	0 / 1 / 2 / 3		Detailed product specifications and pre- or postqualification guidelines for submitting company and product information, including agency evaluation criteria, are stated in the bid invitation or solicitation. At least 1 bid invitation for each health sector product category (pharmaceutical product, medical supply or kit, medical equipment), where an agency procures such products, will be reviewed for comprehensiveness.

3.3.1.2 The pre- and postqualification process is carried out in a fair and transparent manner, and decisions are made promptly.	0 / 1 / 2 / 3	A review of process procedures reveals transparency, and a review of actual procurements shows that they follow prescribed policies and procedures.
3.3.1.3 Pre- or postqualification includes assessment of technical and financial capacity to supply the required value of products.	0 / 1 / 2 / 3	Documentation exists that technical and financial capacity to supply requirements is assessed as part of the pre- or postqualification process.
3.3.2 All evaluations and inspections are carried out by qualified evaluators who have signed a declaration of interest (no situations of real, potential, or apparent conflict of interest are known to them), preferably with the participation of external experts.	0 / 1 / 2 / 3	Pharmaceutical and medical supply inspections are carried out by personnel who are trained to perform such inspections. Inspections are carried out by a team of at least 2 people. Medical equipment evaluation is carried out by a biomedical engineer. Documentation indicates adherence to standard.
3.3.2.1 For drugs and medical supplies and kits, evaluation includes preparation of the manufacturer site master file and product files, including existing certificates of inspection or quality (that is, World Health Organization [WHO] good manufacturing practices [GMPs], Schedule M, International Organization for Standardization standards, most current inspection report).	0 / 1 / 2 / 3	
3.3.3 Planning and preparation for manufacturer inspection includes notification of the inspection date, completion of a site master file by the manufacturer, and agency familiarity with product information submitted by the manufacturer.	0 / 1 / 2 / 3	Documentation is available, and an interview with a representative inspector reveals understanding of planning and preparation procedures.
3.3.4 Inspections are carried out in accordance with written procedures and include all aspects of GMP in line with GMP guidelines.	0 / 1 / 2 / 3	Inspection is carried out by a team of at least 2 inspectors; inspection may be outsourced to a competent agency including the state drug regulatory authority (SDRA).

(continued)

Standard	Compliance rating	Assessor observations and comments	Instructions for assessor
3.3.4.1 Waiving of inspections for procurement of drugs is permissible only if an inspection has been carried out by a stringent drug regulatory authority (International Conference on Harmonisation or Pharmaceutical Inspection Cooperation Scheme member country) in the past 36 months and a GMP certificate has been issued without conditions (copy of inspection report and certificate is on file with the agency) or if the agency has carried out a GMP inspection in line with WHO GMP standards at the manufacturing facility in the past 36 months with a finding of no deficiencies *and* no major changes to premises, equipment, and key personnel have occurred since the inspection (the latter applies to inspections by an SDRA as well).	0 / 3 (mandatory)		Review the waiver policy to determine whether it is in line with the standard and, if waivers have been issued, whether the waiver is appropriately issued.
3.3.5 Once all prequalification data are collected and the evaluation committee (or its equivalent) recommends precertification, final approval is issued by the agency's appointed management authority.	0 / 1 / 2 / 3		The record of prequalification evaluation is available and is approved by the recognized agency's competent authority.
3.3.6 The agency inspection report is communicated to the manufacturer and includes noncompliance observed and recommended corrective actions.	0 / 1 / 2 / 3		Review 3 examples of agency inspection reports, and verify that reports include observed and recommended corrective actions and that reports have been forwarded to the respective manufacturers.

3.3.6.1 Qualitative or physical and laboratory analysis is performed as per drug product specifications on samples for all batches by a laboratory operating in line with WHO good practices for national pharmaceutical control laboratories.	0 / 1 / 2 / 3	Records reveal that, as part of the prequalification process, manufacturer's samples are tested by a laboratory equipped to perform drug analysis and certified as meeting specifications by a national or international organization (for example, WHO) recognized for its certification competency.
3.3.6.2 The agency has records to demonstrate that samples from drug batches supplied by the manufacturer have undergone and passed the same testing used for samples during the prequalification phase. Note: This requirement only applies if prequalification sampling is not carried out and sampling is included. If prequalification sampling is not carried out, the agency has documentation that for batches received, full pharmacopoeial analysis is done on a random basis at a minimum.	0 / 1 / 2 / 3	The procedure for sampling batches received is documented, and records are available that reveal adherence to the procedure.
3.3.6.3 There is evidence that prequalified manufacturers and products are reevaluated at a minimum of every 3 years.	0 / 1 / 2 / 3	Obtain a list of drug or supply manufacturers who have responded to tenders for more than 3 years and verify that records are available documenting reevaluation and inspection of the manufacturing location and products.
3.3.7 The agency maintains a list of registered or qualified suppliers that is updated at least annually.	0 / 1 / 2 / 3	Verify that the list is available and has been updated annually.
3.3.7.1 Evidence is available that over the past 2 years, manufacturers have been added or deleted or have been temporarily disbarred from participation in agency procurements.	0 / 1 / 2 / 3	Documentation is available.
Minimum score for pre- or postqualification	33	
Actual score		

(continued)

189

Standard	Compliance rating	Assessor observations and comments	Instructions for assessor
3.4 Advertisement or sale of the bid documents			
3.4.1 Contracts awarded on the basis of competitive bidding are advertised publicly in at least 1 national newspaper (in addition to local or Internet advertising). If the agency does not have its own Web site, it has access to one that is freely accessible for publishing invitations for bids.	0 / 3 (mandatory)		Written policy (may be included in state legislation) is available that mandates competitive bidding, and a copy of the ad placed in at least 1 national newspaper is available for review. Interviews with procurement personnel confirm adherence to policy.
3.4.2 Sufficient time (at least 4 weeks) is provided to bidders for obtaining documents and preparation of bids.	0 / 1 / 2 / 3		Advertisement of tenders includes sufficient time for bidders to obtain documents.
3.4.3 If an open tender process is used, sale of the bid documents is available to all who request it, and the price of bid documents is reasonable.	0 / 3 (mandatory)		This standard is required.
3.4.3.1 Bid documents are always available on the date specified in the advertised notice.	0 / 3 (mandatory)		This standard is required.
3.4.3.2 Bid documents are available for sale or are available (for example, from an agency Web site) until the day of the bid opening.	0 / 3 (mandatory)		This standard is required.
Minimum score for advertisement or sale of bid documents	13		
Actual score			
3.5 Communications during the bidding process			
3.5.1 Requests for clarifications are promptly and completely provided in writing and shared with all bidders of record.	0 / 1 / 2 / 3		This standard is required by agency policy; sampling of at least 3 procurement records reveals that clarifications or responses to questions are provided within 5 days and shared with all bidders of record (a copy of the response sent to all bidders is available).

3.5.2 Clarifications; minutes of the prebid conference, if any; and modifications to the bid documents are promptly communicated to all prospective bidders.	0 / 1 / 2 / 3	Records are available.
3.5.2.1 Bidders are provided ample opportunity to revise their bids following a modification to bidding documents.	0 / 1 / 2 / 3	When a major bid modification occurs, agency policy provides bidders with additional time to submit bids; confirm that this standard is met during interviews with procurement personnel.
3.5.3 The agency maintains accurate records of all communications with bidders prior to and after deadline submission.	0 / 1 / 2 / 3	Review records.
Minimum score for communications during the bid process	8	
Actual score		
3.6 Receipt of and opening of bids		
3.6.1 Bids received prior to the deadline are securely stored, and procedures are in place to ensure that no tampering can occur.	0 / 3 (mandatory)	A secure "bid box" is available, and access is limited to no more than 2 high-level agency officials.
3.6.2 The time elapsed between final day for submission of bids and the opening of bids is minimal and preferably occurs on the same day.	0 / 1 / 2 / 3	Time elapsed should be no more than 1 week.
3.6.3 All bid openings are conducted publicly, and all firms that submitted a bid receive invitations to attend.	0 / 3 (mandatory)	This standard is required.
3.6.3.1 The names of all bidders and the price quoted by them are read aloud to bid-opening participants or this information is provided in written or electronic form and then recorded in a bid register.	0 / 3 (mandatory)	The bid opening procedure is followed. Bids are recorded in a register and are available for review by all bidders and by the public.
3.6.4 Bids received after the deadline for submission are returned unopened to bidders.	0 / 3 (mandatory)	This standard is required.

(continued)

Standard	Compliance rating	Assessor observations and comments	Instructions for assessor
3.6.5 The bid procedure follows a single-envelope process where technical and price bids are provided unless otherwise permitted by state legislation. If a 2-envelope system is used, the price bid is securely stored until the technical bids are evaluated and opened in the presence of technically qualified bidders.	0 / 3 (mandatory)		If state legislation requires a bid procedure other than a single-envelope process (technical and price together), so state.
Minimum score for receipt and opening of bids	17		
Actual score			
3.7 Bid evaluation			
3.7.1 For every procurement, bid evaluation is conducted by a committee composed of qualified members with expertise in pharmaceuticals or clinical medicine, other health care professionals, educators, and medical equipment technical experts (for equipment procurements). Some external members are desirable.	0 / 1 / 2 / 3		Document the list of committee members and background for evaluating the following types of procurement: (a) drugs, (b) medical supplies or test kits, (c) medical equipment, and (d) consumable supplies. State in the comment section whether external members are on the team. A rating of complete compliance requires external members.
3.7.2 Bid responsiveness is determined solely by meeting all requirements in the bid documents.	0 / 3 (mandatory)		A review of tender documents reveals that a technical responsiveness checklist is available, and the checklist reveals that all technical requirements have been received.
3.7.3 Among all bidders who meet previously specified technical requirements, the lowest bidder is selected for award.	0 / 3 (mandatory)		This standard is required.
3.7.3.1 There will be no negotiations with any bidder, including the lowest bidder, unless this bid exceeds known current market price or is higher than historical pricing or unless such negotiations are otherwise permitted by state law.	0 / 3 (mandatory)		This standard is required.

3.7.3.2 In the event of default or inability to supply as per contract by the lowest bidder, the second-lowest bidder will be notified and awarded the contract. The same system will apply for the third-lowest bidder in the event the second defaults or cannot supply and so on.	0 / 3 (mandatory)	This standard is required unless state law specifies otherwise.
3.7.4 The managing director, tender committee, or other committee charged with this responsibility approves the award. If the principal requires a "no objection," it will be obtained prior to final approval.	0 / 3 (mandatory)	This standard is required.
3.7.5 A bid evaluation report is prepared for all procurements that includes all essential information: a complete description of the evaluation process, reasons for rejecting a bid as nonresponsive, methodology for applying evaluation criteria, and verification of successful bidder's qualifications.	0 / 1 / 2 / 3	Review a minimum of 2 bid evaluation reports, and verify documentation.
3.7.5.1 The bid evaluation report is maintained on file for the duration of the contract at a minimum, and reasons for rejection of bids are provided to unsuccessful bidders, if requested.	0 / 3 (mandatory)	This standard is required.
3.7.6 The agency will provide the following information to the assessor: total number and value of contracts awarded in the past 5 years (less if it is in operation for less than 5 years) through ICB (global tender), NCB (open tender), limited tender, and single tender. Values will be supplied separately for categories of drugs and supplies and for medical equipment and nonmedical supplies.		The assessor assigns the point value as follows: 3 points if there is at least 1 contract within the category annually with a value of at least US$1,000,000; 2 points if there is at least 1 contract within the category annually with a value of US$50,000— US$1,000,000; 1 point if there is at least 1 contract within the category annually with a value of US$50,000; otherwise, 0 points.
3.7.6.1 Drugs and medical supplies or kits	0 / 1 / 2 / 3	Assess on the basis of total value of tender.
3.7.6.2 Medical equipment or nonmedical supplies	0 / 1 / 2 / 3	Assess on the basis of total value of tender.

(continued)

Standard	Compliance rating	Assessor observations and comments	Instructions for assessor
3.7.7 The agency will provide the average time from the date of bid opening to the award of contract for each category *and* the number of contracts awarded under each category within the initial validity period, up to 60 days after the initial bid validity period, and more than 60 days after the initial bid validity period.	0 / 1 / 2 / 3		Scoring is as follows: 1 point awarded if the majority of contracts are awarded 60 days beyond the validity period, 2 points if they are awarded up to 60 days beyond the validity period, and 3 points if they are awarded within the validity period.
Minimum score for bid evaluation	26	Note: The minimum score per standard for 3.7.6.1 and 3.7.6.2 is 1 point.	
Actual score			
3.8 Contract award			
3.8.1 The agency shall have a standard contract form, which is part of the bid document.	0 / 1 / 2 / 3		Verify the availability and use of a standard contract form.
3.8.2 If the agency performs "shopping" (that is, for emergency or very low value procurements), a standard quotation form and purchase order form are available.	0 / 1 / 2 / 3		Verify the availability and use of a standard quotation form.
3.8.3 Procurement rules dictate award to the lowest qualified bidder unless otherwise countermanded by state law (for example, regulation pertaining to state-owned bidder or preference discount for suppliers operating within the state).	0 / 3 (mandatory)		Rules must be in writing, and adherence is evidenced by review of 3 procurement records.
3.8.3.1 Should a low bidder be disqualified, this event is documented in the tender record.	0 / 1 / 2 / 3		During an interview with the management staff, ask if a low bidder has ever been disqualified (that is, because of quality issues). If affirmative, verify that this event is recorded in the tender record.

3.8.4 Unless otherwise directed by state or national legislation, there is no negotiation with bidders regarding technical terms and conditions.	0 / 3 (mandatory)	This standard is required.
3.8.5 Performance security is required in an appropriate amount and format.	0 / 3 (mandatory)	This standard is required.
3.8.6 Rules for a repeat order system limit the increase in contract value to no more than 25% with proper justification.	0 / 3 (mandatory)	This standard is required.
Minimum score for contract award	16	
Actual score		
3.9 Contract administration		
3.9.1 A manual or computerized procurement process exists, and contract monitoring is carried out (that is, monitoring of direct and indirect product costs, receipt monitoring [damage], quality monitoring, monitoring of adherence to delivery schedules, complaint monitoring).	0 / 1 / 2 / 3	Verify that an SOP exists for supplier performance monitoring. Ask the agency to provide examples of companies that were issued a complaint, and verify that the complaint and action taken is documented.
3.9.2 The normal time lapse from invoice submission to final payment indicates that payment is generally made on time.	0 / 1 / 2 / 3	Randomly select 3 awards and determine whether payment was made in accordance with contract terms.
3.9.3 Contract changes or variations are not permitted after the award, unless they are in line with the contract provisions.	0 / 3 (mandatory)	This standard is required
3.9.4 Supplier claims are handled fairly and in accordance with contract terms.	0 / 3 (mandatory)	This standard is required; review complaints register.
3.9.4.1 Procuring entities normally make a good-faith effort to resolve disagreements through informal negotiations, if they are permitted per the dispute resolution procedure included in the contract.	0 / 1 / 2 / 3	Determine, if possible, the number of disagreements handled by formal negotiation or arbitration.
3.9.4.2 If informal negotiations fail, established formal arbitration procedures are described in the contract.	0 / 1 / 2 / 3	Document procedures.

(continued)

Standard	Compliance rating	Assessor observations and comments	Instructions for assessor
3.9.5 Contracts are completed on schedule and within the approved contract price.	0 / 1 / 2 / 3		Review 3 randomly selected contracts and verify adherence.
3.9.6 Rejection of goods because of substandard quality is referred to the Drug Control Authority for disposition.	0 / 3 (mandatory)		This standard is required.
3.9.6.1 Contract terms include rejection of goods with compensation or blacklisting of supplier if evaluation findings of product complaints received from an end user reveal a defective or substandard product (confirmed by Drug Control Authority).	0 / 1 / 2 / 3		There is a product complaints registry or equivalent, and review of records reveals that complaints are handled promptly (that is, within 30 days) and disposition of complaint is recorded; all complaints are thoroughly investigated, as evidenced by a written record, and reported to the Drug Control Authority for further evaluation and disposition.
3.9.7 There is a formal contract closing procedure.	0 / 1 / 2 / 3		The written procedure is available.
Minimum score for contract administration	21		
Actual score			
Minimum total score for procurement cycle management	170 (173 World Bank)		
Actual total score for procurement cycle management			
4.0 Support and control Systems			
4.1 Internal and external auditing arrangements are in place and established and an overall audit plan is available that describes audit goals, schedules, staffing, and reporting; audit reports are available for inspection.	0 / 1 / 2 / 3		An audit plan is available; internal and external audits take place.

Criteria	Score	Scoring
4.1.1 Internal audits include at a minimum (a) operational audits (for example, compliance with procurement policies and procedures); (b) financial audits (for example, a review of the agency's financial statements to determine whether financial statements fairly present the financial position as of a certain date); and (c) information technology audits (assess the controls, accuracy, and integrity of an institution's electronic data processing and computer areas).	0 / 1 / 2 / 3	Document the level of adherence. Scoring is as follows: completely compliant for all 3 audit types = 3 points; substantially compliant for all 3 audits = 2 points; some compliance for 1 or more audit types = 1 point; noncompliant for any type of audit = 0 points.
4.1.2 Audit reports contain a concise summary of key results and conclusions, including identification of root causes of significant weaknesses; audit scope and objectives; detailed audit results; recommendations, if any; and management's commitments to correct material weaknesses.	0 / 1 / 2 / 3	Document the level of adherence.
4.1.2.1 When audit recommendations are provided, appropriate actions are taken and recorded.	0 / 1 / 2 / 3	Document the level of adherence.
4.1.2.2 An external audit program performed by an outside independent auditor provides a financial statement audit, substantiation of internal controls over financial reporting, or other external audit procedures.	0 / 1 / 2 / 3	Document the level of adherence.
4.1.2.3 Procurement audits will be carried out by the accountant general's office or a contracted third party; a copy of all audits is maintained in the agency office and is available for public inspection unless otherwise specified by the auditing authority.	0 / 1 / 2 / 3	Document the level of adherence.

(continued)

Standard	Compliance rating	Assessor observations and comments	Instructions for assessor
4.2 Internal auditors are independent of the activities they audit and possess the necessary knowledge and skill to successfully implement the audit program in a proficient and professional manner. Internal audits encompass compliance with financial, procurement, and information technology procedures.	0 / 3 (mandatory)		This standard is required
4.3 The agency will demonstrate that it has made arrangements for access to quality legal advice and input.	0 / 1 / 2 / 3		The agency will have an attorney of record.
Minimum total score for support and control systems	17		
Actual total score for support and control systems			
5.0 Record keeping			
5.1. The agency maintains a detailed contract award record for all competitive bids, including copies of all public advertisements, prequalification evaluation reports, bidding documents, records of any prebid meetings, minutes of bid openings, bid evaluation reports with reasons for acceptance and rejection of bids, appeals against procedures or award recommendations, signed copies of final contracts, performance and advance payment securities issued, and cross-references to pertinent files.	0 / 1 / 2 / 3		Obtain list of contract awards and randomly select 3 awards for review; document the availability of documents as per the standard.

198

5.2 Contract administration records are maintained and include, at a minimum, contractual notices issued by the supplier; a detailed record of all change or variation orders issued affecting the scope, quantities, timing, or price of the contract; records of invoice and payments; progress reports; certificates of inspection, acceptance, and completion; and records of claims, disputes, and disputes outcome.	0 / 1 / 2 / 3	Review a minimum of 3 contract administration records; document the degree of adherence.
5.3 Periodic management reports are prepared summarizing overall procurement activities for a defined period (for example, quarterly, semiannually, annually), and such reports are available for review.	0 / 1 / 2 / 3	Records are available.
5.4 A record of contract prices is maintained, and the procurement unit regularly conducts periodic supplier market surveys or reviews available survey information (including international price reference sources) to update knowledge of product sources and prices for health sector goods.	0 / 1 / 2 / 3	Verify that the contract price record is maintained; at a minimum, prices should be easily retrieved.
5.5 Historical contract prices, along with adjustments for subsequent changes, are used in evaluation of new bids.	0 / 1 / 2 / 3	Determine from procurement policy or from interviews with personnel.
Minimum score for record keeping	10	
Actual total score for record keeping		

(continued)

Standard	Compliance rating	Assessor observations and comments	Instructions for assessor
6.0 Human resources			
6.1 The procurement agency organization includes sufficient management-level and support positions for all key procurement functions: overall management (managing director or chief executive officer); financial; internal audit; contract administration and contract management; tender process (issue, evaluate, award); quality control personnel; management of administrative staff (management information system, support staff) and reporting lines are clearly delineated (attach an organizational chart).	0 / 1 / 2 / 3		There are offices, departments, committees, or technical experts to carry out the PSA mandate. There is a full-time managing director or the equivalent and at least 1 employee is assigned to each key procurement function (the same employee is not assigned to more than 1 key procurement function).
6.1.1 Personnel responsible for specific procurement functions have a written job description detailing tasks and responsibilities and are familiar with applicable SOPs and policies (see 1.2.1). The staff is updated about changes in rules and thresholds and other issues relevant to assigned responsibilities.	0 / 1 / 2 / 3		The department includes a minimum of 5 key staff members, and 1 is the lead for each of these tasks: management of product specification, pre- or postqualification, tender evaluation, quality assurance, and contract management. Review job descriptions and interview a minimum of 3 procurement employees to determine familiarity with SOPs; if no written SOPs exist, interview employees to determine familiarity with job responsibilities and procurement thresholds.
6.1.2 For each category of commodity procurement (drugs, medical supplies or test kits, medical equipment, consumables), at least 1 employee or contracted outside consultant has requisite expertise to handle each respective commodity category undertaken by the agency.	0 / 1 / 2 / 3		Review curricula vitae of employees or consultants to determine their background and experience, and use interviews to confirm that employee or consultant status is current. If the curriculum vitae is not on file, probe for the individual's background and experience. The assessor will include in the comments any commodity categories not procured by the agency.

Criteria	Score	Notes
6.1.3 Personnel are sufficient for the volume of business; they are appropriately trained, educated, and experienced to perform key activities, including prequalification, quality assurance and management, finance and administration, procurement, and management information services.	0 / 1 / 2 / 3	There is no indication that lack of personnel impedes procurement operations (for example, delays in awarding contracts, supplier complaints regarding contract management, unusual number of emergency procurements). If current staffing is insufficient to satisfy additional procurement volumes, the assessor determines whether the agency has flexibility to hire additional staff members and provide compensation at market-linked remuneration.
6.2 The prequalification or postqualification staff or office is independent from the purchasing staff or office, and pre- and postqualification is carried out by a team of qualified personnel.	0 / 3 (mandatory)	This standard is required.
6.3 The product evaluation staff or office is independent from the manufacturer inspection employee office.	0 / 3 (mandatory)	Product evaluation responsibilities include receipt of product information, screening and evaluation of product information, and communication of the results of product evaluation to the manufacturer.
6.4 On-the-job training programs or outside training exists for all staff members for promotion of professional development.	0 / 1 / 2 / 3	Based on interviews with employees, the assessor determines whether well-organized, somewhat available, or occasional training is provided, or if no training is provided.
6.5 The procurement staff is experienced in international procurement, if it handles global tendering.	0 / 1 / 2 / 3	The assessor determines the level of experience (much experience, moderate experience, little experience, or none).
Minimum total score for human resources	18	
Actual total score for human resources		

(continued)

201

202

Standard	Compliance rating	Assessor observations and comments	Instructions for assessor
7.0 General risk assessment			
7.1 The agency will be able to demonstrate that it has taken steps to curb or control corruption (that is, employees sign conflict of interest statements and provide annual returns of assets they hold).	0 / 1 / 2 / 3		Declaration of interest and codes of ethics and conduct are in place; interviews with minimum of 3 key employees directly involved with procurement reveal that a mechanism exists for employees to report corrupt activities and that there is no fear of repercussion should they do so. A declaration of interest form is available, and inspectors or evaluators have a current, signed declaration on file (assessor to verify), stating that they have no real, potential, or apparent conflict of interest situations known to them and have disclosed whether they have a financial or other interest in, or relationship with, parties with a vested commercial interest in obtaining access to any confidential information disclosed to the inspectors or evaluators.
7.1.1 The agency includes in its bid documents and contracts a provision describing steps that will be taken in the event of a confirmed attempt at bribery or corrupt practice by a contractor or agency employee.	0 / 1 / 2 / 3		Review bid documents for contract terms concerning bribery or corrupt practice.
7.1.2 No unreasonable supplier disqualifications or noncompliance notices are issued.	0 / 1 / 2 / 3		Request a list of manufacturers that have been disqualified from bid consideration or to which notice of noncompliance has been issued. Review records and document reasons for disqualification or noncompliance. Are the actions trivial? Are they authorized by competent authority in the agency?

Item	Score	Guidance
7.1.3 The agency analyzes individual supplier bids for similarities in bid language, bid rotation, and, prices of other bidders.	0 / 1 / 2 / 3	The agency tender analysis SOP discusses analysis of bids for similarities in language and price. If no written policy exists, determine from interviews with at least 2 members of the tender evaluation committee that such similarities are a consideration. Review 3 manufacturer bid proposals for the same tender (look at 3 tenders) and determine if similarities exist in language or price.
7.1.4 Contract prices do not normally exceed agency estimates.	0 / 1 / 2 / 3	For 10 randomly selected contract prices, compare prices to estimates. If the contract price far exceeds the estimate, this may be evidence of profiteering and corruption or lack of skills and information for preparing an estimate.
7.2 Procurement staff members are held in high regard within the agency.	0 / 1 / 2 / 3	Base determination on private sector interviews.
7.3 Powers related to procurement are clearly delegated to the agency carrying out the procurement process, and procurement procedures are clearly defined.	0 / 1 / 2 / 3	Written policy and procedures are available; if the policy and procedures are not written, personnel are aware of where powers are delegated.
7.4 The agency operates independently and is not required to consult or seek guidance from the state government in its day-to-day operation.	0 / 1 / 2 / 3	The agency has operational policies that do not require or include state government approval (except for contract awards or if the state has not authorized an independent procurement agency).
7.4.1 Any violation that comes to the attention of the agency or government is promptly investigated and recorded, and a public record of the complaint and disposition is maintained.	0 / 1 / 2 / 3	A procedure is in place for handling bidder, contractor, and supplier representations or complaints before and after the contract award. All complaints, whether settled informally or formally, are documented.

(continued)

Standard	Compliance rating	Assessor observations and comments	Instructions for assessor
7.4.1.1 A complaints registry exists within the agency.	0 / 1 / 2 / 3		There is an easily retrievable complaints registry or the equivalent, and review of records reveals that complaints are handled promptly (that is, within 30 days); disposition of complaints is recorded. All bidder, contractor, and supplier complaints are recorded in the registry.
7.5 A mechanism is in place that allows for reporting of bribes and solicitation or extortion by procurement officials.	0 / 1 / 2 / 3		A "whistle-blowing" policy or the equivalent is available.
7.6 If the agency has previous experience with World Bank projects, no or only minor issues with Bank-financed contracts have been documented as regards timeliness, transparency, misprocurement, incidence of complaint, or Bank reversal of decisions (objections).	0 / 3 (mandatory for World Bank)		Review previous Bank procurements (3 if possible) for record of complaints.
Minimum total score for general risk assessment	22 (25 World Bank)		
Actual total score for general risk assessment			

8.0 Private sector supplier assessment		Base assessment on interviews with at least 10 private sector organizations that have been successful or unsuccessful in obtaining awards from the agency.
8.1 The agency procurement system is viewed as generally efficient and predictable.	0 / 1 / 2 / 3	
8.2 The procurement process is transparent in all regards.	0 / 1 / 2 / 3	
8.3 Contract management is straightforward and understandable, and the agency has a record of releasing payment within the time period stipulated in the contract.	0 / 1 / 2 / 3	Interviews with private sector organizations confirm that contract management is reasonable, and a review of contract records reveals that payments are made as stipulated in the contract.
8.4 The agency is viewed as free of corruption.	0 / 1 / 2 / 3	
Minimum total score for private sector assessment	8	
Actual score for private sector assessment		
Minimum assessment total score	334 (343 for World Bank)	
Actual assessment total score		

Source: World Bank/Management Sciences for Health 2008.

Note: Scoring methodology is as follows. The minimum score for considering an agency for management of national or international procurement is a substantially compliant rating for all standards and a completely compliant rating for 30 standards. For World Bank procurements, an additional three standards require full compliance.

A possibility exists that an agency does not at present procure drugs (or equipment or nonmedical supplies and medical supplies or test kits) or that the agency uses only a particular procurement method (for example, global tender or limited tender). In such circumstances, the standards that are not applicable should not be assessed, and for each standard not assessed, 2 points should be deducted from the total minimum required score.

Approved agencies are given the responsibility to handle contracts valued in accordance with their experience and personnel expertise—see "Organization, structure, and functions" (standards 1.2.3.1–1.2.3.2), "Bid evaluation" (standards 3.7.6.1–3.7.6.2), and Human Resources (standard 6.1.1)—in carrying out contracts for any given health commodity category (drugs or medical and lab supplies and test kits or medical equipment). Contracts with increasingly higher value may be considered after (a) an agency has a history of successful performance for a given category and contract value and (b) reinspection reveals the organizational capacity to succeed at procurements with a higher value (a sufficient staff and expertise).

A procurement agency may be considered for provisional approval or certification if all mandatory standards are met and a minimum score of at least 1 point has been issued for nonmandatory standards. When the agency submits evidence of substantial compliance for all nonmandatory standards, a reinspection may be requested, and if findings confirm submitted documentation, the certifying agency may grant certification.

An approved agency may request reassessment on an annual basis to maintain its approval status.

Index

Boxes, figures, notes, and tables are indicated by *b, f, n,* and *t* following page numbers.

A

access to medicines. *See also* affordability of medicines; drug prices; essential medicines
  in assessment tool, 172
  definition of, 40–41
  drug companies providing, 72
  drug regulation and, 43, 43*t*
  in election campaigns, 57, 154
  funds, lack or misuse of, 44
  in low-income countries, 8*b*
  supply chains and, 8*b*, 82–93, 93*b*
  TRIPs and, 70*b*
Accountability for Reasonableness (A4R), 103–4
active pharmaceutical ingredients (APIs), 20, 21–22
affordability of medicines. *See also* drug prices; essential medicines
  challenge of providing affordable drugs, xi, 3
  China, 145–46
  dysfunction of pharmaceutical sector and, 39–40
  evaluation of, 60

generics. *See* generic drugs and generics companies
  prescribers taking into consideration, 28
  public vs. private sector, 12
  Russian Federation, 146–47
  substandard or counterfeit drugs and, 118
  U.S., 18
Affordable Medicines Facility–malaria, 34
AIDS. *See* HIV/AIDS
antibiotics, 106, 109, 132, 148
APIs (active pharmaceutical ingredients), 20, 21–22
assessment processes for new drugs, 100–102, 101–2*b*
assessment tool for dysfunction diagnosis, 24, 75–77
  example of, 161–65
  India as example, 175–206
  Turkey as example, 167–73
Austrian Health Institute, 60

B

Bangladesh, doctors' prescription preferences in, 74
"behind-the-counter" drugs, 27–28

benchmarking of drug prices, 24, 93–94,
    95, 158
bidding, 85–86
biologicals and bio-similars, 37*n*3, 155
Bolar provisions, 19, 127, 129*n*2
"bonus" drugs, 64
Brazil
    drug companies in, 156
    TRIPs in, 70*b*
bribery, 51–52, 59
brokers, 22–23, 45
buffer stocks, 50*b*, 88
bundling in drug sales, 64, 153
"bureaucracy avoidance," 58
Burkina Faso, central medical stores in, 89
business practices, unethical, 51–53
"Business-Process Re-engineering" plan
    (Ethiopia), 89
"buyer clubs" for drugs, 93

C

Cameroon, central medical stores in, 89
cardiovascular diseases, 109
central medical stores (CMSs), 12, 26–27,
    32, 35
cGMPs. *See* current good manufacturing
    practices
China
    APIs manufactured in, 20
    doctors' incomes in, 28–29
    drug companies in, 16, 156
    drug expenditures in, 56
    regulatory framework in, 152
    rural poor in, 145–46
    toxic ingredients shipped from, 21*b*
Cipla (Indian generics company), 18
civil society organizations, 32–33, 118, 151
clinical trials, 42, 100
closed-loop control systems, 82–83
CMSs. *See* central medical stores
Code of Pharmaceutical Marketing
    Practices, 16
collusion, 92, 120*n*1
community outreach pharmacies
    (COPs), 148
compulsory rebates, 144
consultants, 36–37
consultations, stakeholder, 133–35, 134*b*
consumers
    pressure for innovation from, 2
    as stakeholders, 29–30

contracts. *See* framework contracts
"control knobs," 4–6, 113
co-payments, 35–36, 52–53, 106, 127, 143
COPs (community outreach pharmacies),
    148
corruption. *See also* bribery; collusion;
    fraud
    access to medicines and, 83
    brokers and, 23
    CMSs and, 27
    formularies and, 154
    good governance and, 117
    in national generics industry, 22
    patterns of, 39, 51–53, 53*b*
cost containment, xiii, 2, 128
    innovation and, 66–70, 69*b*
cost-effectiveness in medicine use,
    107–9, 108*t*
cost of drugs. *See* affordability of medi-
    cines; drug prices
cost-plus pricing, 61
cough syrup, 21*b*
Croatia, Delphi model in, 102
current good manufacturing practices
    (cGMPs), 71, 85, 126. *See also* good
    manufacturing practices

D

DALYs (disability-adjusted life years), 99
Daniels, Norman, 103
data exclusivity rule, 37*n*6
decentralization of health care, 89
Delphi model of consensus building, 102,
    121*n*5
diabetes, 67–68, 74, 107, 109
disability-adjusted life years (DALYs), 99
diseases, xi. *See also specific diseases*
    patterns of, 72
    of the poor, 18, 34
dispensing rights, 28–29
Dr. Reddy's Laboratories, 37*n*5
doctors. *See* physicians
Doha Declaration, 70*b*
domestic manufacturers, 114–15
"do no harm" principle, 75
donors
    access to medicine and, 8*b*
    essential medicines and, 148
    incentives of, 57–58
    R&D support from, 72
    role of, 12, 33–34, 110, 111

essential medicines benefit program
and, 147
health financing and, 110
NGO interaction with, 33
policy diagnosis by, 6
procurement assessment by, 24
World Bank–Harvard Flagship Program on
Health Financing, 4–5
World Health Organization (WHO)
drug control lab prequalification
through, 151
drug prices and, 60
essential medicines concept of, 14,
45, 125
ethics code of, 75

IMS Health data provided to, 61
inventory management systems and, 9
Model Lists of Essential Medicines,
129n1
Model Quality Assurance System, 24
NGO interaction with, 33
policy tools through, 9–10
regulatory capacity support through,
152–53
services provided by, 33
World Trade Organization (WTO), 70b

Y

Yale University, 72

www.ingramcontent.com/pod-product-compliance
Lightning Source LLC
Chambersburg PA
CBHW070904270326
41927CB00011B/2457